The

Climate of

OREGON

From Rain Forest to Desert

The

Climate of

OREGON

From Rain Forest to Desert

George H. Taylor and Chris Hannan

Oregon State University Press

Corvallis

Cover photo (lower) by Bruce B. Johnson (http://www.oregonphotos.com/)

The paper in this book meets the guidelines for permanence and durability
of the Committee on Production Guidelines for Book Longevity of the
Council on Library Resources and the minimum requirements of the
American National Standard for Permanence of Paper for Printed Library
Materials Z39.48-1984.

Library of Congress Cataloging-in-Publication Data
Taylor, George H., 1947-
The climate of Oregon : from rain forest to desert / George H. Taylor and
Chris Hannan.
  p. cm.
Includes bibliographical references and index.
ISBN 0-87071-468-6 (alk. paper)
1. Oregon—Climate. 2. Weather. I. Hannan, Chris. II. Title.
QC984.06T37   1999
551.69795—dc21   99-33928
                                                                    CIP

Oregon State University Press
101 Waldo Hall
Corvallis OR 97331-6407
541-737-3166 •fax 541-737-3170
http://osu.orst.edu/dept/press

Contents

Preface

Oregon's weather and climate have played a major role in shaping the demographics, economics, and ecology of the state. The variety of the climates in Oregon is remarkable. There are coastal mountains with enough rain (up to 200 inches per year) to support rain forests, high mountain peaks that receive upwards of 500 inches per year of snow, parched deserts with as little as 5 inches a year of precipitation, and nearly every climate regime between those extremes. This sheer variety, coupled with a strong reliance on natural resources (agriculture, forestry, and hydroelectric power, for example), has kindled a strong interest in weather and climate among Oregonians. In addition, the people of Oregon are very fond of outdoor recreation, and find that fishing, hunting, skiing, camping, and bicycling are also very much affected by weather and climate.

This book was designed from the start as a companion to *The Oregon Weather Book* (OSU Press, 1999). We believed that a comprehensive reference text on this topic would be of great use to many Oregonians and outsiders. In addition to the data presented here, we have prepared a CD-ROM with *much* more information about Oregon climate. Included are color versions of the graphs, drawings, and photos included here. It's available separately from Oregon Climate Service. Color printing costs prevented us from doing more than two-color maps here, but we hope they're detailed enough to at least give you some ideas about spatial variations in climate. If not, buy the CD-ROM as well!

—*George H. Taylor*
Corvallis, Oregon
June 1999

Acknowledgments

I am blessed with an outstanding wife, Cindy, and three wonderful children, John, Annie, and Tim. Every day I'm grateful for each of you.

Several individuals have helped immensely in my professional growth by providing opportunities:

Einar Hovind hired me twice. The first time, he gave me my first glimpse of meteorology. Years later, he hired me again as a professional. Einar, you embody grace and kindness and I'll always be grateful. Alan Eschenroeder saw something in an inexperienced, just-graduated kid and hired me to my first "professional" job. He was a wonderful mentor and role model. Steve Esbensen offered me the State Climatologist position even though I was new to Oregon and didn't know Molalla from Yoncalla. Steve provided just the right blend of freedom and assistance.

Oregon Climate Service would not have come into existence (in 1991) without the concerted efforts of George H. Keller of OSU and State Senator Cliff Trow. Dr. Keller made repeated efforts to convince legislators that base-level funding was necessary in order to have a strong state climate program. Sen. Trow's bill in the 1991 legislative session, the third such funding attempt, finally passed. I am indebted to you both.

Kelly Redmond of the Western Regional Climate Center, my predecessor as the State Climatologist, continues to help and inspire me. His were big shoes to fill, and I'm not sure I'm worthy even now. Dick Reinhardt, WRCC Director, has also been very supportive of my office. Phil Pasteris and Greg Johnson of the USDA Natural Resources Conservation Service have supported Oregon Climate Service for many years, and have become very good friends as well.

I have been blessed with kind, talented co-workers at Oregon Climate Service. Chris Daly, Wayne Gibson, Chris Hannan, and Tye Parzybok (alphabetically) are my very effective full-time team. Current support staff includes Joy Aikin, Corinne Ruth, Nate DeYoung, and Jen McCannell. In the past, dozens of assistants have worked here. I'll just acknowledge a few: Lexi Bartlett, the first "data babe" and a co-author of many reports; Holly Bohman and Luke Foster, who worked on early data searches and tables for this book; and Mandy Matzke, who's been with us for four summers. Holly, in particular, played a major role in getting this book started.

Warren Slesinger of OSU Press very capably guided us through the initial process of doing a book. Warren's colleague Jo Alexander has done an amazing job of taking two manuscripts and creating actual books! It's been a pleasure to work with you, Jo.

Bruce Johnson supplied the color photos for the cover and also gave me a lot of good advice and feedback on descriptions of weather events, particularly cold weather.

And finally, Jesus Christ is my Lord, Savior, Rock and Shepherd. I give Him glory, honor, and thanks for His role in my life.

—George Taylor

I am grateful to the Oregon Climate Service (OCS) staff for all the support in the day-to-day operations of our office, which eventually led to the completion of this book. George Taylor, State Climatologist and co-author of this book, first hired me at OCS in 1992. Through the years, George has become more than just a boss or mentor, but rather a friend. I consider myself very fortunate to have such an interesting job. OCS has been involved in so many exciting projects. Just like the weather can be very different from one day to the next, the variety in this profession is what I find most fascinating. George has mentioned all those who have supported our office and those who contributed to and aided in the completion of this book. I would like to extend my thanks to those same individuals.

—*Chris Hannan*

Introduction

Weather in Oregon varies a lot across the state, from generally cloudy and wet near the coast to wet, snowy, and cold in the mountains, and mostly sunny and dry east of the Cascades. Then again, weather varies from season to season, with Oregon having generally cool, wet winters and warm, dry summers. But weather also changes from day to day, and sometimes from hour to hour.

Put all these variations together, average them over thirty years or so, and you get *climate*, the long-term average of weather conditions. That's what this book is all about. *Not* clouds and rain and heat waves and ice storms—those are in the companion book, *The Oregon Weather Book*—but rather numbers, statistics, graphs, and maps. Dry, maybe (no pun intended), but that's climate for you: much less exciting than weather.

Less exciting, but very useful. Every week Oregon Climate Service's Web site (www.ocs.orst.edu) gets over 40,000 "hits" (data requests). Farmers, scientists, engineers, students, attorneys—plus all those folks who just *love* weather and climate, and whose favorite TV station is the Weather Channel—log on, look around, grab data and images, and go away satisfied (we hope!). And more often than not, it's climate information they need, for making climate-oriented decisions: what to plant, when to plant it, where to build, how big to make it, when to vacation, where to vacation, and so on, and so on. The fact is, climate affects *lots* of people in *lots* of ways.

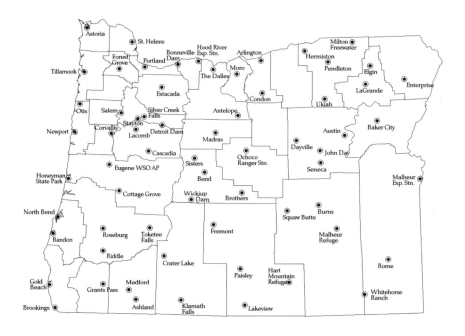

Selected NOAA Weather Reporting Stations in Oregon

Station name	Station number	Latitude (N) Degrees	Minutes	Longitude (W) Degrees	Minutes	Elevation (feet)	County
Antelope	197	44	55	120	43	2680	Jefferson
Arlington	265	45	43	120	12	290	Gilliam
Ashland	304	42	13	122	43	1780	Jackson
Astoria WSO AP	328	46	9	123	52	10	Clatsop
Austin 3 S	356	44	34	118	30	4210	Grant
Baker FAA AP	412	44	49	117	49	3370	Baker
Bandon 2 NNE	471	43	9	124	24	20	Coos
Bend	694	44	4	121	19	3650	Deschutes
Bonneville Dam	897	45	37	121	57	60	Multnomah
Brookings	1055	42	3	124	16	70	Curry
Brothers	1067	43	48	120	36	4640	Deschutes
Burns WSO AP	1175	43	34	118	57	4140	Harney
Cascadia	1433	44	24	122	28	860	Linn
Condon	1765	45	13	120	10	2830	Gilliam
Corvallis St Univ	1862	44	37	123	12	230	Benton
Cottage Grove 1 S	1897	43	46	123	4	650	Lane
Crater Lake Nps Hq	1946	42	54	122	7	6480	Klamath
Dayville 8 NW	2173	44	33	119	39	2260	Grant
Detroit Dam	2292	44	43	122	15	1220	Marion
Elgin	2597	45	34	117	55	2660	Union
Enterprise 2 S	2675	45	24	117	16	3880	Wallowa
Estacada 2 SE	2693	45	16	122	19	410	Clackamas

Eugene WSO AP	2709	44	7	123	13	360	Lane
Forest Grove	2997	45	31	123	6	180	Washington
Fremont	3095	43	19	121	10	4510	Lake
Gold Beach R S	3356	42	24	124	25	50	Curry
Grants Pass	3445	42	25	123	19	930	Josephine
Hart Mountain Refuge	3692	42	33	119	39	5620	Lake
Hermiston 2 S	3847	45	49	119	16	620	Umatilla
Honeyman State Pk	3995	43	55	124	6	120	Lane
Hood River Exp Stn	4003	45	40	121	31	500	Hood River
John Day	4291	44	25	118	57	3060	Grant
Klamath Falls 2 SSW	4506	42	12	121	46	4100	Klamath
La Comb 3 NNE	4606	44	37	122	43	520	Linn
La Grande	4622	45	19	118	4	2760	Union
Lakeview 2 NNW	4670	42	13	120	22	4780	Lake
Madras 2 N	5142	44	40	121	9	2440	Jefferson
Malheur Branch Exp St	5160	43	58	117	1	2230	Malheur
Malheur Refuge Hdq	5162	43	16	118	49	4110	Harney
Medford WSO AP	5429	42	22	122	52	1310	Jackson
Milton Freewater	5593	45	57	118	25	970	Umatilla
Moro	5734	45	28	120	43	1870	Sherman
Newport	6032	44	34	124	3	140	Lincoln
North Bend FAA AP	6073	43	25	124	15	10	Coos
Ochoco R S	6243	44	24	120	25	3980	Crook
Otis 2 NE	6366	45	1	123	55	150	Lincoln
Paisley	6426	42	42	120	31	4360	Lake
Pendleton WSO AP	6546	45	40	118	51	1490	Umatilla
Portland WSO AP	6751	45	36	122	36	20	Washington
Riddle	7169	42	57	123	21	680	Douglas
Rome 2 Nw	7310	42	52	117	39	3410	Malheur
Roseburg Kqen	7331	43	12	123	21	470	Douglas
St Helens RFD	7466	45	52	122	49	100	Columbia
Salem WSO AP	7500	44	55	123	1	200	Marion
Seneca	7675	44	7	118	58	4660	Grant
Silver Creek Falls	7809	44	52	122	39	1350	Marion
Sisters	7857	44	18	121	33	3180	Deschutes
Squaw Butte Exp Stn	8029	43	28	119	43	4660	Harney
Stayton	8095	44	46	122	49	430	Marion
The Dalles	8407	45	36	121	12	100	Wasco
Tillamook 1 W	8494	45	27	123	52	10	Tillamook
Toketee Falls	8536	43	16	122	27	2060	Douglas
Ukiah	8726	45	7	118	55	3360	Umatilla
Whitehorse Ranch	9290	42	19	118	13	4200	Harney
Wickiup Dam	9316	43	40	121	40	4360	Deschutes

Oregon Weather Records

Highest temperature: 119°F	Pendleton	July 29, 1898
	Prineville	August 10, 1898
Lowest temperature: -54°F	Seneca	February 10, 1933
	Ukiah	February 9, 1933
Wettest day: 11.65 inches	Port Orford 5E	November 19, 1996
Wettest month: 52.78 inches	Glenora	December 1917
Wettest year: 204.12 inches	Laurel Mountain	1996
Driest year: 3.33 inches	Warm Springs Reservoir	1939
Greatest 1-day snowfall: 39 inches	Bonneville Dam	January 9, 1980
Greatest 1-month snowfall: 313 inches	Crater Lake	January 1950
Greatest annual snowfall: 903 inches	Crater Lake	1950
Highest wind speed: 131 mph	Mt. Hebo	October 12, 1962
Lowest pressure: 28.51 inches	Astoria	December 12, 1995

—Port Orford 5E is the station 5 miles east of Port Orford

PART 1

Large-scale Influences on Oregon's Weather and Climate

O   regon's weather and climate result from an interplay of
            warm and cold air, marine and continental air, and the
            large-scale circulation of the atmosphere. On any given
day, one or more of these influences may predominate, but over longer
periods of time they become more consistent. The climate is affected by the
general circulation of the atmosphere on a planetary scale; but local
weather conditions can be very significantly affected by regional and local
influences.

General Circulation of the Atmosphere

The circulation of the atmosphere is driven by differences in temperature
between the tropics and the poles. Since the sun shines more directly on the
tropical latitudes, temperatures there are consistently warm throughout the
year. Near the poles, however, the sun's rays are much less direct. This is
especially true in winter, when the sun is very low on the horizon (in mid-
winter, above the Arctic and Antarctic Circles, the sun does not rise at all).
Summer temperatures in these latitudes are generally quite mild, however,
due to a higher sun angle and very long days.

In the atmosphere, temperature differences create air flow. The
atmosphere continually attempts to reach equilibrium, with warm air
moving to colder areas and cold air to warmer, keeping the atmosphere in a
somewhat steady, though imbalanced, state. Were it not for this fact, the
tropics would get warmer and warmer and the poles colder and colder. The
greater the difference in temperature, the greater the tendency for
temperature balance to occur, and thus the greater the north-south air flow.

North-south temperature differences also result in changes in wind
speeds. In general, the greater the temperature difference, the higher the
wind speeds. Winds are caused by differences in atmospheric pressure,
which generally coincide with differences in temperature. The highest
temperature differences (which occur in winter) thus produce the highest
wind speeds (on a global basis). In mid-latitudes, where Oregon lies, these
winds blow generally from west to east.

Often there is a very strong demarcation line between the colder polar air
and warmer tropical air. The more sudden the transition, and the greater
the difference in temperature, the stronger the winds tend to be. The
strongest winds of all occur in the upper atmosphere above these transition
areas, and are known as "jet streams." Typical jet streams are swift air
currents hundreds (or even thousands) of miles long, less than 100 miles
wide, and less than a mile thick. Speeds often exceed 115 mph and
sometimes surpass 275 mph. The highest speeds usually occur at the top of
the troposphere, the lowest layer in the atmosphere, at roughly 40,000 feet
above sea level. The jet stream is also significant because (1) it delineates the
"line" between the cold polar and warm tropical air; and (2) it represents
the path along which storms tend to travel, and thus is often called the
"storm track."

Seasonal Changes

North-south variations in temperature are not constant throughout the year, however. In winter, the temperature difference between the equator and the pole is very high. In the Northern Hemisphere, consider, for example, Guayaquil, Ecuador (very near the equator) and Fairbanks, Alaska. In July, Guayaquil's average temperature is 79°F and Fairbanks' is 63°F, a difference of 16°F. In January, on the other hand, the difference is huge: steady Guayaquil averages 78°F and Fairbanks - 10°, a difference nearly six times larger than in July. These differences are typical of winter months, and promote very active movement of warm air northward and cold air southward. Greater temperature differences also cause a more vigorous jet stream, yielding more storms and stronger west-to-east winds than during the warm season.

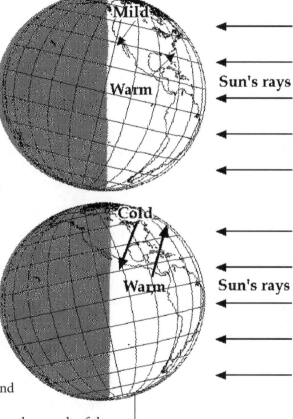

In summer, on the other hand, the temperature difference between the tropics and polar regions reaches an annual minimum. The prevailing west-to-east winds decrease in intensity and high pressure forms at the surface over the eastern Pacific west of Oregon. The only real temperature contrast is between the perpetually frozen polar regions and high latitudes, such as Fairbanks. Thus, the jet stream and storm track remain far to the north of Oregon, and are usually rather passive. Another result of the lower temperature gradient is that the tropics and poles have very little influence on Oregon's weather due to reduced north-south circulation. During summer, most of Oregon's weather comes from locations at similar latitudes, such as the North Pacific.

Figure 1 illustrates the contrast between the angle of the sun's rays in summer and in winter, which produces seasonal changes in temperature. North-south air movement is much more vigorous during the high-contrast winter months. Figure 2 shows the typical position of the high pressure area offshore during summer, as well as average wind directions surrounding the high; a corresponding high off the east coast

Figure 1. Seasonal changes in the angle of the sun's rays and resulting effects on temperatures and circulation. In the Northern Hemisphere summer (top), high-latitude temperatures are mild, and north-south air flow minimal because of low temperature gradient. In winter (bottom), very cold polar temperatures cause a large temperature gradient and thus very active north-south air flow.

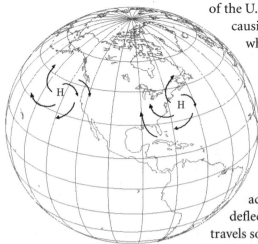

Figure 2. Typical position of the semi-permanent high-pressure cells over the North Atlantic and North Pacific in summer, and resultant wind directions.

of the U.S. brings warm, moist air from the subtropics, causing the often uncomfortable high humidity for which that area is renowned. Oregon, however, is affected predominantly by cooler air from the North Pacific.

Ocean surface currents off Oregon respond primarily to surface winds, just as they do throughout the world. The clockwise air flow around the oceanic summer high-pressure cell leads to a southward-moving current along the West Coast. "Coriolis" acceleration caused by the earth's rotation deflects surface water to the right—offshore—as it travels southward along the coast. As a result, cool subsurface water is pulled up along the shoreline, a process known as "upwelling." This cool water is rich in nutrients, supporting abundant marine life. It also exerts a strong influence on the coastal summer climate, causing it to be generally very mild (sometimes downright cold!), with frequent fog and cool sea breezes.

Oregon Climate and the Seasons

As the seasons change, so does Oregon's climate.

Inland during summer the daytime air temperatures are usually much warmer than along the coast. High temperatures in the Willamette Valley and in much of eastern Oregon average in the low 80s, but in some low-elevation valleys temperatures 5-10°F higher are common (Medford, Pendleton, Roseburg, and Ontario are often the warmest cities in Oregon during summer). The warm inland temperatures create low pressure near the surface, which strengthens the offshore-onshore pressure gradient and helps to maintain the typical sea breeze circulation.

At night in summer, the land cools off much more quickly than does the water, which remains nearly the same temperature. In most cases, onshore minimum temperatures are lower than ocean temperatures. For example, the average low temperature in July in Salem is 50.9°, which is cooler than average ocean temperatures at that time of year. This reversal of the temperature gradient causes a pressure gradient shift as well, with lower pressure offshore and higher pressure onshore. The result is an offshore, or "land" breeze blowing generally from east to west at night. These nighttime summer land breezes are typically much weaker than daytime sea breezes because the temperature/pressure gradients are much lower at night than during the day.

As autumn approaches there are strong changes in atmospheric circulation in the Northern Hemisphere. Offshore, the subtropical high-pressure cells move southward and become weaker. Southward-flowing coastal currents weaken and eventually stop, and are replaced by winter currents that flow northward along the coast. Upwelling no longer occurs.

As the season progresses to winter, the storm track becomes more active and migrates south. In October, Washington is often hit with storms which merely brush by Oregon. But October is a big transition month in Oregon. Early in the month, mild "Indian summer" days are common, and the probability of precipitation in western Oregon is only about 30%. By the end of the month, however, early winter has usually arrived. Precipitation probabilities have risen to 60%, temperatures have dropped considerably, and there is a 50-50 chance that the first frost of the season has occurred.

As winter progresses, the month of greatest precipitation steadily moves southward. In northern Washington, October is generally the wettest month; in Oregon, December and January are the wettest, while in California the maximum average occurs in February.

As the season further progresses to spring, the most active weather zone (the storm track) begins to slowly move back toward high latitudes and decrease in intensity. This is a very gradual process, taking several months to complete, during which time the frequency of storms diminishes. Sometimes spring seems agonizingly long, and compared with autumn it is very slow indeed. While the autumn transition lasts about a month (the month of October), spring extends from the end of February until late May or early June, at least in western Oregon.

Air Masses

An air mass is a large body of air that has similar moisture and temperature characteristics. Oregon is affected by air masses arriving from each compass direction, and our weather results largely from the nature and origin of the air mass that is present at any given time. There are six primary source regions for Oregon air masses (Figure 3 shows their approximate location relative to Oregon). The air masses, and their typical influence on Oregon weather, are:

Pacific. Western Oregon is dominated by Pacific marine air. This is consistently true near the coast, often true in the Willamette Valley, but less true as one moves farther inland. Nonetheless, storms from the Pacific produce the vast majority of Oregon's precipitation and the influence of mild maritime air causes temperatures to be much more moderate, by and large, than they are in inland states. Oregon is often under the influence of weather from this direction for weeks at a time in winter, with storm after storm affecting the area. Typically, storms arrive here about every three days.

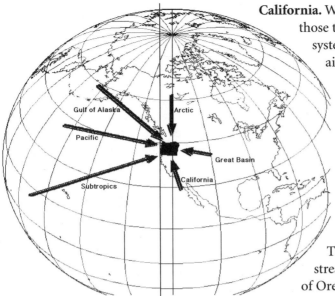

Figure 3. Air masses affecting Oregon, and their source regions.

California. Winds from the south (such as those that occur in advance of a storm system) bring generally warm, dry air to Oregon. In summer, air masses reaching Oregon by way of California often produce thunderstorms, especially in eastern Oregon.

The subtropics. When upper-level winds are strong and from the southwest, Oregon may be under the influence of warm, moist air from the subtropics. The results of the subtropical jet stream can be very wet; in fact, most of Oregon's wettest weather, and many of its winter floods, result from subtropical moisture. Recent examples include the very large floods of February and November, 1996 (see Flood chapter). Many people call these subtropical air masses the "Pineapple Express," since they appear to originate near Hawaii, although often the moisture comes from beyond Hawaii, much farther south and west. The mild air raises freezing levels (sometimes over 10,000 feet), causing snow to melt rapidly. Combined with high rainfall, the snowmelt contributes significantly to big flood events.

Gulf of Alaska. Occasionally the upper-level winds bring modified polar air into Oregon from the northwest. This is air from the Arctic regions, tempered slightly by the North Pacific, but still cold and damp.

Inland polar regions. Oregon's coldest temperatures occur when cold, dry air from the Arctic moves into the state. Most of the time, the Cascades and other mountain ranges prevent this air from reaching western Oregon, and the coldest temperatures remain east of the Cascades. Occasionally, however, the arctic air penetrates the westside areas, either through the Columbia Gorge or by way of Puget Sound, producing cold, often snowy weather.

Great Basin. During summer, air from the Great Basin can be hot and dry (if it comes from the east or southeast) or warm and moist (if it brings moisture from the south by way of Arizona or Nevada). Winter air from this direction is cold and dry (although generally milder than the arctic air masses).

PART 2

Climate Elements

Precipitation

Moist air moving into Oregon from the Pacific brings abundant precipitation (by definition, rain plus melted snow and ice) to the Oregon coast. As a result, coastal areas average 70-90 inches a year at sea level, and some of the Coast Range peaks approach 200 inches per year. As air crosses the Coast Range and drops into the Willamette Valley, it warms slightly and gets a bit drier, and annual precipitation is reduced to about 30-60 inches per year. The steep ascent up the very high Cascades barrier cools the air, causing condensation (and precipitation) averaging 80 to 120 inches per year, much of it in the form of snow. By the time Pacific air reaches eastern Oregon, most of the water has already fallen as rain or snow in western Oregon. For that reason, most of Oregon east of the Cascades is rather dry: valley locations generally receive 8-15 inches of precipitation per year, while the highest peaks exceed 30 inches (a few get more than 50 inches). Figure 4 shows an idealized cross-section of Oregon, illustrating the generalized west-to-east distribution in precipitation.

Seasonal Characteristics

Unlike subtropical regions, where the wet season tends to occur during summer, the mid-latitude coastal areas and inland valleys of Oregon receive the bulk of their annual precipitation during winter. In western Oregon, the wettest months are generally from November through March. Although significant precipitation can occur during the warm season, average totals during those months are generally lower than during winter. East of the

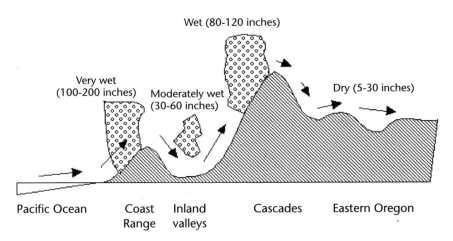

Figure 4. Cross-section of Oregon, showing west-to-east distribution of precipitation.

Wet (80-120 inches)

Very wet (100-200 inches)

Moderately wet (30-60 inches)

Dry (5-30 inches)

Pacific Ocean   Coast Range   Inland valleys   Cascades   Eastern Oregon

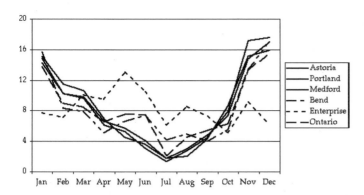

Figure 5. Percentage of annual precipitation for each month at six Oregon sites.

Cascades, however, the seasonal distribution is quite different. Relatively low winter totals are nearly matched by rain from summer thunderstorms, which are much more common than in western areas. Thus, much of eastern Oregon receives almost uniform precipitation throughout the year.

This is illustrated in Figure 5, which shows the percentage of annual precipitation occurring each month at six sites throughout the state. Notice how all three western Oregon stations (Astoria, Medford, and Portland) have similar distributions, with very low precipitation in the warm season, while the three eastern Oregon locations (Bend, Enterprise, and Ontario) receive significant precipitation during late spring and summer. Table 1 shows the percentage of annual precipitation occurring each month at sites throughout the state. Table 2 shows the actual monthly averages.

Spatial Distribution

The most important factors influencing annual average precipitation in the region are elevation and distance from the coast. Locally, elevation is the most important factor; on a regional basis, however, distance from the coast becomes increasingly important.

Although air masses in the Northwest contain sufficient amounts of water to allow precipitation to occur at sea level and over flat terrain, the effects of the mountain ranges—known as orographic influences—on precipitation are very significant. The primary effect is to cause precipitation to increase with elevation, so in general, the higher the elevation, the greater the precipitation. Orographic effects typically operate at large spatial scales, responding to smoothed topographic features rather than detailed variations in terrain. Thus, a major terrain barrier such as the Coast Range or Cascades results in abundant orographic precipitation, even though small ridges and valleys embedded in a mountain range may not show demonstrable effects.

Table 1. Average precipitation in selected Oregon cities (by climate zone) showing percentage of annual precipitation each month

Zone	Station	County	Elev. (ft)	Jan	Feb	Mar	Apr	May	Jun	Jul	Aug	Sep	Oct	Nov	Dec
1	Astoria	Clatsop	10	15	11	11	7	5	4	2	2	4	9	15	16
1	Brookings	Curry	70	15	12	13	7	5	2	1	2	3	8	16	17
2	Corvallis	Benton	225	16	12	11	6	5	3	1	2	4	7	16	18
2	Eugene	Lane	364	15	12	11	8	5	3	1	2	3	7	16	17
2	Portland	Multnomah	20	15	10	10	7	6	4	2	3	5	7	15	17
3	Ashland	Jackson	1750	12	9	10	8	7	5	2	3	5	8	15	16
3	Medford	Jackson	1300	14	10	10	6	5	3	1	3	5	8	17	18
3	Roseburg	Douglas	465	16	11	11	7	4	3	1	2	4	7	17	17
4	Detroit Dam	Marion	1220	15	12	11	8	6	4	1	2	4	7	15	16
4	Government Camp	Hood River	3980	16	12	10	8	5	4	1	2	4	7	14	16
4	McKenzie Bridge RS	Lane	1478	15	11	11	8	5	4	1	2	4	8	15	16
5	Crater Lake	Klamath	6475	15	12	12	7	5	3	1	2	4	7	16	17
5	Silver Lake RS	Lake	4380	10	7	8	7	9	9	5	7	6	7	13	12
6	Hood River	Hood River	500	15	12	8	8	4	3	1	1	2	9	20	17
6	Moro	Sherman	1870	13	9	9	7	7	5	3	4	5	7	15	16
6	Pendleton	Umatilla	1492	13	9	10	9	8	5	3	4	5	7	13	14
7	Bend	Deschutes	3660	16	8	8	5	7	7	4	5	4	6	13	17
7	Burns	Harney	4140	7	10	14	7	9	6	5	4	5	7	12	12
7	Klamath Falls	Klamath	4098	13	9	10	6	6	5	3	5	4	8	15	16
8	Enterprise	Wallowa	3880	8	7	10	9	13	10	6	9	7	5	9	6
8	John Day	Grant	3063	9	6	8	9	12	10	4	7	6	7	11	10
8	La Grande	Union	2755	12	9	9	8	10	8	4	5	6	7	11	11
9	Ontario	Malheur	2145	14	9	8	7	8	7	2	5	5	6	13	15
9	Rome	Malheur	3410	7	6	10	9	13	13	4	6	7	7	10	8

Averages are based on 1961-1990 data

Table 2. Average precipitation in selected Oregon cities (by climate zone) showing total monthly precipitation (in inches)

Zone, station (co.)	Elev. (ft)	Jan	Feb	Mar	Apr	May	Jun	Jul	Aug	Sep	Oct	Nov	Dec	Year
1 Astoria (Clatsop)	10	10.00	7.59	7.07	4.61	3.02	2.40	1.16	1.33	2.91	5.73	10.05	10.55	66.42
1 Brookings (Curry)	70	10.85	9.03	9.49	5.30	3.64	1.55	.53	1.31	2.15	5.84	11.52	12.23	73.44
2 Corvallis (Benton)	225	6.82	5.04	4.55	2.56	1.95	1.23	.52	.87	1.51	3.11	6.82	7.72	42.70
2 Eugene (Lane)	364	7.03	5.38	5.17	3.60	2.20	1.22	.46	.80	1.32	3.35	7.51	7.86	45.90
2 Portland (Multnomah)	20	5.35	3.68	3.54	2.39	2.06	1.48	.63	1.09	1.75	2.66	5.34	6.13	36.10
3 Ashland (Jackson)	1750	2.37	1.72	1.95	1.61	1.29	.91	.32	.58	.95	1.60	2.82	3.06	19.18
3 Medford (Jackson)	1300	2.69	1.93	1.82	1.16	1.00	.58	.26	.52	.86	1.49	3.23	3.32	18.86
3 Roseburg (Douglas)	465	5.13	3.70	3.56	2.24	1.43	.83	.43	.73	1.24	2.23	5.36	5.47	32.35
4 Detroit Dam (Marion)	1220	12.79	10.24	9.42	6.54	4.87	3.27	.90	1.60	3.56	6.42	13.21	13.98	86.80
4 Government Camp (Hood River)	3980	13.65	10.01	8.92	7.15	4.75	3.42	1.13	1.83	3.90	6.13	11.92	14.01	86.82
4 McKenzie Bridge RS (Lane)	1478	9.88	7.33	7.03	5.02	3.58	2.59	.85	1.44	2.93	5.08	10.01	10.76	66.50
5 Crater Lake (Klamath)	6475	9.66	7.78	8.09	4.60	3.01	1.98	.68	1.29	2.38	4.75	10.56	10.84	65.62
5 Silver Lake RS (Lake)	4380	.89	.68	.76	.63	.86	.85	.50	.61	.58	.63	1.20	1.10	9.29
6 Hood River (Hood River)	500	4.56	3.59	2.50	2.47	1.10	.91	.44	.27	.64	2.69	5.95	5.28	30.40
6 Moro (Sherman)	1870	1.49	.98	1.04	.78	.77	.59	.28	.47	.54	.75	1.66	1.74	11.09
6 Pendleton (Umatilla)	1492	1.51	1.14	1.16	1.04	.99	.64	.35	.53	.59	.86	1.58	1.63	12.02
7 Bend (Deschutes)	3660	1.83	.97	.92	.60	.77	.86	.49	.58	.47	.65	1.57	1.99	11.70
7 Burns (Harney)	4140	.81	1.17	1.60	.80	1.07	.67	.52	.43	.62	.78	1.41	1.41	11.29
7 Klamath Falls (Klamath)	4098	1.81	1.28	1.35	.75	.85	.69	.35	.62	.55	1.07	1.97	2.23	13.52
8 Enterprise (Wallowa)	3880	1.26	1.17	1.65	1.55	2.15	1.72	1.00	1.40	1.19	.84	1.50	1.00	16.43
8 John Day (Grant)	3063	1.15	.82	1.12	1.21	1.56	1.40	.53	.95	.84	.92	1.47	1.40	13.37
8 La Grande (Union)	2755	1.96	1.47	1.48	1.42	1.61	1.43	.63	.92	.97	1.24	1.86	1.86	16.85
9 Ontario (Malheur)	2145	1.33	.87	.82	.63	.73	.72	.20	.44	.53	.61	1.30	1.50	9.68
9 Rome (Malheur)	3410	.58	.50	.83	.69	1.01	1.05	.36	.46	.58	.55	.82	.63	8.06

Averages are based on 1961-1990 data

11

There are many methods of interpolating precipitation from monitoring stations to grid points. Some provide estimates of acceptable accuracy in flat terrain, but none have been able to adequately explain the complex variations in precipitation that occur in mountainous regions. Inadequacies in these methods are typically overcome by adding numerous estimated "pseudo-stations" to the data set and tediously modifying the resulting output by hand. Even then, there is no provision for easily updating precipitation maps with new data or developing maps for other years or months.

Significant progress in mapping precipitation has recently been achieved through the development of PRISM (Precipitation-elevation Regressions on Independent Slopes Model) by Chris Daly of Oregon State University. PRISM is an analytical model that uses point data and a digital elevation model to generate gridded estimates of monthly and annual precipitation. PRISM is uniquely suited to regions with mountainous terrain, because it incorporates a conceptual framework that allows the spatial scale and pattern of orographic precipitation to be quantified and generalized (Daly, et al. 1994).

PRISM is currently being used to produce new precipitation maps for every state in the U.S. Unfortunately, maps for British Columbia and Alaska are not in preparation at this time, but new maps of southern Oregon are already available. Figure 6 shows a simplified map of annual average precipitation in Oregon. As can be seen, the immediate coastal areas are quite wet (averaging 60 to 80 inches per year), but much higher precipitation amounts occur somewhat inland at higher elevations. Some high elevation sites in the Coast Range receive over 150 inches per year.

Long-term Distribution

Precipitation in Oregon can vary significantly from year to year. However, the records indicate a number of longer-term cyclical patterns, with relatively dry years and relatively wet years bunched together. Figure 6 shows annual precipitation at Astoria since 1855. Two lines are shown: the thinner represents annual total for the Water Year, October through September, ending on the year shown, while the thicker line is a 5-year (centered) running average of the annual values. The annual variations are clearly seen, as are the multi-year trends. For example, the early 1930s had a number of wet years in a row, causing a notable peak in the 5-year values. Other unusually wet periods occurred around 1880, 1900, 1920, and 1950. The early 1990s were among the driest on record, with the lowest 5-year average during the entire period.

Although many of the long-term trends at other sites in the study area are somewhat different from Astoria's, one fact is common to the whole state: every site experiences periods of generally wet conditions and generally dry conditions spanning multiple years. In addition, variations from one year to the next tend to be fairly large.

Figure 6. Water year precipitation, Astoria, 1854-1996. Thin line shows annual totals, thick line 5-year running averages.

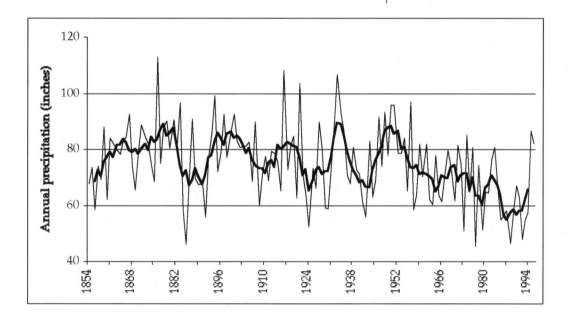

Stream Flows

Especially on an annual basis, undisturbed stream flows are highest during the wettest years, and reach their minimum values during dry periods. During this century, many of the rivers and streams in the state have been dammed, for hydroelectric or flood control purposes (or both). This has served to make stream flows more uniform, by mitigating the highest flows in winter and spring and maintaining higher minimum flows in summer and autumn.

Over the past fifty years, increases in reservoir storage capacity on the Columbia River system have intercepted the huge spring snowmelt peak, reducing the large late spring pulse of fresh water emptied into the sea near Astoria, and through this delay increasing the amount of fresh water sent to the sea in autumn and early winter. The freshwater plume that used to travel south on summer ocean currents has been reduced, and the northward-flowing plume in winter has increased. Decreases in salinity along the coast have consequently been noted as far as six hundred miles north of the mouth of the Columbia River. The consequences to estuarine environments are unknown.

Frequency of Precipitation

Although the entire state can be considered "wet" by most standards, sites in the south experience significantly fewer days with measurable precipitation than those farther north. Table 3 shows the average number of days with measurable precipitation for stations throughout the state. While the southernmost stations receive about 120 days per year with .01 inches or more, the more northerly locations receive nearly double that amount.

Table 3. Average number of days with measurable precipitation (.01 inch or more) at selected Oregon locations.

Station (number)	Zone	Jan	Feb	Mar	Apr	May	Jun	Jul	Aug	Sep	Oct	Nov	Dec	Year
Astoria WSO AP (328)	1	22	19	21	18	15	12	8	8	10	15	21	22	190
Bandon 2 NNE (471)	1	20	18	20	16	12	9	4	6	8	12	20	21	167
Brookings (1055)	1	17	16	18	13	9	6	4	5	6	11	18	18	141
Newport (6032)	1	20	18	21	17	14	11	7	8	10	15	21	22	187
North Ben (6073)	1	19	17	20	16	12	9	4	6	7	12	20	20	160
Tillamook 1 W (8494)	1	21	19	21	18	15	10	7	7	11	15	21	23	187
Bonneville Dam (897)	2	20	18	20	17	14	10	5	6	9	13	20	21	172
Eugene WSO AP (2709)	2	17	15	16	12	10	6	3	4	6	10	17	18	134
Forest Grove (2997)	2	19	17	17	14	12	8	4	4	7	12	19	20	154
Portland WSO AP (6751)	2	18	15	17	14	12	9	4	5	8	12	19	19	151
Salem WSO AP (7500)	2	17	15	17	13	11	7	3	4	7	11	18	19	143
Silver Creek Falls (7809)	2	19	16	19	16	13	9	4	5	8	13	19	19	163

Station (number)	Zone	Jan	Feb	Mar	Apr	May	Jun	Jul	Aug	Sep	Oct	Nov	Dec	Year
Grants Pass (3445)	3	15	14	16	11	7	4	2	3	5	9	16	17	118
Medford WSO AP (5429)	3	13	11	12	10	7	5	2	3	4	7	14	14	101
Riddle (7169)	3	16	15	16	13	8	6	2	3	5	9	17	17	126
Roseburg KQEN (7331)	3	18	15	17	14	9	6	2	3	6	10	18	18	137
Toketee Falls (8536)	3	17	16	19	16	11	8	3	4	7	11	18	18	149
Belknap Springs (652)	4	18	16	19	17	13	9	4	5	8	13	19	19	160
Detroit Dam (2292)	4	20	18	20	18	15	10	5	5	9	13	21	21	176
Government Camp (3402)	4	20	18	20	18	15	10	5	6	9	13	20	20	172
Santiam Pass (7559)	4	20	18	18	16	12	10	5	6	9	12	18	21	164
Crater Lake (1946)	5	17	16	19	14	10	8	3	5	6	10	17	18	142
Fremont 5 NW)3095)	5	8	7	9	6	5	6	2	3	3	5	9	9	74
Wickiup Dam (9316)	5	13	11	12	8	7	6	4	4	5	7	13	13	103
Antelope 1 NW (197)	6	10	9	11	8	7	6	3	4	4	6	12	11	91
Hermiston 2 S (3847)	6	11	9	9	7	6	5	3	4	4	6	12	12	87
Hood River Exp Stn (4003)	6	16	14	14	12	8	6	3	4	6	10	18	17	128
Moro (5734)	6	11	9	11	8	7	5	3	4	4	7	13	11	91
Pendleton WSO AP (6546)	6	12	11	11	9	7	6	3	4	5	6	12	12	96
The Dalles (8407)	6	12	12	11	7	5	4	2	4	4	7	14	13	94
Bend (694)	7	10	7	8	6	5	5	3	4	4	5	9	10	75
Burns WSO (1175)	7	9	9	13	8	9	6	3	4	5	6	12	10	99
Hart Mountain Refuge (3692)	7	7	7	9	8	8	7	3	4	5	6	9	8	80
Klamath Falls (4506)	7	11	9	11	7	6	5	2	3	3	6	11	12	86
Lakeview (4670)	7	11	10	11	9	8	6	3	3	4	6	11	11	93
Madras (5139)	7	8	8	7	6	5	5	3	3	4	5	9	9	73
Ochoco Ranger Station (6243)	7	9	8	6	6	6	6	3	5	4	6	9	9	75
Sisters Ranger District (7857)	7	10	8	9	7	5	4	3	3	4	6	11	10	82
Squaw Butte Exp. Stn. (8029)	7	8	6	8	5	7	6	3	4	4	5	8	7	69
Austin (356)	8	14	12	13	9	10	8	4	6	6	8	14	15	115
Elgin (2597)	8	14	13	14	11	11	9	5	6	6	9	14	15	130
Enterprise 2 S (2675)	8	11	11	14	12	13	11	7	7	7	7	14	10	120
John Day (4291)	8	11	9	10	10	10	9	3	5	5	7	11	12	101
LaGrande (4622)	8	12	9	12	11	10	9	4	5	6	8	11	11	108
Seneca (7675)	8	10	9	10	8	8	7	3	4	4	6	10	12	88
Ukiah (8726)	8	13	10	11	10	9	8	3	5	5	7	12	12	104
Burns Junction (1174)	9	7	8	7	7	6	5	3	4	4	4	8	7	68
Malheur Branch Exp Stn (5160)	9	9	8	8	6	6	6	2	3	4	5	10	10	76
Rome 2 NW (7310)	9	4	3	4	4	4	4	2	2	3	3	5	4	41

Values represent 1961-1990 averages. WSO AP = Weather Service office, Airport.

Maps

Simplified maps of monthly precipitation in Oregon appear on the
following pages. These were produced by Chris Daly using PRISM (see page
12) and represent the 1961-1990 climate normals.

Figure 7. Oregon precipitation— January

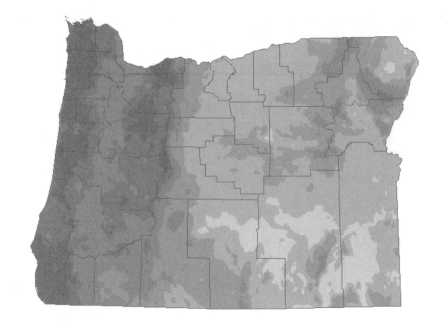

Figure 8. Oregon precipitation— February

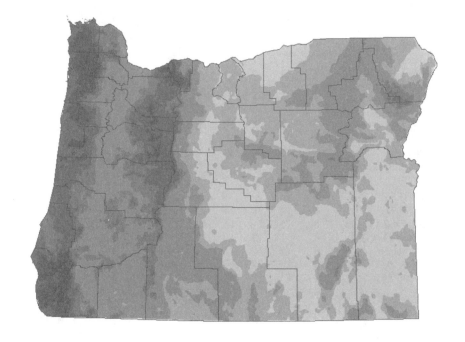

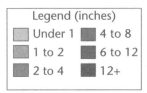

Legend (inches)
- Under 1
- 1 to 2
- 2 to 4
- 4 to 8
- 6 to 12
- 12+

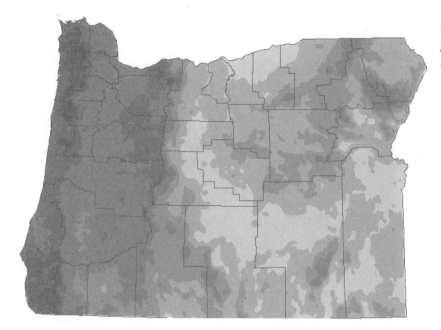

Figure 9. Oregon precipitation— March

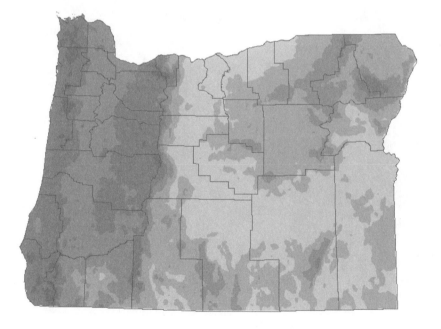

Figure 10. Oregon precipitation—April

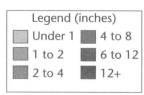

Legend (inches)
Under 1   4 to 8
1 to 2   6 to 12
2 to 4   12+

Figure 11. Oregon precipitation—May

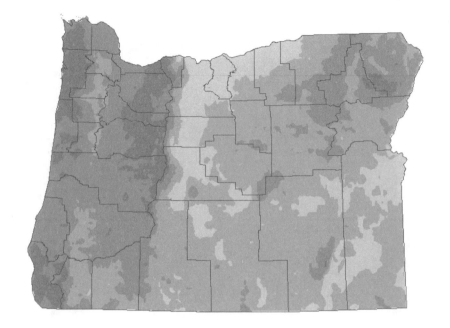

Figure 12. Oregon precipitation—June

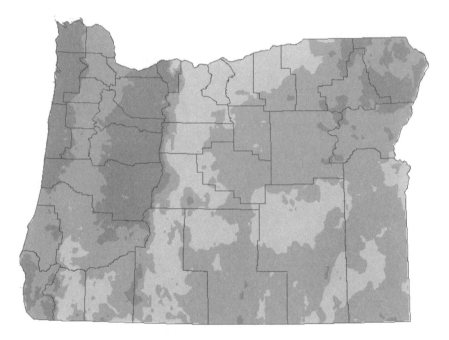

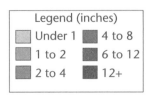

Legend (inches)

	Under 1		4 to 8
	1 to 2		6 to 12
	2 to 4		12+

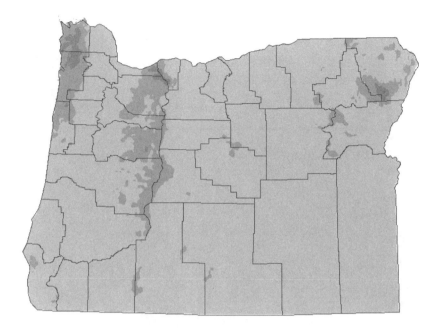

Figure 13. Oregon precipitation—July

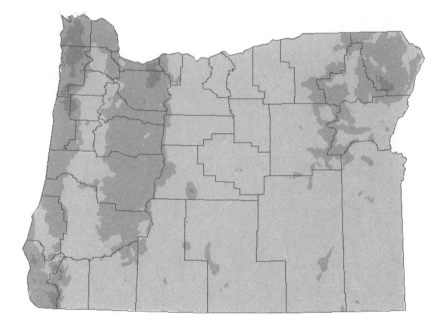

Figure 14. Oregon precipitation— August

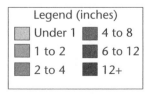

Legend (inches)	
Under 1	4 to 8
1 to 2	6 to 12
2 to 4	12+

Figure 15. Oregon precipitation— September

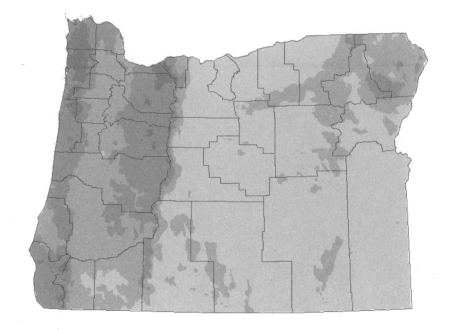

Figure 16. Oregon precipitation— October

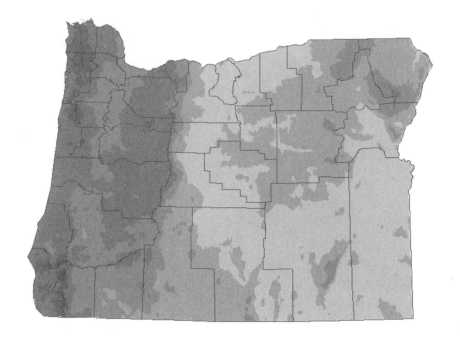

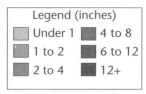

Legend (inches)

Under 1	4 to 8
1 to 2	6 to 12
2 to 4	12+

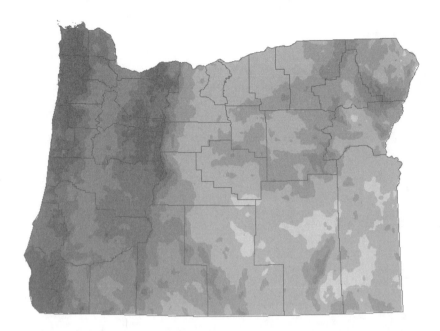

Figure 17. Oregon precipitation— November

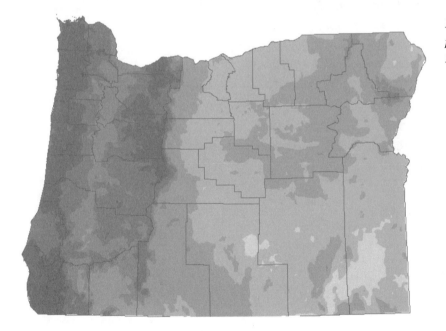

Figure 18. Oregon precipitation— December

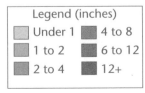

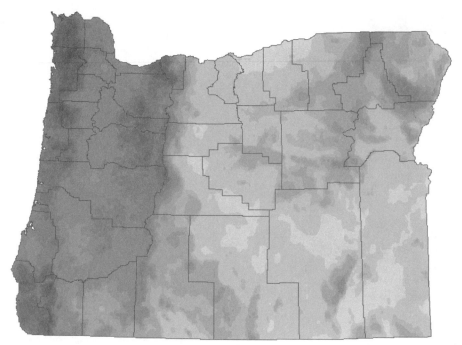

*Figure 19.
Annual average
precipitation in
Oregon.*

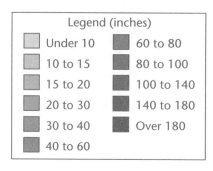

Legend (inches)

	Under 10		60 to 80
	10 to 15		80 to 100
	15 to 20		100 to 140
	20 to 30		140 to 180
	30 to 40		Over 180
	40 to 60		

Temperature

O ut-of-state residents have a stereotype of Oregon's weather: it rains a lot and temperatures are mild. In reality, Oregon has some of the most extreme ranges of temperatures and precipitation anywhere in the United States.

Seasonal and Diurnal Characteristics

The strong marine influence near the coast causes both seasonal and diurnal temperatures to be mild and relatively uniform compared with inland areas. There is a gradual transition from the mild, wet coastal sites to the drier, milder inland valleys. The biggest climatic transition occurs at the Cascade crest. The Cascades effectively divide Oregon into two states: the generally wet, relatively mild western third and the generally dry, more extreme eastern two-thirds. Table 4 lists temperature parameters for three Oregon sites at the same latitude: Newport, on the coast; Corvallis, in the Willamette Valley between the Coast Range and Cascades; and Madras, east of the Cascades. The Coast Range causes temperatures in Corvallis to be more extreme than those at Newport, while the much more significant barrier of the Cascade Mountains causes Madras to be even more extreme than Corvallis.

Table 5 lists monthly and annual mean maximum and minimum temperatures at locations throughout Oregon.

Table 4. Temperature parameters (°F) for three Oregon locations.

Parameter	Newport	Corvallis	Madras
Mean maximum in warmest month	65.1	81.2	87.2
Mean minimum in coldest month	50.0	33.0	21.1
Days with maximum 90°F or more	0.5	13.5	33.3
Days with maximum 32°F or less	0.6	2.7	13.8
Record high temperature	100	108	112
Record low temperature	1	-14	-40
Annual heating degree days @ 65°F	5132	4818	6444
Annual cooling degree days @ 65°F	0	203	277

Table 5. Mean monthly maximum and minimum temperatures (°F), Oregon locations. Values represent 1961-1990 averages.

Station (number)	Jan	Feb	Mar	Apr	May	Jun	Jul	Aug	Sep	Oct	Nov	Dec	Year
Antelope (0197), Zone 6													
Mean max	39.4	45.7	51.6	58.1	66.5	75.8	84.1	83.7	74.8	63.4	48.1	39.9	60.9
Mean min	23.3	27.1	29.8	32.8	38.5	45.8	50.5	50.6	43.8	36.5	29.9	24.5	36.1
Ashland (0304), Zone 3													
Mean max	46.0	52.1	56.1	61.8	69.7	78.5	86.6	85.6	78.5	66.6	52.2	45.3	64.9
Mean min	28.7	31.1	33.1	36.0	41.4	47.8	51.6	51.5	45.3	38.7	33.3	29.5	39.0
Astoria (0328), Zone 1													
Mean max	47.8	51.0	53.2	56.0	60.1	64.1	67.5	68.8	67.8	61.1	53.5	48.2	58.3
Mean min	35.9	37.3	38.1	40.3	44.8	49.5	52.4	52.6	49.0	44.0	40.2	36.6	43.4
Bandon (0471), Zone 1													
Mean max	53.4	55.1	55.6	57.1	60.4	63.7	66.1	67.0	67.1	63.1	57.4	53.5	60.0
Mean min	38.2	39.4	39.7	40.7	43.9	48.1	50.4	50.4	47.7	44.3	41.8	38.7	43.6
Belknap Springs (0652), Zone 4													
Mean max	39.1	44.4	49.6	56.4	64.5	72.8	80.7	80.7	73.9	62.7	47.1	39.0	59.2
Mean min	27.2	29.0	30.6	33.4	38.4	45.0	48.3	48.3	43.5	37.6	32.8	28.4	36.9
Bend (0694), Zone 7													
Mean max	41.6	46.3	51.2	57.5	65.1	73.6	81.4	80.8	73.1	63.1	48.4	41.6	60.3
Mean min	21.8	24.8	26.3	29.3	34.8	41.2	45.2	44.8	37.8	31.6	27.4	22.4	32.3
Brookings (1055), Zone 1													
Mean max	54.8	56.3	57.3	59.6	63.3	66.5	67.7	67.6	68.6	64.4	58.5	54.8	61.6
Mean min	40.9	41.9	41.9	42.8	46.1	49.5	51.2	52.1	51.1	48.2	44.7	41.2	46.0
Burns (1175), Zone 7													
Mean max	33.6	39.5	47.7	56.5	65.6	74.4	85.1	83.3	73.6	61.8	45.2	35.2	58.5
Mean min	13.0	19.3	24.9	29.0	35.9	41.6	47.2	45.0	36.3	28.1	22.0	15.1	29.8
Corvallis OSU (1862), Zone 2													
Mean max	45.5	50.4	54.9	59.5	66.1	73.1	80.2	81.1	75.4	64.3	52.2	45.6	62.4
Mean min	33.0	35.1	37.0	39.2	43.1	48.6	51.0	51.2	47.8	41.7	38.0	33.9	41.6
Crater Lake N.P. (1946), Zone 5													
Mean max	34.5	35.2	36.5	41.7	49.2	58.1	68.0	68.5	61.7	52.0	38.5	34.4	48.2
Mean min	17.5	17.9	18.1	21.1	27.0	33.8	39.8	40.2	35.5	30.1	22.5	18.3	26.8
Drain (2406), Zone 3													
Mean max	47.8	53.2	57.6	62.4	69.1	75.9	82.8	83.1	77.9	66.8	53.9	47.4	64.8
Mean min	33.5	35.4	36.8	38.7	42.8	48.0	49.9	50.2	46.1	42.4	39.0	34.7	41.5
Dufur (2440), Zone 6													
Mean max	40.6	47.6	55.1	62.0	70.3	78.0	85.0	84.5	76.6	64.4	48.7	40.5	62.8
Mean min	24.4	27.8	30.4	33.4	38.4	44.6	48.2	48.3	42.6	35.3	30.3	24.8	35.7
Elgin (2597), Zone 8													
Mean max	36.7	43.7	51.3	59.9	68.9	77.6	87.4	86.9	77.6	64.6	47.4	38.2	61.7
Mean min	20.5	24.2	27.9	31.7	37.4	43.8	45.9	44.9	37.8	30.9	27.8	22.2	32.9
Enterprise (2675), Zone 8													
Mean max	32.8	37.2	47.1	56.1	61.6	70.6	77.6	78.2	68.6	59.0	42.6	31.3	55.4
Mean min	12.2	14.3	23.3	27.9	33.4	39.6	41.5	41.1	33.0	26.5	20.8	10.1	27.1
Eugene (2709), Zone 2													
Mean max	46.4	51.4	55.9	60.5	67.1	74.2	81.7	81.8	76.2	64.6	52.4	46.2	63.2
Mean min	35.2	37.0	38.9	40.6	44.5	49.7	52.8	53.2	49.3	43.5	39.7	35.9	43.4
Forest Grove (2997), Zone 2													
Mean max	45.2	50.7	55.6	60.8	67.8	74.8	80.9	81.9	75.9	64.9	52.2	45.2	63.0
Mean min	31.9	34.3	36.6	39.1	43.8	49.4	52.7	52.4	47.9	41.1	37.1	32.9	41.6
Government Camp (3402), Zone 4													
Mean max	35.4	38.5	40.6	45.1	52.2	60.0	67.7	68.1	62.0	53.4	40.7	36.2	50.0
Mean min	23.6	25.4	26.6	29.6	34.2	40.8	45.5	46.1	41.4	35.7	29.1	24.7	33.6

Station (number)	Jan	Feb	Mar	Apr	May	Jun	Jul	Aug	Sep	Oct	Nov	Dec	Year
Grants Pass (3445), Zone 3													
Mean max	47.6	54.9	60.5	67.0	74.6	82.9	90.1	89.8	83.1	70.3	53.8	46.2	68.4
Mean min	32.7	34.4	36.0	38.4	43.6	49.7	53.1	52.7	46.7	41.2	37.9	33.7	41.7
Hart Mountain Refuge (3692), Zone 7													
Mean max	39.2	41.9	45.0	52.9	62.4	71.5	81.2	80.0	71.4	60.9	46.1	39.6	57.7
Mean min	18.0	21.0	22.2	26.0	32.2	39.1	43.9	43.6	37.0	30.6	24.2	18.4	29.7
Heppner (3827), Zone 6													
Mean max	41.3	47.6	53.7	60.4	69.0	77.9	85.7	84.8	75.4	64.3	50.1	42.0	62.7
Mean min	25.8	29.8	33.2	36.1	42.1	48.6	52.5	52.9	46.1	38.7	32.5	26.4	38.7
Hillsboro (3908), Zone 2													
Mean max	45.3	50.6	55.5	60.3	67.1	73.6	79.7	80.2	74.8	64.2	52.3	45.5	62.4
Mean min	32.5	34.5	36.4	38.8	43.1	49.2	51.8	51.4	46.6	40.6	36.9	33.2	41.3
Honeyman State Park (3995), Zone 1													
Mean max	50.8	53.9	55.8	58.7	62.9	67.0	70.3	70.9	70.8	64.2	55.4	50.5	60.9
Mean min	37.0	38.4	38.6	39.8	43.2	47.9	49.7	50.8	48.8	45.2	41.3	37.6	43.2
Hood River Exp. Stn (4003), Zone 6													
Mean max	40.7	46.8	53.7	60.0	67.5	74.2	80.1	80.5	74.0	63.4	49.3	41.2	61.0
Mean min	28.3	31.2	34.4	38.4	43.8	50.0	53.4	52.8	45.8	38.1	34.4	29.4	40.0
John Day (4291), Zone 8													
Mean max	40.4	47.0	52.7	60.0	68.7	78.3	88.1	87.2	77.6	66.0	50.1	41.8	63.2
Mean min	21.0	25.0	28.4	32.3	38.6	45.2	48.6	47.8	40.4	33.2	28.2	22.1	34.2
Klamath Falls (4506), Zone 7													
Mean max	38.8	45.0	50.3	58.0	67.1	76.2	84.6	83.4	75.5	63.8	47.1	39.0	60.7
Mean min	20.3	24.8	27.7	31.0	38.2	45.6	50.8	49.7	42.7	34.4	27.4	21.6	34.5
Klamath Exp. Stn. (4510), Zone 7													
Mean max	39.2	45.2	50.6	58.3	67.6	76.5	84.9	83.8	76.2	64.1	47.4	39.2	61.2
Mean min	20.4	24.9	27.8	31.1	38.2	45.6	50.9	49.7	42.8	34.6	27.6	21.8	34.7
Lakeview (4670), Zone 7													
Mean max	37.9	42.3	47.4	55.7	65.0	74.1	83.5	82.0	73.8	62.6	46.6	39.0	59.2
Mean min	19.0	23.1	26.3	30.6	37.3	44.6	50.2	48.2	41.1	33.2	26.4	20.6	33.4
Leaburg (4811), Zone 2													
Mean max	46.6	51.8	56.0	60.8	67.2	74.2	81.5	82.1	75.8	65.0	52.5	46.2	63.3
Mean min	32.9	34.8	36.4	38.9	43.1	48.2	50.5	50.5	47.1	42.4	38.1	33.8	41.4
Madras (5142), Zone 7													
Mean max	43.2	49.8	56.2	62.8	71.2	79.8	87.4	87.0	78.4	66.5	51.4	43.2	64.7
Mean min	23.6	26.3	28.2	31.0	36.9	43.2	46.4	45.7	39.2	32.3	28.8	23.7	33.8
Malheur Br. Exp. Stn. (5160), Zone 9													
Mean max	33.4	42.4	54.0	63.4	73.0	82.3	91.1	89.2	78.3	64.7	47.5	35.5	62.9
Mean min	17.9	24.1	30.8	37.0	45.0	52.9	58.1	55.8	46.0	35.6	28.1	20.3	37.6
Malheur NWR HQ (5162), Zone 7													
Mean max	37.3	43.9	50.1	58.5	67.6	76.1	84.9	83.3	75.0	63.4	47.6	38.0	60.5
Mean min	17.3	22.4	25.8	30.0	37.4	44.4	49.3	47.6	38.5	29.9	24.5	17.8	32.1
Medford Exp. Stn. (5424), Zone 3													
Mean max	44.9	52.6	57.7	63.8	71.6	79.9	87.8	87.1	79.9	67.5	51.3	44.1	65.7
Mean min	28.5	30.9	33.8	36.4	41.2	47.6	50.7	50.7	43.9	37.2	33.5	29.7	38.7
Medford (5429), Zone 3													
Mean max	45.7	53.3	58.5	64.6	72.9	82.1	90.5	89.9	82.8	69.4	52.6	44.3	67.2
Mean min	30.4	32.2	35.4	38.0	43.4	50.7	55.2	55.1	48.2	40.4	35.5	31.2	41.3
Moro (5734), Zone 6													
Mean max	37.6	43.7	50.8	57.1	65.1	73.8	81.6	81.3	72.8	61.6	46.7	38.3	59.2
Mean min	24.0	28.3	31.8	35.7	41.5	48.5	53.7	53.2	45.4	36.7	31.0	25.0	37.9
North Bend (6073), Zone 1													
Mean max	51.8	54.0	54.8	56.5	60.2	63.8	66.3	67.1	66.9	63.0	56.9	52.4	59.5
Mean min	38.9	40.5	41.1	42.4	46.6	50.7	52.5	53.0	50.5	46.7	43.2	39.7	45.5

Station (number)	Jan	Feb	Mar	Apr	May	Jun	Jul	Aug	Sep	Oct	Nov	Dec	Year
North Willamette Exp. Stn. (6151), Zone 2													
Mean max	46.1	51.0	55.3	59.7	66.3	73.3	79.8	80.3	74.5	63.9	52.8	46.2	62.4
Mean min	32.4	34.4	36.5	39.5	44.1	49.6	52.4	52.3	48.4	41.4	37.4	33.1	41.8
Ochoco Ranger Station (6243), Zone 7													
Mean max	35.7	41.6	47.8	55.3	63.6	72.8	81.4	81.9	73.1	61.3	43.7	35.6	57.8
Mean min	15.9	19.5	23.0	26.2	31.6	37.7	40.2	40.0	33.7	28.2	23.8	17.5	28.1
Ontario (6294), Zone 9													
Mean max	35.2	44.5	56.2	66.0	76.2	85.9	95.4	93.0	81.5	67.2	49.1	36.8	65.6
Mean min	19.1	24.8	30.6	36.2	44.0	51.6	57.4	54.4	44.2	34.3	28.3	20.5	37.1
Paisley (6426), Zone 7													
Mean max	41.6	47.0	51.3	58.9	67.5	76.0	84.6	83.7	76.1	65.4	49.4	41.7	61.9
Mean min	21.6	25.2	27.3	31.4	38.2	45.3	49.1	48.3	40.6	33.4	26.4	21.8	34.1
Pendleton Br. Exp. Stn. (6540), Zone 6													
Mean max	40.0	46.9	54.1	61.3	69.5	78.8	88.3	87.2	77.3	65.2	49.8	41.1	63.3
Mean min	24.8	29.1	32.4	35.7	41.4	47.5	51.4	51.0	42.9	34.4	31.4	25.6	37.3
Pendleton (6546), Zone 6													
Mean max	39.7	46.9	54.2	61.3	70.0	79.5	87.8	86.2	76.3	63.7	48.9	40.5	62.9
Mean min	27.2	31.6	35.4	39.4	45.8	52.9	58.0	57.7	49.9	41.0	34.1	27.9	41.7
Portland (6751), Zone 2													
Mean max	45.4	51.0	56.0	60.6	67.1	74.0	79.9	80.3	74.6	64.0	52.6	45.6	62.6
Mean min	33.7	36.1	38.6	41.3	47.0	52.9	56.5	56.9	52.0	44.9	39.5	34.8	44.5
Rome 2 NW (7310), Zone 9													
Mean max	39.8	47.9	54.9	63.4	72.9	82.5	92.6	90.7	80.4	68.2	51.5	41.0	65.5
Mean min	17.3	23.3	25.8	30.1	38.4	46.3	51.3	48.6	39.0	30.2	24.2	18.5	32.8
Roseburg KQEN (7331), Zone 3													
Mean max	48.5	53.4	57.8	62.9	69.3	76.5	83.6	84.1	78.1	67.0	54.3	48.0	65.3
Mean min	33.9	35.8	37.7	39.7	44.5	50.3	53.5	54.3	49.3	43.8	39.3	34.8	43.1
Salem (7500), Zone 2													
Mean max	46.4	51.5	55.7	60.4	67.0	74.5	81.6	82.0	76.0	64.2	52.4	46.4	63.2
Mean min	32.7	34.1	35.6	37.7	42.2	48.3	50.9	51.4	47.1	41.1	37.5	33.6	41.0
Seaside (7641), Zone 1													
Mean max	51.1	54.1	55.6	58.0	61.9	65.3	68.2	69.2	69.9	64.4	56.3	51.4	60.5
Mean min	36.7	38.2	38.4	40.6	44.7	48.9	51.6	52.1	49.1	44.7	40.7	37.2	43.6
Silverton (7823), Zone 2													
Mean max	45.7	50.7	54.9	59.1	65.4	72.1	78.6	79.2	73.8	63.3	52.3	45.8	61.7
Mean min	32.8	35.2	37.4	40.1	44.9	50.3	53.4	53.9	49.9	43.4	38.2	33.4	42.7
Squaw Butte Exp. Stn. (8029), Zone 7													
Mean max	35.2	40.8	46.4	54.7	63.6	73.7	82.8	82.3	72.6	61.2	45.0	36.4	57.9
Mean min	18.0	22.5	25.5	29.4	35.8	43.9	50.2	49.7	42.1	34.3	26.0	19.6	33.1
Tillamook (8494), Zone 1													
Mean max	50.0	53.0	54.6	57.0	60.9	64.8	67.3	68.6	68.8	62.9	54.7	49.8	59.4
Mean min	35.7	36.9	36.9	38.5	42.4	46.7	49.2	49.6	46.4	42.2	39.1	36.1	41.6
Toketee Falls (8536), Zone 3													
Mean max	42.0	48.1	53.5	60.8	69.5	78.0	85.7	85.4	77.0	62.9	47.8	41.3	62.7
Mean min	28.8	30.6	32.5	35.4	40.5	46.9	49.9	49.3	43.9	37.9	33.5	29.6	38.2
Union Exp St (8746), Zone 8													
Mean max	36.4	43.0	50.4	57.9	65.6	74.1	83.4	83.7	73.8	62.4	47.3	38.1	59.7
Mean min	23.5	27.4	29.9	33.8	39.4	45.9	49.5	48.7	41.0	34.0	30.6	24.8	35.7
Whitehorse Ranch (9290), Zone 7													
Mean max	40.2	46.3	51.5	59.1	67.8	76.7	86.2	84.1	74.9	65.2	49.7	41.1	61.9
Mean min	17.8	22.0	25.4	30.1	37.4	44.9	50.8	49.9	41.2	33.4	25.0	18.4	33.0
Wickiup Dam (9316), Zone 5													
Mean max	37.7	42.0	46.0	53.2	62.3	71.2	79.9	79.8	71.8	60.9	44.9	37.9	57.3
Mean min	16.9	19.9	23.5	27.8	33.6	40.3	43.6	42.1	35.0	29.0	25.3	18.9	29.7

Long-term Characteristics

Like precipitation, temperature shows significant year-to-year variations as well as noticeable longer-term trends. Figure 20 shows annual average temperatures in Corvallis since 1889. This location has several distinct advantages for evaluation of long-term temperature trends: there has been very little urban development near the station; data records are seldom missing; and there have been very few station relocations.

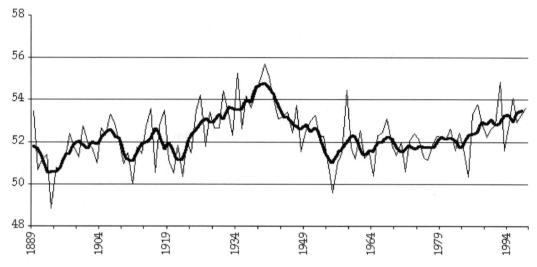

Figure 20. Annual average temperatures (°F) in Corvallis, 1889-1997. Thin line represents annual average. Thick line represents 5-year average.

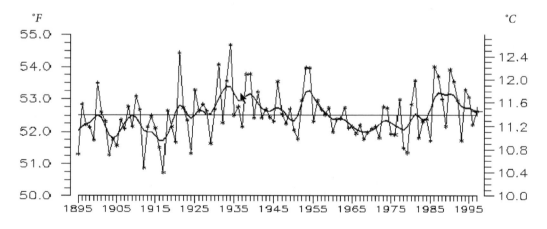

Figure 21. U.S. annual average temperatures, 1895-1997.

Corvallis data show a trend that is commonly seen in U.S. stations that are not subject to local biases, such as urban growth: the warmest temperatures of the century occurred in the late 1930s and early 1940s. This was followed by a cooler period in the next several decades, and warming in the last twenty years; however, temperatures have remained below those observed sixty years ago.

Figure 21 shows U.S. average temperatures from 1985 to 1997 for all Historical Climate Network (HCN) stations. HCN stations (of which Corvallis is one) are long-term, reliable observing sites which have had few moves and little or no nearby changes that would interfere with the recorded data. Notice the similarity between the Corvallis trend and the nationwide data.

Spatial Distribution

Figures 22 through 29 show average maximum and minimum temperatures in Oregon during four months: January, April, July, and October. Note the very mild temperatures throughout the year near the coast: relatively warm in January, when the interior is coldest, and relatively cool in summer.

The maps also demonstrate the effects of the two most significant influences on temperature: elevation and distance from the coast. As one moves upward in elevation, average temperature drops by about 3°F per 1,000 feet. As one moves away from the coast, the daily and annual temperature variation becomes greater and greater.

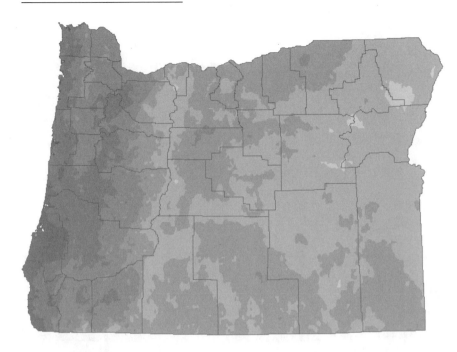

*Figure 22.
Oregon
maximum
temperatures
1961-1990—
January*

*Figure 23.
Oregon
maximum
temperatures
1961-1990—
April*

Legend °F	
Under 42	54 to 58
42 to 50	58 to 62
50 to 54	62+

*Figure 24.
Oregon
maximum
temperatures
1961-1990—July*

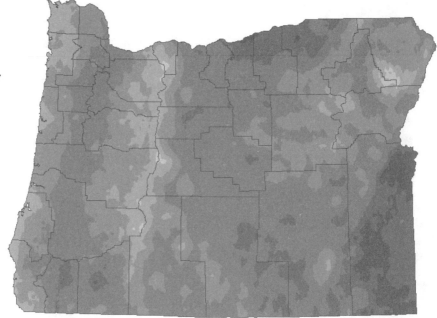

*Figure 25.
Oregon
maximum
temperatures
1961-1990—
October*

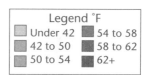

Legend °F
Under 42   54 to 58
42 to 50   58 to 62
50 to 54   62+

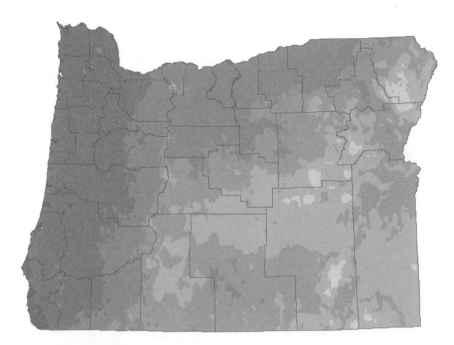

*Figure 26.
Oregon
minimum
temperatures
1961-1990—
January*

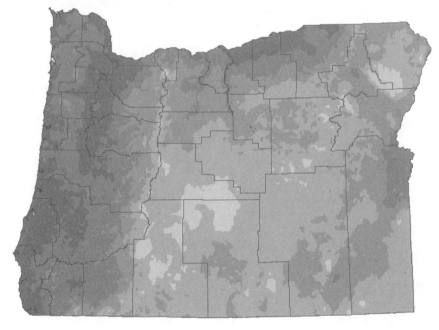

*Figure 27.
Oregon
minimum
temperatures
1961-1990—
April*

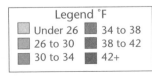

Figure 28. Oregon minimum temperatures 1961-1990—July

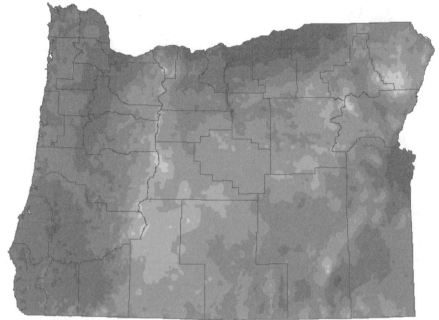

Figure 29. Oregon minimum temperatures 1961-1990— October

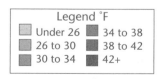

Legend °F	
Under 26	34 to 38
26 to 30	38 to 42
30 to 34	42+

Winds

Local winds in Oregon are dominated by large-scale pressure patterns over the North Pacific and onshore. During winter (and, to a lesser extent, autumn and spring), frequent synoptic-scale cyclonic storms reach the area from the west, greatly influencing winds and other weather elements. Summer months see fewer strong storms, and are more typically characterized by sea and land breezes.

Storm Winds

When the state is under the influence of cyclonic storms, large-scale winds tend to follow a particular pattern, although local terrain influences, and the location and intensity of the storms, can alter this pattern significantly. A typical succession prior to and following the arrival of a storm is as follows:

—As the storm approaches, winds begin to blow from the south or southeast. Wind speeds generally increase as the front associated with the storm gets nearer. For most coastal areas, these pre-frontal periods produce the highest wind speeds observed during the year.

—If passage of a warm front occurs, wind direction often changes, approaching from the southwest. Wind speeds may not change significantly.

—Passage of the cold front causes a sudden increase in pressure, decrease in wind speeds, and change in wind direction. Post-frontal winds are generally from the west and often gusty. Localized disturbances such as thunderstorms often produce local wind effects. These are generally miniature versions of the patterns described here: southerly winds prior to arrival, west winds following passage.

—As the frontal system continues moving eastward, high pressure builds onshore, causing steady decreases in wind speeds and gustiness. If storms are very close together, this step may be skipped entirely.

—Impending arrival of another storm system causes south winds to blow (see first step above) and the process repeats.

During summer, the North Pacific High, a quasi-stationary area of high pressure off the coast, exerts a significant influence on weather in the western U.S. The High moves northward in summer as the jet stream weakens and moves toward the pole. As a result, Pacific storms, which are already less vigorous than those in winter, tend to be diverted to the north.

Extreme Winds

Several times each year, very strong winds hit the coast. Wantz and Sinclair (1981) have published estimates of extreme winds in the Northwest. They estimate that speeds along the coast (sustained for an average of one minute and recurring on average every two years) are as high as 56 mph, while fifty-year events would produce winds of approximately 74 mph. Peak gusts would be about 40% higher. The most damaging storm in recent decades was the Columbus Day storm of October 11-13, 1962, which affected the entire state. During that storm, Naselle, Washington, reported a peak gust of 160 mph, while Mt. Hebo, Oregon, reported 131 mph and Portland, Oregon (Morrison St. Bridge), 116 mph. The storm caused an estimated $250 million and took fifty lives.

Fortunately, the Columbus Day storm was a very rare event. Storms of much lesser magnitude, however, can cause major damage, especially along the coast. This can include the downing of large trees ("wind throw") and other property damage. Although some areas near the coast are sheltered by the terrain, most of the coastal vicinity is quite exposed to wind damage during strong storms.

Prevailing Winds

Prevailing, or average, winds in Oregon vary with the seasons. In winter, the most common wind directions are from the south and east; in summer, they are from the west or northwest. However, local topography plays a significant role in affecting wind direction. For example, winds in the Columbia Gorge follow the east-west orientation of the valley, with general flow from the east in winter and west in summer. In the Willamette Valley, the north-south orientation channels the winds much of the time, causing north and south winds to predominate.

Wantz, J.W., and R.E. Sinclair, 1981. Distribution of Extreme Winds in the Bonneville Power Administration Service Area. *Journal of Applied Meterology*, 20, 1400-11.

Humidity

The presence of the Pacific, combined with generally mild temperatures, causes average relative humidity throughout Oregon to be quite high in the cool season; in coastal areas, it remains high all year. Table 6 shows average relative humidities at 4 p.m. (in general, the minimum values for the day) at several locations in Oregon. The values are quite similar around the state, with the lowest values during summer. During the warm season, the actual amount of water vapor in the air (as measured by dew point temperature rather than relative humidity) is quite low, especially compared with the eastern U.S. Oregon summers are among the most pleasant in the nation due to typically mild temperatures and low humidity.

Table 7 shows average relative humidities four times per day at National Weather Service first-order stations.

Table 6. Average 4 p.m. relative humidity (percent)

Site	Jan	Feb	Mar	Apr	May	Jun	Jul	Aug	Sep	Oct	Nov	Dec	Year
Astoria	78	74	71	69	70	71	69	70	69	73	77	80	73
Baker	78	74	58	46	47	49	36	36	40	51	67	78	55
Bend	64	60	45	39	36	38	32	30	32	47	64	69	46
Burns	68	61	47	35	35	30	21	22	24	36	54	68	42
Eugene	80	73	64	58	54	49	38	39	43	62	79	84	60
Klamath Falls	70	62	51	37	39	37	26	31	33	43	59	74	47
LaGrande	66	64	55	39	42	43	28	31	32	45	59	71	48
Meacham	80	76	71	60	57	54	35	36	45	65	79	84	62
Medford	71	57	50	45	39	33	26	27	29	43	68	76	47
North Bend	80	79	74	73	73	74	73	74	75	79	80	82	76
Ontario	78	61	42	30	30	29	22	23	27	37	58	76	43
Pendleton	75	65	49	42	37	32	23	26	32	46	69	78	48
Portland	75	67	60	55	53	49	45	45	48	62	74	78	59
Redmond	65	56	49	37	38	36	25	28	31	45	57	66	44
Roseburg	78	68	59	52	49	46	38	39	45	61	76	82	58
Salem	79	71	63	54	52	50	39	40	47	64	76	81	60
Sexton Summit	75	65	67	64	52	52	42	40	42	57	77	76	59

Table 7. Average relative humidity (percent), monthly and annual

Station/time	J	F	M	A	M	J	J	A	S	O	N	D	Year
Astoria													
0400 LST	86	87	88	89	90	90	90	91	91	90	88	87	89
1000 LST	84	82	78	74	74	75	75	77	75	81	83	85	79
1600 LST	78	74	71	69	70	71	69	70	69	73	77	80	73
2200 LST	85	86	86	85	85	85	86	88	88	88	87	86	86
Eugene													
0400 LST	92	92	92	91	91	90	88	88	89	94	93	93	91
1000 LST	88	86	78	71	66	63	57	60	65	80	87	89	74
1600 LST	80	73	64	58	54	49	38	39	43	62	79	84	60
2200 LST	91	90	86	83	82	79	73	73	77	88	92	92	84
Medford													
0400 LST	90	88	86	84	83	79	74	75	79	86	92	91	84
1000 LST	88	83	73	63	56	48	45	47	53	69	87	89	67
1600 LST	71	57	50	45	39	33	26	27	29	43	68	76	47
2200 LST	87	82	75	70	65	59	51	52	60	76	88	89	71
Pendleton													
0400 LST	81	79	74	71	69	66	54	54	61	72	79	82	70
1000 LST	78	71	59	51	47	42	34	36	42	55	72	78	55
1600 LST	75	65	49	42	37	32	23	26	32	46	69	78	48
2200 LST	80	77	69	63	58	52	39	41	51	66	78	81	63
Portland													
0400 LST	85	86	86	86	85	84	82	94	87	90	88	87	86
1000 LST	82	80	73	69	66	65	62	64	67	78	82	83	73
1600 LST	75	67	60	55	53	49	45	45	48	62	74	78	59
2200 LST	83	81	78	75	73	71	68	70	75	94	84	85	77

LST = Local Standard Time

Relative humidity is only part of the picture, however. In general, the air over Oregon actually holds relatively small amounts of moisture, at least compared with some other parts of the U.S. Relative humidity is the actual amount of water vapor, compared with how much the air can hold when it's "saturated." And air is saturated when it is holding all the water vapor it can possibly hold. If air is saturated, the relative humidity is 100%.

But saturation depends on air temperature. The warmer the air, the more water the air can hold before reaching saturation. Think of a sponge: the bigger the sponge, the more water it can hold. And warmer air is like having a bigger sponge.

Off the coast of Oregon, the water is always cool (or downright cold). Thus the air over the water is also cool, and its capacity to hold water vapor is restricted. Evaporation is also reduced by the cool water temperatures—the cooler the water, the less evaporation there is. But the water off the southern and eastern U.S. is *much* warmer, especially in summer. Warm water and warm air result in high rates of evaporation, and a high capacity to hold water vapor (a "big sponge").

The best way to actually measure this is by means of "dew point" (or dew point temperature), which represents the actual amount of water vapor in the air. Dew point tells us precisely how much water vapor is in the air, and the greater the amount of water vapor, the higher the dew point. In western Oregon, typical dew points are in the 40s and 50s. In Florida or Georgia, they're often in the 70s. There's more than twice as much water vapor in the air when the dew point is 70 than when it's 50. And that's why it feels so sticky in the east during the summer.

But though dew point is a precise measure of water vapor, relative humidity can be misleading. Consider a rainy winter day in Oregon (easy to imagine), with a temperature of 36°F and 100% relative humidity; thus, a dew point of 36. Now compare that with a hot, dry summer day in Death Valley, with a temperature of 122°F and a bone-dry relative humidity of 7%. If we computed the dew point we'd find it to be 37. But wait, that's *higher* than on the rainy Oregon day. There is actually *more* water vapor in the air on a hot summer day in Death Valley than on a rainy winter day in Oregon, even though the relative humidity is much, much lower in Death Valley.

Table 8 shows average monthly dew point in Oregon and at several stations in the eastern half of the United States. Notice in particular the contrast in the summer dew points.

Table 8. Average monthly dew point (°F).

City	Jan	Feb	Mar	Apr	May	Jun	Jul	Aug	Sep	Oct	Nov	Dec
Portland	**33**	**36**	**37**	**41**	**46**	**50**	**53**	**54**	**51**	**47**	**40**	**36**
Medford	**32**	**34**	**35**	**38**	**42**	**46**	**49**	**49**	**45**	**43**	**37**	**34**
Pendleton	**24**	**30**	**30**	**34**	**40**	**42**	**43**	**43**	**41**	**39**	**33**	**29**
Miami	57	59	61	63	68	72	73	74	74	69	63	58
Atlanta	34	34	39	48	57	65	68	67	62	51	40	34
St. Louis	22	25	30	42	52	62	66	64	56	46	33	26
Washington, D.C.	25	25	29	40	52	61	65	64	59	48	36	26
New York	22	23	27	38	47	57	62	62	56	46	35	26
Boston	19	19	25	34	44	55	60	60	53	44	34	22
Minneapolis	6	10	20	32	43	55	60	59	50	40	25	13

Cloud Cover and Solar Radiation

Near the coast, there is frequent and persistent cloud cover throughout the year. However, cloudiness often drops significantly within a few miles of the coast, especially during the warm season, as a result of air temperature increases. During winter, when the area is dominated by large-scale storm systems, cloud cover tends to be much more uniform throughout the state.

Table 9 shows average monthly cloud cover in Oregon, while Table 10 shows the percentage of possible sunshine for three sites: Portland and Roseburg in western Oregon and Baker in extreme eastern Oregon.

Table 9. Average cloud cover (percent) for selected Oregon stations

Site	Jan	Feb	Mar	Apr	May	Jun	Jul	Aug	Sep	Oct	Nov	Dec	Year
Astoria	85	84	81	81	77	78	67	66	63	74	80	86	77
Baker	69	67	63	59	57	50	28	28	38	45	60	67	53
Burns	76	72	67	63	61	50	25	34	33	49	65	73	56
Eugene	85	81	79	72	67	62	36	44	49	71	83	89	68
Klamath Falls	84	66	64	59	67	43	13	29	25	43	65	75	51
La Grande	81	79	80	64	47	58	20	36	40	58	71	85	61
Meacham	85	84	80	76	62	61	31	39	47	65	80	84	67
Medford	82	76	72	66	69	48	21	23	33	56	75	86	58
North Bend	86	76	75	66	59	61	46	56	55	63	73	82	67
Pendleton	82	80	72	66	61	52	26	33	40	57	77	84	61
Portland	85	84	82	77	60	68	46	53	56	72	81	89	72
Redmond	80	70	70	56	73	53	15	34	30	45	68	72	51
Roseburg	87	84	80	72	50	57	30	38	48	71	85	89	67
Salem	83	82	79	73	68	65	40	47	51	69	80	88	69
Sexton Summit	77	77	77	68	70	48	23	28	35	56	73	77	58
Troutdale	81	84	86	72	62	68	49	52	52	75	81	87	71

Table 10. Monthly percent of possible sunshine

Site	Jan	Feb	Mar	Apr	May	Jun	Jul	Aug	Sep	Oct	Nov	Dec	Year
Baker	41	49	56	61	63	67	83	81	74	62	46	37	60
Portland	24	32	37	47	51	47	67	61	58	38	29	21	45
Roseburg	26	30	39	49	52	61	79	74	68	42	25	20	50

Snow

now is relatively rare along the immediate coastline; as one moves inland or to higher elevation, the amount of snowfall reported per year increases steadily. For example, Laurel Mountain, in the Coast Range at 3590 feet above sea level, averages 110 inches of snow per year. Assuming a ratio of snow to water of 10:1, this represents about 10% of Laurel Mountain's average annual precipitation of 116 inches.

The mildness of the Willamette Valley and other western Oregon inland valleys causes snow to be rare. In the Cascades, however, snow is frequent and significant. Eastern Oregon also receives a significant percentage of its winter precipitation in the form of snow, although the lower annual precipitation makes the actual snowfall amounts much lower than in the Cascades. Table 11 lists average monthly and annual snowfall at various Oregon stations.

Figure 30 shows the average annual snowfall (1961-90 averages) across Oregon. While the Cascades, and mountains in northeast and southwest Oregon, show up as expected, it may surprise many to see the high amounts in the Coast Range; despite their proximity to the ocean, the higher peaks in the Coast Range (in excess of 3,000 feet in some places) pick up significant snowfall amounts.

Crater Lake is legendary for its high snowfall totals. Located at 6,480 feet elevation at the state park headquarters, the Crater Lake measurement site has seen more snow more often than any other long-term weather station in the state. Although Crater Lake is south of the typical path of the main winter storm track, it still receives significant snow during most winter storms. In addition, it frequently picks up abundant moisture from subtropical systems arriving from the southwest, often receiving more snow than at Cascade peaks farther north.

Winter comes early at Crater Lake. In 50% of all years, the first snow comes prior to September 29, and by the end of the snow season (generally some time in June), an average of 98 days will have had measurable snowfall. Table 12 lists daily, monthly, seasonal, and annual snowfall records at Crater Lake.

The National Weather Service defines several categories of snowfall, based on the rate of fall and the prevailing winds or visibility:

Snow flurries. *Light snow falling for short durations. No accumulation or just a light dusting is all that is expected.*

Snow showers. *Snow falling at varying intensities for brief periods of time. Some accumulation is possible.*

Squalls. *Brief, intense snow showers accompanied by strong, gusty winds. Accumulation may be significant. Snow squalls are best known in the Great Lakes region.*

Blowing snow. *Wind-driven snow that reduces visibility and causes significant drifting. Blowing snow may be snow that is falling and/or loose snow on the ground picked up by the wind.*

Blizzard. *Winds over 35 mph with snow and blowing snow reducing visibility to near zero.*

Table 11. Average monthly and annual snowfall (in inches) at selected Oregon stations.

Station (Zone)	Jan	Feb	Mar	Apr	May	Jun	Jul	Aug	Sep	Oct	Nov	Dec	Year
Astoria WSO AP (1)	2.2	.4	.4	.1							.2	1.4	4.7
Brookings (1)	.2	.3	.1									.1	.4
Corvallis (2)	2.2	1.3	.2								.2	1.6	5.7
Eugene WSO AP (2)	3.1	.9	.2								.2	1.7	6.1
Portland WSO AP (2)	1.8	.9	.1								.5	2.0	5.4
Ashland (3)	2.7	1.2	1.0	.5		.					.3	2.4	8.4
Medford WSO AP (3)	3.0	.8	.7	.2							.4	2.3	7.5
Roseburg KQEN (3)	2.3	.6	.1								.0	.7	4.0
Belknap Springs (4)	24.4	15.9	13.3	2.7	.2					.3	6.8	22.3	88.0
Detroit Dam (4)	7.9	3.7	2.2	.4							1.0	3.5	18.2
Government Camp (4)	61.6	44.6	49.2	29.8	7.5	.2			.3	6.4	34.1	52.7	278.2
McKenzie Bridge (4)	13.2	6.9	4.3	.4						.3	2.6	8.8	40.1
Crater Lake (5)	85.3	73.2	87.5	43.0	19.3	4.0	.5	.2	4.1	21.3	69.1	84.0	495.0
Silver Lake (5)	5.0	2.7	3.1	1.4	.7					.3	2.2	6.4	18.6
Hood River Exp Stn (6)	14.0	6.4	1.5								3.4	9.9	36.5
Moro (6)	6.0	2.7	1.2	.2						.2	2.5	6.2	19.3
Pendleton WSO AP (6)	6.1	2.1	1.0	.2						.2	2.2	5.2	17.0
Bend (7)	10.0	3.9	4.1	2.0	.3					.2	5.6	9.5	34.8
Burns WSO (7)	6.6	6.9	4.6	1.0	.3	.1				.6	6.4	10.4	42.3
Klamath Falls (7)	9.3	4.7	3.7	.9	.1					.5	4.5	10.0	34.9
Enterprise 2 S (8)	12.0	8.2	8.1	5.0	1.4				.2	1.3	7.6	9.4	52.6
John Day (8)	6.2	3.7	3.2	1.2	.1					.3	2.5	7.1	24.0
LaGrande (8)	9.0	4.7	1.7	.7						.2	3.0	7.4	28.7
Ontario (9)	7.2	2.8	.7	.1						.1	2.2	6.7	20.3
Rome 2 NW (9)	4.4	.8	1.4	.5	.2					.2	1.7	3.7	13.5

Values represent 1961-1990 averages. Blank cells indicate 0 or negligible snow for that month.

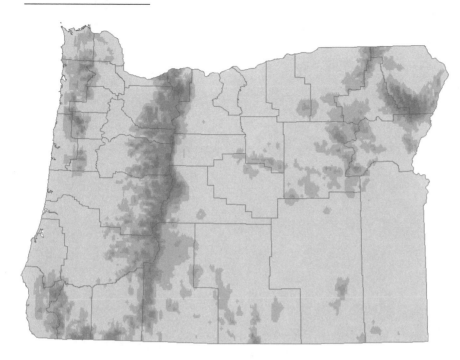

*Figure 30.
Annual snowfall
for Oregon
(water
equivalent).
1961-1990
averages.*

Legend (inches)
- less than 10
- 10 to 20
- 20 to 30
- 30 to 50
- 50 to 110
- 110 to 180

Table 12. Crater Lake snowfall records.

1-day total		Monthly total		Season (July-June)		Calendar year	
(inches)	Date	(inches)	Month	(inches)	Season	(inches)	Year
37	Jan. 27, 1937	313	Jan. 1950	836	1951-52	903	1950
37	Jan. 17, 1951	248.5	Feb. 1949	830	1932-33	819	1948
37	Feb. 28, 1971	241.6	Jan. 1933	824	1949-50	766	1933
34	Nov. 17, 1994	216	Jan. 1904	822	1948-49	740	1932
31.5	Jan. 13, 1947	213.4	Jan. 1937	789	1931-32	735	1964
31.5	Oct. 30, 1956	198.7	Feb. 1938	677	1937-38	732	1951
31	Jan. 2, 1933	196	Dec. 1948	677	1936-37	726	1937
31	Jan. 26, 1954	195.5	Dec. 1996	672	1970-71	717	1996
31	Jan. 20, 1964	194.1	Mar. 1938	660	1955-56	703	1952
30	Dec. 25, 1931	194	Jan. 1952	651	1947-48	698	1971

PART 3

Oregon Climate Zones

Introduction

Climate zones for the entire United States have been established by the National Climatic Data Center. Each zone represents an area with similar precipitation and temperature characteristics, obtained by averaging values for all NOAA cooperative stations available for a given month. Descriptions of Oregon's nine climate zones follow.

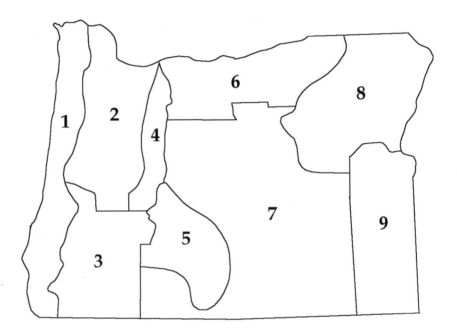

Zone 1: The Coastal Area
Zone 2: The Willamette Valley
Zone 3: Southwestern Interior
Zone 4: Northern Cascades
Zone 5: The High Plateau
Zone 6: The North Central Area
Zone 7: The South Central Area
Zone 8: The Northeast Area
Zone 9: The Southeast Area

Zone 1. The Coastal Area

Stretching along Oregon's Pacific border, the coastal zone is characterized by wet winters, relatively dry summers, and mild temperatures throughout the year. The features of the coastal terrain include a coastal plain (extending from less than a mile to a few tens of miles in width), numerous coastal valleys, and the western slopes of the Coast Range, the peaks of which range from 2,000 to 5,500 feet above sea level and extend down the full length of the state. Rivers such as the Coquille, Umpqua, and Yaquina dissect the Coast Range and drain its slopes. The zone's heavy precipitation results from moist air masses moving off the Pacific Ocean onto land, especially during winter months. The abundant moisture supports lush pastures for dairy and animal production as well as valley crops of grass seed, flower bulbs, nuts, and fruit.

Along the lower elevations of the immediate coast, normal annual precipitation is between 65 and 90 inches. However, spots high on the west slopes of the Coast Range may get up to 200 inches. Several days of abundant rainfall can cause strong flood events, though flood control dams have greatly reduced the incidence of damaging floods in some locations. As is typical of western Oregon, the highest monthly precipitation for the coast occurs in the winter months of November, December, and January. Table 13 is a summary of mean monthly and annual precipitation for recording stations in the coastal zone.

Snowfall in the vicinity of the coast is minimal, usually only 1 to 3 inches, though some of the higher elevations receive significant amounts. For example, Laurel Mountain (elevation 3,589 feet) received 55 inches of snow in January of 1982. At Mary's Peak (elevation 4,097 feet), the highest peak in the Coast Range, snow often lasts into May.

The months of July, August, and September tend to be the warmest, but average summer temperatures are only about 15°F above the coldest month, January. Table 14 lists mean maximum, mean minimum, and mean average temperatures for each month in various Zone 1 locations. Average heating and cooling degree days (base 65°F) are lower for the coastal region than any other Oregon region as a result of the mild temperatures.

Extremely high or low temperatures are rare, and the annual temperature range is lower than that of any other Oregon climate zone.

Temperatures of 90°F or above occur, on the average, less than once per year, and freezing temperatures are infrequent (except at higher elevations in the Coast Range). Newport, for example, records temperatures of 32°F or below an average of thirty times per year. Killing frosts are even less frequent; most of the area averages more than three hundred days between the last occurrence (in spring) and the first occurrence (in fall) of 28°F temperatures. Median dates of low temperature thresholds in spring and fall are listed in Table 15, and Table 16 gives the length of the growing season at each station.

Occasional strong winds strike the Oregon coast, usually in advance of winter storms. Wind speeds can exceed hurricane force, and in rare cases have caused significant damage to structures or vegetation. Damage is most likely at exposed coastal locations, but it may extend into inland valleys as well. Such events are typically short lived, lasting less than one day.

Skies are likely to be cloudy during winter, and only partly cloudy during summer. At Astoria, average winter cloud cover is over 80%, dropping only to about 65% in summer. Summer cloud cover is due mostly to fog and low clouds. As a result of the persistent cloudiness, total solar radiation is lower here than in any other part of the state.

Table 13. Monthly and annual precipitation (in inches). 1961-1990 means.

Station/Elevation (feet)	Jan	Feb	Mar	Apr	May	Jun	Jul	Aug	Sep	Oct	Nov	Dec	Year
Alsea Fish Hatchery (230)	14.87	11.80	11.04	6.39	4.03	2.25	.74	1.31	3.02	6.17	14.15	16.24	92.00
Astoria WSO (10)	10.01	7.59	7.07	4.61	3.02	2.40	1.16	1.33	2.91	5.73	10.05	10.55	66.42
Bandon 2 NNE (20)	9.29	7.20	7.47	4.36	2.76	1.50	.40	.97	1.69	4.11	9.30	9.86	58.91
Brookings (45)	10.85	9.03	9.65	5.30	3.64	1.55	.53	1.31	2.15	5.84	11.89	12.23	74.78
Cloverdale (20)	12.84	9.38	9.77	5.82	4.28	3.24	1.51	1.65	3.62	6.59	12.24	13.11	84.04
Elkton 3 SW (120)	8.53	6.52	6.29	3.52	1.96	.99	.30	.73	1.44	3.49	8.81	9.71	52.17
Gold Beach (120)	12.02	10.31	10.75	5.98	3.85	1.62	.47	1.18	2.42	5.73	12.64	13.43	80.40
Honeyman State Park (120)	11.48	9.38	9.23	5.23	3.79	2.37	.86	1.34	2.49	5.92	11.50	12.41	76.01
Nehalem 9 NE (140)	18.62	15.34	13.49	7.83	5.32	3.85	2.20	1.80	5.48	8.52	18.16	20.54	121.74
Newport (140)	11.11	8.13	8.24	4.84	3.50	2.69	1.04	1.26	2.63	5.36	10.88	12.03	71.72
North Bend (10)	9.73	7.76	7.81	4.65	2.89	1.60	.45	.96	1.80	4.59	10.27	10.97	63.48
Otis 2 NE (150)	14.88	11.11	11.11	6.77	4.84	3.69	1.68	1.92	3.91	7.58	14.25	15.55	97.27
Port Orford (30)	11.72	8.44	9.02	5.00	3.27	1.95	.61	1.44	1.96	4.90	11.15	12.36	71.49
Powers (230)	9.67	7.66	7.90	4.74	2.62	1.02	.30	.73	1.71	3.82	9.39	10.43	59.99
Seaside (10)	10.88	9.13	8.19	5.11	3.56	2.85	1.55	1.45	3.15	6.17	10.90	11.52	74.46
Summit (750)	10.99	8.54	8.09	4.88	3.17	2.01	.77	1.04	2.33	4.88	10.33	11.84	68.86
Tidewater (50)	14.81	11.34	11.32	6.67	4.15	2.55	.83	1.25	2.88	6.24	13.85	15.54	91.42
Tillamook 1 W (10)	13.58	9.94	10.19	6.05	4.45	3.20	1.60	1.75	3.76	7.12	13.08	13.93	88.65
Willamina S (240)	7.93	6.27	6.03	3.15	1.79	1.18	.50	.69	1.74	3.65	7.50	9.54	49.96

Table 14. Monthly temperatures (°F). 1961-1990 means.

Station	Code	Jan	Feb	Mar	Apr	May	Jun	Jul	Aug	Sep	Oct	Nov	Dec	Year
Astoria	MMXT	47.9	51.1	53.2	55.9	60.2	64.4	67.8	69.0	67.7	61.2	53.5	48.3	58.4
	MMNT	35.9	37.4	37.9	40.1	44.5	49.5	52.5	52.7	49.1	44.1	40.2	36.6	43.4
	MNTM	41.9	44.2	45.6	48.0	52.3	56.9	60.2	60.9	58.4	52.7	46.9	42.4	50.9
Bandon	MMXT	53.4	55.2	55.7	57.2	60.4	63.7	66.1	67.0	67.4	63.2	57.5	53.6	59.9
	MMNT	38.2	39.5	39.8	40.7	43.9	48.1	50.4	50.4	47.6	44.3	41.8	38.7	43.6
	MNTM	45.8	47.3	47.7	48.9	52.1	55.9	58.3	58.7	57.5	53.7	49.6	46.1	51.8
Brookings	MMXT	54.7	56.3	57.1	59.6	63.2	66.4	67.7	67.5	68.7	64.4	58.4	54.7	61.6
	MMNT	40.9	42.0	41.8	42.5	46.0	49.5	51.2	52.0	51.2	47.9	44.6	41.2	46.0
	MNTM	47.8	49.1	49.4	51.0	54.6	57.9	59.4	59.8	59.9	56.2	51.5	47.9	53.8
Cloverdale	MMXT	50.2	53.5	55.0	57.6	62.4	66.4	70.3	71.2	70.4	64.2	55.4	50.5	60.5
	MMNT	37.2	38.6	38.6	39.7	43.3	47.4	49.5	50.2	48.5	44.6	41.1	37.5	43.0
	MNTM	43.7	46.1	46.8	48.7	52.8	56.9	59.9	60.7	59.4	54.4	48.2	44.0	51.8
Elkton	MMXT	49.0	54.2	58.7	63.9	70.2	76.9	83.5	84.2	79.2	67.3	54.5	48.0	65.8
	MMNT	36.1	37.8	38.9	40.6	44.3	49.1	51.3	51.8	48.3	45.1	41.4	36.8	43.4
	MNTM	42.6	46.0	48.8	52.2	57.3	63.0	67.3	68.0	63.6	56.2	47.9	42.2	54.7
Gold Beach	MMXT	54.6	55.8	56.2	58.1	61.2	65.1	67.8	68.3	67.7	63.8	57.7	54.6	60.9
	MMNT	40.3	41.4	41.5	42.7	45.4	49.3	51.0	51.8	50.6	47.2	43.9	40.8	45.6
	MNTM	47.4	48.6	48.9	50.4	53.3	57.2	59.3	60.1	59.2	55.5	50.8	47.5	53.2
Honeyman State Park	MMXT	50.3	52.9	55.5	58.6	62.7	66.0	68.8	69.1	69.3	63.1	54.1	49.9	60.1
	MMNT	37.4	38.6	39.5	40.5	44.0	47.8	50.2	51.0	49.1	45.5	41.6	37.5	43.7
	MNTM	43.8	45.8	47.5	49.6	53.4	56.9	59.5	60.0	59.2	54.3	47.8	43.7	51.9
Newport	MMXT	50.3	52.7	53.6	55.2	58.6	62.0	64.6	65.3	65.5	61.1	54.8	50.4	57.9
	MMNT	37.3	38.5	38.7	39.7	43.4	47.7	49.6	49.9	48.2	44.6	41.5	37.8	43.1
	MNTM	43.8	45.6	46.1	47.5	51.0	54.8	57.1	57.6	56.9	52.8	48.1	44.1	50.5
North Bend	MMXT	51.9	54.0	54.8	56.5	60.2	63.8	66.3	67.1	66.9	63.0	56.9	52.6	59.5
	MMNT	38.9	40.5	41.1	42.4	46.6	50.7	52.5	53.0	50.5	46.7	43.2	40.1	45.5
	MNTM	45.4	47.3	48.0	49.5	53.4	57.3	59.4	60.1	58.7	54.8	50.1	46.3	52.5
Otis	MMXT	47.1	51.2	53.9	56.7	61.3	65.6	69.3	70.8	69.1	61.4	52.3	46.9	58.8
	MMNT	36.0	37.6	38.1	39.4	43.1	47.5	49.5	50.3	48.4	44.3	40.3	36.5	42.6
	MNTM	41.5	44.4	46.0	48.0	52.2	56.5	59.4	60.5	58.7	52.9	46.3	41.7	50.7
Port Orford	MMXT	53.6	55.1	56.1	58.2	61.7	65.3	68.3	69.1	68.5	63.7	57.3	53.8	60.9
	MMNT	39.5	40.2	40.9	41.7	45.1	49.3	51.6	51.7	50.2	46.6	42.9	39.8	45.1
	MNTM	46.6	47.5	48.5	49.9	53.4	57.3	60.0	60.4	59.4	55.3	50.1	46.8	53.1
Powers	MMXT	52.8	55.8	58.1	61.7	66.8	72.3	77.7	78.8	76.3	68.5	57.8	52.3	65.0
	MMNT	34.5	35.7	37.5	39.6	43.6	48.4	50.9	50.6	46.7	42.5	38.9	35.1	42.0
	MNTM	43.6	45.8	47.8	50.7	55.2	60.4	64.3	64.7	61.5	55.5	48.4	43.7	53.5
Seaside	MMXT	51.0	53.8	55.2	57.6	61.5	65.1	67.9	68.9	69.5	63.8	55.9	51.3	60.0
	MMNT	36.7	38.2	38.4	40.5	44.7	48.9	51.6	52.0	49.0	44.6	40.6	37.2	43.4
	MNTM	43.9	46.0	46.7	49.0	53.1	57.0	59.8	60.4	59.2	54.2	48.2	44.2	51.7
Tidewater	MMXT	50.1	54.9	57.4	60.6	65.4	70.1	74.2	75.7	74.6	66.8	55.7	49.7	62.9
	MMNT	36.4	37.9	38.6	40.0	44.0	48.6	51.9	52.3	49.9	45.7	41.1	37.1	43.6
	MNTM	43.3	46.4	48.0	50.3	54.7	59.4	63.1	64.0	62.3	56.3	48.4	43.4	53.2
Tillamook	MMXT	49.9	52.9	54.5	56.9	60.8	64.7	67.3	68.5	68.6	62.8	54.6	49.8	59.3
	MMNT	35.7	36.9	36.9	38.5	42.4	46.7	49.2	49.5	46.4	42.2	39.1	36.1	41.6
	MNTM	42.8	44.9	45.7	47.7	51.6	55.7	58.2	59.0	57.5	52.5	46.8	42.9	50.4

Table 15. Median frost dates. 1961-1990 means.

	Median dates of last occurrence in spring of				Median dates of first occurrence in fall of			
	24°F	28°F	32°F	36°F	24°F	28°F	32°F	36°F
Astoria	21 Jan	3 Mar	14 Apr	7 May	***	11 Dec	9 Nov	13 Oct
Bandon	***	9 Feb	10 Apr	12 May	***	15 Dec	22 Nov	10 Oct
Brookings	***	***	3 Feb	18 Apr	***	***	***	26 Nov
Cloverdale	***	3 Feb	15 Apr	17 May	***	18 Dec	23 Nov	18 Oct
Coquille	10 Feb	10 Feb	24 Apr	23 May	11 Nov	27 Nov	3 Nov	14 Oct
Dora	30 Jan	20 Feb	28 Apr	20 May	21 Dec	28 Nov	20 Oct	8 Oct
Elkton 3 SW	10 Jan	9 Feb	27 Mar	7 May	***	17 Dec	16 Nov	17 Oct
Falls City	3 Feb	2 Apr	5 May	26 May	6 Dec	13 Nov	27 Oct	4 Oct
Gold Beach	***	***	3 Mar	20 Apr	***	***	14 Dec	19 Nov
Honeyman State Park	9 Jan	2 Feb	5 Apr	5 May	***	19 Dec	27 Nov	2 Nov
Illahe	5 Jan	10 Feb	10 Apr	11 May	***	13 Dec	9 Nov	16 Oct
Newport	***	9 Feb	19 Apr	13 May	***	19 Dec	27 Nov	30 Oct
North Bend	***	29 Jan	6 Mar	12 Apr	***	28 Dec	29 Nov	31 Oct
Otis	10 Jan	6 Feb	24 Apr	15 May	***	12 Dec	15 Nov	13 Oct
Port Orford 2	***	28 Jan	14 Mar	5 May	***	23 Dec	27 Nov	8 Nov
Powers	23 Jan	21 Feb	19 Apr	17 May	23 Dec	28 Nov	1 Nov	9 Oct
Seaside	16 Jan	19 Feb	13 Apr	8 May	30 Dec	28 Nov	3 Nov	16 Oct
Tidewater	3 Jan	9 Feb	15 Apr	6 May	***	12 Dec	13 Nov	22 Oct
Tillamook	10 Feb	6 Apr	9 May	7 Jun	13 Dec	8 Nov	8 Oct	17 Sep

Table 16. Growing season. 1961-1990 means

	Average days between occurrences of			
	24° F	28° F	32° F	36° F
Astoria	***	283	209	160
Bandon	***	310	226	152
Brookings	***	***	***	223
Cloverdale	***	319	222	155
Coquille	275	292	193	145
Dora	327	283	175	142
Elkton 3 SW	***	312	235	163
Falls City	307	225	175	132
Gold Beach	***	***	287	213
Honeyman State Park	***	321	237	181
Illahe	***	307	213	158
Newport	***	314	222	170
North Bend	***	334	268	203
Otis	***	310	205	151
Port Orford 2	***	330	259	187
Powers	335	281	196	145
Seaside	349	284	205	161
Tidewater	***	307	212	169
Tillamook	308	216	152	102

Codes for Table 14

MMXT = mean maximum

MMNT = mean minimum

MNTM = monthly mean

Tables 15, 16

*** Did not occur

Zone 2. The Willamette Valley

The Willamette Valley is the most diverse agricultural area in the state, and also the home of the majority of the population. Oregon's three largest cities, Portland, Salem, and Eugene, are located in the north, central, and south portions of the Valley, respectively, but these urban areas are surrounded by varied and productive ranches, orchards, and farms. Among the crops grown in significant quantities are tree fruits, nuts, berries, mint, grains, and hay. Livestock operations are also common, including the dairy and poultry industries.

The climate of the Valley is relatively mild throughout the year, characterized by cool, wet winters and warm, dry summers. The climatic conditions closely resemble the Mediterranean climates that occur in California, although Oregon's winters are somewhat wetter and cooler. Growing seasons in the Willamette Valley are long, and moisture is abundant during most of the year (although summer irrigation is common).

Like the remainder of western Oregon, the Valley has a predominant winter rainfall climate. Typical distribution of precipitation includes about 50% of the annual total from December through February, lesser amounts in the spring and fall, and very little during summer. Rainfall tends to vary inversely with temperatures— the cooler months are the wettest, the warm summer months the driest.

There is considerable variation in precipitation in the Valley, ranging from annual totals below 40 inches in the Portland area to upwards of 80 inches in the Cascade and Coast Range foothills. Elevation is the single most important determinant of precipitation totals. Portland, for example, at 21 feet above sea level, receives an average of 37.4 inches (30-year normal), while Salem (196 feet) receives 40.4 inches and Eugene (359 feet) receives 46.0 inches. Thus, a change of only 338 feet of elevation produces an increase of 23% above Portland's total.

Extreme temperatures in the Valley are rare. Days with maximum temperature above 90°F occur only five to fifteen times per year on average, and below zero temperatures occur only about once every 25 years.

Scale of miles
0   10   20   30   40   50

Mean high temperatures range from the low 80s in the summer to about 40°F in the coldest months, while average lows are generally in the low 50s in summer and low 30s in winter. The mean growing season (days between 32°F temperatures) is 150-180 days in the lower portions of the Valley, and 110-130 days in the foothills (above about 800 feet).

Although snow falls nearly every year, amounts are generally quite low. Valley floor locations average 5-10 inches per year, mostly during December through February, although higher totals are observed at greater elevations in the foothills.

Severe storms are rare in the Valley. Ice storms occasionally occur in the north, resulting from cold air flowing westward through the Columbia Gorge. High winds occur several times per year in association with major weather systems.

Relative humidity is highest during early morning hours, and is generally 80-100% throughout the year. During the afternoon, humidities are generally lowest, ranging from 70 to 80% during January to 30-50% during summer. Annual pan evaporation is about 35 inches, mostly occurring during the period April-October.

Winters are likely to be cloudy. Average cloud cover during the coldest months exceeds 80%, with an average of about 26 cloudy days in January (with three partly cloudy and two clear days). During summer, however, sunshine is much more abundant, with average cloud cover less than 40%; more than half of the days in July are clear.

Table 17 is a summary of average precipitation conditions at selected stations in the Willamette Valley, while temperature conditions are summarized in Table 18. Median dates of low temperature thresholds in spring and fall are listed in Table 19, and Table 20 gives the length of the growing season at each station.

Table 17. Monthly and annual precipitation (in inches). 1961-1990 means.

Station/Elevation (feet)	Jan	Feb	Mar	Apr	May	Jun	Jul	Aug	Sep	Oct	Nov	Dec	Year
Beaverton (270)	5.74	4.40	3.90	2.49	2.15	1.57	.68	1.04	1.85	2.66	6.56	6.72	39.77
Bonneville Dam (60)	11.37	9.17	7.87	5.53	3.66	2.57	.99	1.58	3.24	5.60	11.07	12.35	74.99
Cascadia (262)	8.48	6.82	6.79	5.28	4.10	2.83	.90	1.40	2.65	4.88	9.29	9.37	61.70
Corvallis (230)	6.82	5.04	4.55	2.56	1.95	1.20	.55	.87	1.51	3.11	6.77	7.73	42.67
Corvallis Water Bureau (590)	11.73	8.64	7.87	3.95	2.50	1.38	.43	.78	1.76	4.26	10.44	12.39	66.13
Cottage Grove 1 S (650)	6.53	5.09	5.24	3.59	2.43	1.39	.52	.97	1.65	3.47	7.46	7.20	45.54
Dallas 2 NE (290)	8.08	6.00	5.64	2.71	1.98	1.22	.50	.70	1.55	3.28	7.65	9.11	48.42
Dilley (170)	7.15	5.43	5.07	2.50	1.76	1.35	.53	.90	1.58	3.37	6.87	8.26	44.20
Dorena Dam (820)	6.27	5.02	5.22	3.95	2.80	1.81	.72	1.14	1.94	3.52	7.31	6.96	46.65
Estacada 2 SE (410)	8.53	6.40	6.23	4.77	3.73	2.58	1.03	1.49	2.63	4.55	8.44	8.90	59.28
Eugene WSO AP (360)	7.91	5.65	5.52	3.11	2.16	1.43	.52	1.08	1.67	3.30	8.32	8.61	49.25
Fern Ridge (490)	6.45	5.02	4.53	2.63	1.84	1.20	.39	.75	1.32	2.94	6.92	7.65	41.63
Forest Grove (180)	7.10	5.26	4.86	2.46	1.70	1.29	.48	.93	1.60	3.31	6.91	7.98	43.86
Foster Dam (550)	7.13	5.89	5.42	3.94	3.34	2.38	.74	1.33	2.00	3.79	7.95	7.86	51.77
Haskins Dam (760)	12.19	9.53	9.08	4.15	2.72	1.51	.53	.91	2.27	5.21	11.85	13.58	73.52
Headworks (750)	11.01	8.74	8.36	6.67	5.04	3.81	1.54	2.18	4.02	6.09	10.49	11.55	79.50
Hillsboro (160)	5.87	4.25	4.02	2.15	1.62	1.39	.54	1.07	1.51	2.82	5.74	6.59	37.57
Lacomb (520)	7.40	5.70	6.27	4.52	3.57	2.50	1.06	1.55	2.16	4.34	8.53	8.32	55.93
Leaburg 1 SW (680)	8.86	7.17	7.16	5.11	3.72	2.50	.78	1.29	2.71	4.99	10.15	9.67	64.11
N. Willamette Exp. St. (150)	5.84	4.34	4.06	2.64	2.28	1.70	.66	1.02	1.93	2.98	6.39	6.94	40.78
Noti 1 NW (450)	10.18	7.68	7.26	3.93	2.38	1.32	.39	.80	1.66	4.06	9.86	11.14	60.65
Oregon City (170)	7.13	5.21	4.78	3.41	2.54	1.91	.78	1.16	2.05	3.44	6.87	7.79	47.06
Portland KGW-TV (160)	6.66	4.62	4.51	2.89	2.23	1.57	.69	1.13	2.01	3.20	6.40	7.23	43.15
Portland WSFO AP (20)	5.36	3.85	3.56	2.39	2.06	1.48	.63	1.09	1.75	2.67	5.34	6.13	36.32
Rex (520)	6.28	4.49	4.21	2.59	2.18	1.56	.63	1.00	1.82	3.18	6.41	7.02	41.37
ST Helens (100)	5.91	4.61	4.66	2.53	2.41	1.64	.70	1.37	1.84	3.45	6.70	6.96	42.76
Salem WSO AP (200)	5.91	4.50	4.17	2.42	1.88	1.34	.58	.76	1.56	2.98	6.28	6.87	39.24
Silver Creek Falls (1350)	11.47	9.06	9.10	6.37	4.78	3.21	1.15	1.73	3.12	6.02	11.58	12.09	79.69
Silverton (410)	6.50	4.82	4.85	3.37	2.76	1.90	.84	1.11	2.05	3.41	6.90	7.35	45.85
Stayton (430)	7.12	5.72	5.31	3.65	2.91	2.16	.86	1.28	2.22	3.97	8.04	8.23	51.48

Table 18. Monthly temperatures (°F). 1961-1990 means.

Station	Code	Jan	Feb	Mar	Apr	May	Jun	Jul	Aug	Sep	Oct	Nov	Dec	Year
Beaverton	MMXT	46.2	50.2	56.1	61.3	66.8	73.3	78.9	79.7	74.5	64.3	52.5	46.0	62.6
	MMNT	32.5	34.7	37.2	40.0	44.4	49.7	53.0	52.7	49.1	42.2	37.1	33.1	42.3
	MNTM	39.3	42.5	46.6	50.6	55.6	61.5	65.9	66.2	61.8	53.3	44.8	39.5	52.4
Bonneville	MMXT	42.6	47.8	53.7	58.6	65.9	72.1	78.0	78.8	72.6	62.5	50.7	43.7	60.6
Dam	MMNT	32.6	36.0	38.0	41.3	46.6	52.4	56.3	56.2	52.4	46.2	40.0	34.4	44.4
	MNTM	39.2	41.6	45.9	50.6	56.2	62.4	67.3	67.7	62.9	54.7	45.7	39.0	52.8
Cascadia	MMXT	45.4	51.0	54.2	58.4	64.7	71.5	78.3	79.9	73.7	63.8	51.7	45.0	61.5
	MMNT	30.9	32.8	34.4	36.8	41.3	46.7	48.4	47.9	43.6	38.5	35.8	32.2	39.1
	MNTM	38.2	41.8	44.4	48.0	52.9	59.1	63.3	63.8	58.7	51.3	43.7	38.5	50.3
Corvallis	MMXT	45.4	50.8	54.8	59.0	66.1	73.1	80.1	81.1	75.0	64.2	52.1	45.8	62.3
	MMNT	32.9	35.4	37.0	38.8	43.0	48.5	50.9	51.2	47.7	41.6	37.8	34.1	41.6
	MNTM	39.3	42.8	46.0	49.3	54.6	60.9	65.7	66.2	61.6	53.0	45.2	39.8	52.0
Corvallis	MMXT	44.9	49.8	54.4	58.6	65.8	72.2	78.4	79.4	73.6	63.5	51.2	44.9	61.4
Water	MMNT	31.7	33.9	35.6	37.3	41.8	47.4	50.1	50.4	47.4	41.1	36.4	32.6	40.5
Bureau	MNTM	38.4	41.4	45.0	48.3	53.7	59.7	64.2	64.8	60.5	52.3	43.9	38.5	50.9
Cottage	MMXT	47.7	53.4	56.7	60.9	67.6	74.2	81.2	81.8	75.9	65.4	53.4	47.8	63.8
Grove	MMNT	32.4	34.7	35.4	36.5	40.8	45.7	47.4	47.8	43.9	40.2	37.3	33.6	39.6
	MNTM	40.3	43.7	46.2	49.2	54.2	60.0	64.4	64.7	60.1	53.0	45.5	40.5	51.8
Dallas	MMXT	46.2	51.5	55.9	60.8	68.6	75.6	82.6	82.8	76.6	65.3	52.3	45.9	63.7
	MMNT	32.8	34.9	36.2	37.8	42.1	46.9	48.9	48.8	46.2	41.2	37.1	33.4	40.5
	MNTM	39.5	43.0	46.0	49.6	55.4	61.3	65.6	65.8	61.6	53.4	44.8	39.4	52.1
Dorena Dam	MMXT	46.6	51.7	55.1	59.2	65.3	71.9	78.9	79.8	74.4	64.4	52.4	46.6	62.2
	MMNT	31.7	33.2	34.9	37.4	41.6	47.1	49.5	49.5	45.6	40.6	36.7	32.7	40.0
	MNTM	39.2	42.4	44.9	48.3	53.5	59.5	64.2	64.6	60.0	52.5	44.6	39.6	51.1
Estacada	MMXT	45.2	50.3	54.9	59.8	66.9	73.0	78.9	79.0	72.4	61.0	51.0	45.5	61.5
	MMNT	33.3	36.1	37.2	39.3	43.9	48.8	51.7	51.7	48.3	42.9	38.3	34.3	42.2
	MNTM	39.4	42.8	46.1	49.8	55.3	60.9	65.3	65.4	60.6	52.1	44.8	39.7	51.9
Eugene WSO	MMXT	46.2	51.7	55.8	60.1	67.2	74.5	82.0	82.0	75.8	64.5	52.3	46.3	63.2
	MMNT	33.2	35.7	37.1	38.5	42.7	48.0	51.2	51.7	47.8	41.9	38.0	34.5	41.7
	MNTM	39.9	43.4	46.6	49.8	55.0	61.4	66.7	67.0	62.0	53.3	45.4	40.3	52.6
Fern Ridge	MMXT	46.2	51.3	55.3	59.3	66.2	73.3	80.3	80.9	75.3	64.5	52.6	46.6	62.6
	MMNT	32.6	35.0	36.5	38.6	43.1	48.7	51.7	52.3	48.7	43.0	38.0	34.1	41.8
	MNTM	39.4	43.1	45.9	49.0	54.6	61.0	66.0	66.6	62.0	53.7	45.2	40.3	52.2
Forest Grove	MMXT	45.7	51.5	56.1	61.0	68.5	75.2	81.6	82.7	76.4	65.1	52.7	45.8	63.5
	MMNT	32.3	35.2	36.7	38.9	43.6	49.2	52.5	52.4	48.0	41.3	37.3	33.7	41.8
	MNTM	39.2	43.0	46.5	50.3	56.2	62.3	67.2	67.5	62.3	53.4	45.1	39.5	52.7
Foster Dam	MMXT	47.3	51.4	55.9	60.0	66.1	72.5	79.4	80.1	74.3	64.8	52.9	47.1	62.6
	MMNT	33.1	35.1	37.2	39.4	43.4	48.3	50.5	50.2	46.4	41.5	38.2	34.2	41.5
	MNTM	40.2	43.3	46.6	49.8	54.8	60.4	65.0	65.2	60.3	53.2	45.6	40.7	52.1
Headworks	MMXT	44.9	49.7	53.5	58.5	66.0	72.0	77.8	78.1	72.1	63.2	51.3	45.1	61.0
	MMNT	33.9	36.3	37.1	39.2	43.8	48.8	52.1	53.0	49.9	44.7	38.9	34.8	42.7
	MNTM	39.5	42.7	45.3	49.3	55.0	60.5	65.1	65.7	61.5	54.1	45.2	39.8	52.0
Hillsboro	MMXT	45.6	51.3	55.7	60.3	67.6	73.9	80.1	80.7	74.8	64.5	52.5	45.9	62.7
	MMNT	33.0	35.5	36.8	38.7	43.3	49.0	51.8	51.6	47.0	40.8	37.2	33.9	41.6
	MNTM	39.4	43.0	46.3	49.9	55.4	61.5	66.0	66.1	61.1	52.7	45.0	39.7	52.2
Lacomb	MMXT	46.2	51.1	55.5	59.7	65.9	72.2	77.8	79.2	74.2	64.5	51.9	46.8	62.1
	MMNT	31.5	34.4	36.0	38.1	42.4	47.3	49.8	49.4	45.6	40.3	36.3	34.1	40.4
	MNTM	39.1	42.1	45.9	49.5	54.3	59.9	64.1	64.4	60.3	52.5	44.3	39.8	51.4

Table continues on next page

Station	Code	Jan	Feb	Mar	Apr	May	Jun	Jul	Aug	Sep	Oct	Nov	Dec	Year
Leaburg	MMXT	46.9	52.2	56.0	60.4	67.4	74.2	81.5	82.3	75.5	65.0	52.6	46.5	63.4
	MMNT	33.2	34.9	36.5	39.0	43.1	48.2	50.4	50.5	47.2	42.4	38.2	34.0	41.4
	MNTM	40.2	43.5	46.3	49.9	55.2	61.2	66.0	66.4	61.5	53.8	45.4	40.2	52.5
N. Willam-	MMXT	45.8	51.3	55.4	59.4	66.8	73.1	79.6	80.2	74.1	64.0	52.7	46.3	62.4
ette Exp.	MMNT	32.2	34.6	36.5	39.0	44.0	49.5	52.4	52.2	48.4	41.2	37.3	33.3	41.7
St.	MNTM	39.2	42.7	46.0	49.7	55.4	61.5	66.1	66.2	61.6	52.8	45.2	39.6	52.2
Oregon City	MMXT	46.6	52.4	56.7	61.7	69.4	76.0	81.9	82.0	76.0	64.9	53.2	46.7	64.0
	MMNT	34.6	37.3	38.9	41.0	46.2	51.6	54.8	55.0	51.2	44.7	39.5	35.5	44.2
	MNTM	40.8	44.7	47.9	51.8	57.9	63.9	68.4	68.5	63.9	55.0	46.6	40.9	54.2
Portland	MMXT	45.7	50.3	56.2	60.9	67.0	73.6	79.4	79.1	73.8	63.6	51.3	46.1	62.3
KGW	MMNT	35.8	38.0	40.7	43.5	48.0	53.2	56.5	57.0	53.7	47.4	41.1	36.0	45.9
	MNTM	40.9	45.4	48.4	51.9	58.0	63.8	68.3	68.7	64.0	56.0	47.0	41.6	54.5
Portland	MMXT	45.2	51.2	56.0	59.9	67.1	73.6	79.8	80.1	74.0	63.8	52.4	45.8	62.4
WSO	MMNT	33.6	36.5	38.5	41.0	46.8	52.8	56.4	56.8	51.7	44.7	39.2	34.9	44.4
	MNTM	39.6	43.6	47.3	51.0	57.1	63.3	68.1	68.5	63.2	54.5	46.1	40.2	53.5
St Helens	MMXT	45.8	51.4	57.9	62.6	68.2	74.9	79.7	81.2	74.5	65.3	51.8	45.5	63.2
	MMNT	32.3	36.6	39.3	41.1	46.0	51.6	54.5	55.4	51.1	44.1	38.1	33.9	43.7
	MNTM	39.6	43.3	48.4	52.4	57.1	63.4	67.5	68.4	63.6	54.9	45.5	39.5	53.6
Salem WSO	MMXT	46.2	51.6	55.7	59.9	67.0	74.4	81.5	82.0	75.6	64.3	52.3	46.4	63.1
	MMNT	32.6	34.5	35.6	37.3	42.2	47.9	50.6	51.1	46.8	40.8	37.0	33.8	40.9
	MNTM	39.5	42.7	45.8	49.1	54.7	61.3	66.2	66.6	61.5	52.7	44.9	39.9	52.1
Silver Creek	MMXT	45.1	48.6	52.6	58.0	64.8	71.2	77.1	77.4	72.8	61.9	49.7	44.0	60.6
	MMNT	30.4	31.7	33.1	35.2	40.0	45.0	47.2	47.5	43.0	38.5	34.5	31.1	38.3
	MNTM	37.8	40.2	42.9	46.5	52.1	57.8	62.1	62.1	58.0	50.4	42.2	37.7	49.5
Silverton	MMXT	45.4	51.2	55.0	58.6	65.8	71.9	78.4	79.3	73.6	63.4	52.3	46.0	61.7
	MMNT	32.4	35.5	37.4	39.5	44.7	50.2	53.2	53.6	49.8	43.3	38.0	33.6	42.6
	MNTM	39.2	43.0	46.2	49.6	55.3	61.1	66.0	66.5	62.0	53.4	45.4	39.5	52.3
Stayton	MMXT	46.6	51.6	55.7	60.3	66.9	73.6	80.1	80.8	75.0	64.3	52.9	46.5	63.0
	MMNT	32.5	35.2	37.4	39.5	43.7	48.9	51.1	51.0	47.6	42.4	38.1	33.7	41.7
	MNTM	39.6	43.4	46.6	49.9	55.3	61.2	65.6	65.9	61.3	53.4	45.5	40.1	52.3

Codes for Table 18

MMXT = mean maximum

MMNT = mean minimum

MNTM = monthly mean

Table 19. Median frost dates. 1961-1990 means.

	Median dates of last occurrence in spring of				Median dates of first occurrence in fall of			
	24°F	28°F	32°F	36°F	24°F	28°F	32°F	36°F
Beaverton	3 Feb	9 Mar	19 Apr	10 May	19 Dec	26 Nov	26 Oct	15 Oct
Bonneville Dam	22 Jan	16 Feb	18 Mar	20 Apr	***	19 Dec	24 Nov	13 Nov
Cascadia	13 Feb	4 Apr	13 May	25 May	28 Nov	3 Nov	3 Oct	17 Sep
Corvallis	28 Jan	8 Mar	24 Apr	17 May	20 Dec	26 Nov	25 Oct	6 Oct
Corvallis Water Bureau	29 Jan	16 Feb	27 Apr	20 May	10 Dec	26 Nov	4 Nov	13 Oct
Cottage Grove	18 Feb	14 Apr	20 May	4 Jun	17 Dec	10 Nov	28 Sep	8 Sep
Dallas	4 Feb	23 Mar	2 May	27 May	9 Dec	12 Nov	16 Oct	24 Sep
Dorena Dam	12 Feb	29 Mar	29 Apr	22 May	19 Dec	18 Nov	16 Oct	2 Oct
Estacada	29 Jan	16 Feb	13 Apr	10 May	24 Dec	3 Dec	7 Nov	13 Oct
Fern Ridge	28 Jan	19 Feb	21 Apr	8 May	21 Dec	1 Dec	7 Nov	20 Oct
Forest Grove	4 Feb	13 Mar	25 Apr	13 May	9 Dec	12 Nov	18 Oct	3 Oct
Foster Dam	31 Jan	20 Feb	10 Apr	15 May	28 Dec	27 Nov	24 Oct	12 Oct
Headworks	24 Jan	10 Feb	12 Apr	4 May	***	14 Dec	18 Nov	22 Oct
Hillsboro	3 Feb	6 Mar	29 Apr	13 May	19 Dec	16 Nov	18 Oct	3 Oct
Lacomb	4 Feb	16 Mar	2 May	22 May	25 Dec	22 Nov	20 Oct	2 Oct
Leaburg	18 Jan	21 Feb	19 Apr	15 May	24 Dec	8 Dec	10 Nov	14 Oct
North Willamette Exp. Stn.	2 Feb	13 Mar	22 Apr	16 May	18 Dec	14 Nov	21 Oct	10 Oct
Oregon City	30 Jan	21 Feb	5 Apr	28 Apr	30 Dec	6 Dec	6 Nov	16 Oct
Portland KGW	9 Jan	3 Feb	3 Mar	14 Apr	31 Dec	20 Dec	30 Nov	14 Nov
Portland WSO	29 Jan	16 Feb	26 Mar	25 Apr	28 Dec	3 Dec	10 Nov	22 Oct
St. Helens	31 Jan	20 Feb	10 Apr	15 May	28 Dec	27 Nov	24 Oct	12 Oct
Salem	4 Mar	12 Apr	4 May	25 May	29 Nov	2 Nov	16 Oct	2 Oct
Scotts Mills	23 Feb	13 Apr	12 May	3 Jun	4 Dec	15 Nov	18 Oct	25 Sep
Silver Creek Falls	1 Mar	17 Apr	14 May	8 Jun	24 Nov	23 Oct	4 Oct	12 Sep
Silverton	29 Jan	5 Mar	11 Apr	29 Apr	20 Dec	26 Nov	4 Nov	16 Oct
Stayton	1 Feb	15 Mar	20 Apr	11 May	14 Dec	26 Nov	22 Oct	3 Oct

***Did not occur

Table 20. Growing season. 1961-1990 means.

	Average days between occurrences of			
	24° F	28° F	32° F	36° F
Beaverton	320	262	190	158
Bonneville Dam	***	308	252	207
Cascadia	289	213	143	116
Corvallis	326	263	184	142
Corvallis Water Bureau	316	284	191	146
Cottage Grove	303	210	131	96
Dallas	310	235	168	120
Dorena Dam	311	235	170	133
Estacada	330	292	209	157
Eugene WSO	308	259	176	135
Fern Ridge	328	286	200	165
Forest Grove	309	245	177	143
Foster Dam	331	280	198	150
Headworks	***	308	220	171
Hillsboro	320	255	173	144
Lacomb	325	251	171	133
Leaburg	342	291	205	152
North Willamette Exp. Stn.	321	246	182	147
Oregon City	336	290	215	172
Portland KGW	356	320	272	214
Portland WSO	333	290	230	180
St. Helens	331	280	198	150
Salem WSO	270	204	165	130
Silver Creek Falls	268	189	143	96
Silverton	326	266	207	170
Stayton	317	256	185	145

*** Did not occur

Zone 3. Southwestern Interior

T he southwestern interior of Oregon is one of the more rugged parts of the state. Mountains and ridges are separated by deeply indented river valleys, with most of the rivers flowing westward toward the Pacific Ocean. Although much of the area lies in something of a rain shadow, sheltered from the Pacific by the Coast Range to the west, many of the higher elevation sites receive abundant precipitation with some locations receiving in excess of 120 inches per year.

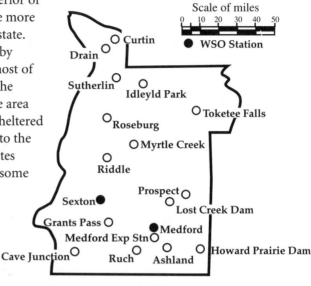

Due to the ruggedness of the terrain, much of Zone 3 remains sparsely settled. The only major urban areas lie in the broader valley areas, particularly the Rogue and Umpqua valleys. Ashland, Medford, and Grants Pass are the major cities in the Rogue valley; Roseburg is the primary urban area in the Umpqua valley.

Long an important area for forestry, southwestern Oregon is perhaps best known for its fruit crops, particularly the Rogue River pear industry, which covers more than 10,000 acres. Additional agricultural and livestock commodities of importance include hay, grain, seed crops, beef cattle, poultry, sheep, and the dairy industry.

As is the case in the rest of western Oregon, most precipitation in Zone 3 falls during the months of November through March. Of Medford's average annual precipitation of 18.85 inches, about 75% falls during that five-month period. Occasional summer thunderstorms cause precipitation during the warmer months, but average monthly totals during summer are quite low.

Total precipitation is strongly influenced by elevation, and Zone 3 is no exception; in general, the driest areas are those at the lowest valley locations, while precipitation increases steadily at higher elevations. The driest area in Zone 3 extends from Central Point through Medford and nearly to Ashland, all of which receive less than 20 inches per year. Not far south of Ashland, however, is Mount Ashland at 7,500 feet, which receives an excess of 50 inches per year. Perhaps the wettest area in Zone 3 is in the remote, mountainous area east of Roseburg near Quartz Mountain. Although precipitation data in that area are scarce, it has been estimated that some of the higher peaks receive in excess of 120 inches of rain per year. Another very wet area lies in the Klamath Mountains near Cave Junction in the southwestern part of Zone 3. Some of the higher peaks, such as Onion

Mountain and Squaw Mountain, probably receive more than 120 inches per year, although lack of precipitation measurement stations makes this somewhat uncertain. Table 21 lists monthly and annual precipitation values for several Zone 3 stations.

Snow falls nearly every winter in southwestern Oregon. In the valleys, the annual total is about 20 to 30 inches per year, although snow on the ground seldom lasts more than a few days at a time. Nonetheless, these valleys do receive more snow than the Willamette Valley, although they are farther south. Zone 3 valleys are less influenced by marine air due to higher,more rugged coastal mountains in southern Oregon. As a result,temperatures are often lower and snowfall more plentiful in southernvalleys, despite their lower latitude.

At higher elevations, a great deal more snow is reported. At Sexton Summit (3,836 feet), for example, the average annual snowfall is about 100 inches. The frequency of snowstorms also varies widely with elevation differences. Medford, for example, has an average of three days per year with at least 1 inch of snow while Sexton Summit averages thirty days.

Due to its effective separation from the coast, Zone 3 has greater temperature extremes than the remainder of western Oregon. During summer, it is often the warmest part of the state. Medford, for example, averages about 55 days per year with maximum temperatures of 90°F or above; in fact, the average daily maximum for July is above 90°F. Winter temperatures can be quite cold. The average extreme low temperature in Medford during December and January is about 18°F, and an average of twenty days in January have low temperatures of 32°F or below. Medford's monthly mean temperature ranges from 72.5°F in July to 37.7°F in December, a range greater than most other stations west of the Cascades. Table 22 lists mean maximum, mean minimum, and mean average temperatures for each month at several stations in the zone.

Table 23 lists median dates of the last occurrence in spring and first occurrence in fall of four low temperature thresholds. Table 24 lists the average number of days between occurrences of those same four temperatures. Valley locations such as Riddle, Drain, and Grants Pass have longer growing seasons than higher elevation sites such as Howard Prairie Dam and Prospect. Most of the valley locations have at least 140 days between spring and fall 32°F temperatures. Length of time between 28°F temperatures is generally more than two hundred days.

Cloud cover is greatest during the winter months, averaging more than 80% of total potential cloud cover during December and January. Mid-latitude storms generally produce extensive middle and high clouds, while fair weather periods between storms often produce extensive valley fog, sometimes lasting for many days. Summers, however, are mostly cloud-free, averaging only about 20% mean sky cover.

Table 21. Monthly and annual precipitation (in inches). 1961-1990 means.

Station/Elevation (feet)	Jan	Feb	Mar	Apr	May	Jun	Jul	Aug	Sep	Oct	Nov	Dec	Year
Ashland (1750)	2.37	1.72	1.95	1.61	1.29	.91	.32	.58	.92	1.60	2.82	3.06	19.16
Cave Junction (1280)	10.95	7.94	7.43	3.50	1.79	.57	.20	.67	1.36	4.00	9.90	11.25	59.84
Curtin (400)	5.74	6.57	4.86	3.88	2.53	1.63	.84	1.01	1.90	3.31	8.21	7.40	49.82
Drain (292)	7.04	5.50	5.27	3.34	2.14	1.14	.45	.87	1.42	3.47	7.76	7.82	46.17
Grants Pass (960)	5.16	3.82	3.52	1.84	1.16	.49	.22	.48	.90	2.45	5.31	5.69	31.67
Howard Prairie Dam (4570)	4.75	3.53	3.72	2.27	1.83	1.25	.41	.80	1.08	2.12	5.04	5.82	33.04
Idelyld Park (1080)	9.24	7.20	7.12	4.61	2.96	1.72	.61	.97	2.34	4.88	10.78	10.47	63.54
Lost Creek Dam (1580)	4.40	4.11	4.10	2.18	1.81	.82	.36	.77	1.30	2.45	5.56	5.44	33.04
Medford Exp. St. (1457)	2.87	2.05	2.07	1.38	1.11	.75	.29	.61	1.03	1.68	3.34	3.64	21.45
Medford WSO (1300)	2.69	1.93	1.82	1.16	1.00	.58	.26	.52	.86	1.49	3.23	3.32	18.85
Prospect (2482)	5.98	4.67	4.62	2.75	2.21	1.03	.38	.99	1.44	3.31	6.84	6.83	41.16
Riddle (680)	4.78	3.42	3.46	1.99	1.24	.64	.29	.63	1.10	2.14	5.36	5.56	30.11
Roseburg KQEN (465)	5.13	3.70	3.56	2.24	1.43	.83	.43	.73	1.24	2.23	5.36	5.47	32.44
Ruch (1550)	4.27	2.79	2.89	1.59	1.04	.77	.37	.58	1.05	1.73	4.19	4.73	26.01
Sutherlin (600)	4.80	5.75	4.08	3.26	2.25	1.27	.71	.91	1.76	2.86	6.31	5.89	41.13
Toketee Falls (2060)	6.71	5.25	5.42	3.58	2.64	1.51	.57	1.16	1.74	3.65	7.77	7.47	48.17

Table 22. Monthly temperatures (°F). 1961-1990 means.

Station	Code	Jan	Feb	Mar	Apr	May	Jun	Jul	Aug	Sep	Oct	Nov	Dec	Year
Ashland	MMXT	46.3	52.3	56.2	62.1	70.0	78.7	86.8	85.7	78.6	66.6	52.3	45.4	65.0
	MMNT	29.6	31.9	33.7	36.2	41.6	48.0	51.7	51.6	45.7	39.1	34.1	30.0	39.4
	MNTM	38.0	42.1	45.0	49.1	55.8	63.4	69.3	68.7	62.2	52.8	43.2	37.7	52.2
Cave	MMXT	46.7	53.3	58.0	64.0	72.7	80.7	88.5	87.9	81.5	69.0	52.7	46.0	66.8
Junction	MMNT	31.9	33.1	34.3	36.0	40.6	46.5	49.7	49.0	44.1	39.1	36.7	32.7	39.5
	MNTM	39.3	43.2	46.1	50.0	56.7	63.6	69.1	68.5	62.8	54.0	44.7	39.3	53.1
Drain	MMXT	47.9	53.3	57.6	62.5	69.2	75.9	83.0	83.2	78.0	66.9	53.9	47.5	64.8
	MMNT	33.7	35.5	36.7	38.8	42.8	48.0	49.9	50.1	46.0	42.3	39.1	34.9	41.4
	MNTM	40.8	44.4	47.2	50.6	56.0	62.0	66.4	66.7	62.0	54.6	46.5	41.2	53.1
Grants Pass	MMXT	47.6	54.9	60.5	66.8	74.7	83.0	90.1	89.8	83.1	70.0	53.8	46.3	68.4
	MMNT	32.6	34.4	36.0	38.3	43.6	49.8	53.1	52.7	46.7	41.2	37.9	33.6	41.7
	MNTM	40.1	44.6	48.3	52.5	59.1	66.4	71.6	71.3	64.9	55.6	45.9	39.9	55.1
Howard	MMXT	37.5	42.4	45.9	52.2	61.0	70.2	78.6	78.4	71.6	60.7	43.7	36.5	56.5
Prairie	MMNT	18.9	21.1	23.8	27.5	33.1	40.0	43.6	43.2	37.7	32.3	26.7	21.1	30.7
Dam	MNTM	28.2	31.8	34.8	39.8	47.1	55.1	61.1	60.8	54.7	46.5	35.2	28.8	43.6
Idelyld Park	MMXT	46.4	52.4	56.4	62.0	69.0	75.8	82.6	82.4	76.6	65.5	52.0	45.7	63.6
	MMNT	31.9	33.6	35.0	37.0	41.0	46.4	48.4	48.1	44.5	40.0	36.9	32.7	39.5
	MNTM	39.2	43.0	45.7	49.5	55.0	61.1	65.5	65.3	60.5	52.8	44.5	39.2	51.6
Lost Creek	MMXT	47.4	52.5	57.0	63.3	71.3	80.1	88.9	88.9	81.4	70.4	52.6	46.0	66.6
Dam	MMNT	28.2	30.1	33.0	36.1	40.5	46.4	50.0	49.4	43.1	36.7	33.1	29.1	38.0
	MNTM	37.8	41.3	45.0	49.7	55.9	63.2	69.5	69.1	62.3	53.6	42.9	37.5	52.3
Medford	MMXT	46.2	53.6	58.5	65.0	73.0	81.5	88.8	88.3	81.5	68.3	52.6	45.1	66.7
Exp. St.	MMNT	30.1	32.0	34.3	36.5	41.3	47.7	50.6	50.7	44.2	37.7	34.6	30.9	39.1
	MNTM	38.2	42.8	46.4	50.8	57.1	64.6	69.7	69.5	62.9	53.0	43.6	38.0	52.9
Medford	MMXT	45.7	53.3	58.1	64.1	72.5	82.1	90.5	89.9	82.5	69.1	52.3	44.3	67.0
WSO	MMNT	30.1	32.0	34.8	37.5	42.8	49.9	54.3	54.3	47.5	39.8	34.8	31.0	40.7
	MNTM	37.9	42.7	46.4	50.8	57.6	66.0	72.4	72.1	65.0	54.4	43.5	37.7	53.9
Prospect	MMXT	46.7	51.9	55.4	61.7	70.0	78.3	86.8	86.9	80.7	68.6	52.0	45.6	65.2
	MMNT	27.6	29.6	31.1	33.2	38.1	44.1	47.4	46.9	41.8	36.5	32.6	28.6	36.4
	MNTM	37.2	40.7	43.2	47.4	54.0	61.2	67.1	66.9	61.3	52.5	42.3	37.1	50.8
Riddle	MMXT	49.0	54.8	58.7	63.4	69.6	76.8	83.4	83.7	78.7	68.6	54.7	48.3	65.8
	MMNT	33.9	35.7	37.1	39.1	43.7	49.5	52.6	52.5	47.0	42.3	39.3	34.9	42.3
	MNTM	41.4	45.2	47.9	51.3	56.6	63.1	68.0	68.1	62.9	55.4	47.0	41.6	54.0
Roseburg	MMXT	48.5	53.4	57.8	62.9	69.3	76.5	83.6	84.1	78.1	67.0	54.3	48.0	65.3
KQEN	MMNT	33.9	35.8	37.7	39.7	44.5	50.3	53.5	54.3	49.3	43.8	39.3	34.8	43.1
	MNTM	41.2	44.6	47.8	51.3	56.9	63.4	68.6	69.2	63.7	55.4	46.8	41.4	54.2
Ruch	MMXT	48.6	54.9	59.4	65.3	74.1	81.9	89.3	88.8	82.3	70.4	54.3	47.0	68.2
	MMNT	29.7	30.8	33.1	35.4	40.6	46.8	49.9	49.7	44.5	38.6	34.1	30.3	38.7
	MNTM	39.1	42.8	46.2	50.3	57.3	64.3	69.6	69.4	63.4	54.5	44.2	38.7	53.4
Toketee Falls	MMXT	42.5	48.5	53.7	61.1	69.9	78.3	86.0	85.7	77.5	63.3	48.1	41.8	63.0
	MMNT	29.0	30.8	32.6	35.5	40.6	46.9	49.9	49.3	44.1	38.1	33.7	29.8	38.3
	MNTM	35.7	39.6	43.2	48.3	55.2	62.6	68.0	67.5	60.8	50.7	40.9	35.8	50.7

Codes for Table 22

MMXT = mean maximum

MMNT = mean minimum

MNTM = monthly mean

Table 23. Median frost dates. 1961-1990 means.

	Median dates of last occurrence in spring of				Median dates of first occurrence in fall of			
	24°F	28°F	32°F	36°F	24°F	28°F	32°F	36°F
Ashland	13 Mar	19 Apr	11 May	27 May	24 Nov	5 Nov	12 Oct	27 Sep
Cave Junction	3 Mar	19 Apr	12 May	1 Jun	12 Dec	18 Nov	12 Oct	14 Sep
Drain	1 Feb	9 Mar	26 Apr	16 May	26 Dec	4 Dec	18 Oct	2 Oct
Grants Pass	11 Feb	24 Mar	29 Apr	20 May	15 Dec	27 Nov	15 Oct	3 Oct
Howard Prairie Dam	25 Apr	22 May	17 Jun	12 Jul	1 Nov	10 Oct	13 Sep	24 Aug
Idleyld Park	12 Feb	5 Apr	16 May	5 Jun	11 Dec	10 Nov	4 Oct	13 Sep
Lost Creek Dam	3 Mar	13 Apr	16 May	28 May	18 Nov	2 Nov	6 Oct	19 Sep
Medford Expt. Stn.	1 Mar	31 Mar	17 May	30 May	23 Nov	27 Oct	4 Oct	15 Sep
Medford WSO	27 Feb	5 Apr	3 May	20 May	28 Nov	6 Nov	15 Oct	4 Oct
Prospect	9 Apr	9 May	1 Jun	1 Jul	23 Nov	13 Oct	20 Sep	5 Sep
Riddle	19 Jan	6 Mar	20 Apr	13 May	28 Dec	11 Dec	20 Oct	5 Oct
Roseburg	5 Jan	1 Mar	7 Apr	6 May	24 Dec	25 Nov	12 Nov	21 Oct
Ruch	22 Mar	30 Apr	20 May	7 Jun	25 Nov	27 Oct	4 Oct	13 Sep
Toketee Falls	2 Mar	14 Apr	14 May	1 Jun	2 Dec	30 Oct	1 Oct	13 Sep

Table 24. Growing season. 1961-1990 means.

	Average days between occurrences of			
	24°F	28°F	32°F	36°F
Ashland	257	201	154	124
Cave Junction	284	213	153	105
Drain	329	270	175	140
Grants Pass	308	248	169	137
Howard Prairie Dam	190	141	88	43
Idleyld Park 4 NE	303	219	141	100
Lost Creek Dam	260	203	143	114
Medford Experiment Station	267	210	140	109
Medford WSO Airport	276	216	166	137
Prospect 2 SW	228	158	111	66
Riddle	344	281	183	146
Roseburg	353	269	219	168
Ruch	248	181	137	98
Toketee Falls	275	200	141	104

Zone 4. Northern Cascades

The Cascade Mountains, the dominant terrain feature in Oregon, stretch the entire length of the state from the California border to Washington. With average elevations in excess of 4,000 feet, the Cascades are crowned with a number of very high peaks. Mount Hood, near the Washington border, exceeds 11,000 feet, while Mt. Jefferson and the Three Sisters exceed 10,000 feet. Mt. McLoughlin near Medford is approximately 9,500 feet, but the Cascades are a higher and more imposing topographic feature in the northern part of Oregon. Average elevations and the number of peaks over 9,000 feet are higher north of about 43.5°N latitude. The region extending from this latitude northward to the Columbia River and encompassing high elevations west of the Cascade crest is the fourth of nine Oregon climatic zones.

The northern Cascades exert a profound effect on Oregon climate and weather. Mid-latitude storms approaching from the west are forced to rise as they encounter the Cascades, resulting in large amounts of orographic precipitation on the western slopes. So effective are the Cascades in removing moisture from the Pacific air masses that most of Oregon east of the Cascades lies in a rain shadow, resulting in large areas with annual precipitation less than 12 inches. Most of the northern Cascades, on the other hand, receive in excess of 80 inches per year; the highest peaks collect more than 150 inches per year, most of it in the form of snow. As is the case in the rest of western Oregon, most of the precipitation in the northern Cascades falls during the winter months, with November through March accounting for more than 75% of the total annual precipitation. Spring and fall rain and snow and summer thunderstorms contribute to the annual total, but they are dwarfed by the winter precipitation totals.

Monthly mean snowfall totals vary significantly according to elevation; since precipitation tends to increase with increasing elevation, more potential moisture for snowfall is available at higher elevations. And since temperatures generally decrease with increasing elevation, those high precipitation amounts are more likely to be in the form of snow. As an example, McKenzie Bridge (elevation 1,400 feet) receives an average of about 42 inches of snow per year, while Marion Forks (2,500 feet) receives about 150 inches, and Government Camp (3,980 feet) about 300 inches per year.

Scale of miles
0 10 20 30 40 50

Government Camp

Three Lynx

Detroit Dam

Marion Forks Fish Hatchery

Santiam Junction

Belknap Springs

McKenzie Bridge RS

Oakridge Fish Hatchery

Table 25 lists mean monthly and annual precipitation for Zone 4. The highest totals, near the Cascade crest, are in excess of 100 inches. Significant variations can be seen at some of the lower elevations, especially in valleys on the lee side of sizable ridges.

Mean monthly temperature data appear in Table 26. The correlation of temperature with elevation is quite strong, with the highest station (Government Camp) having consistently lower temperatures than the other sites. McKenzie Bridge has by far the highest annual mean maximum temperatures in the zone, but its annual average temperature is only slightly higher than Detroit Dam because of lower minimum temperatures at McKenzie.

Median dates of the last occurrence in spring and first occurrence in fall of four low temperature thresholds appear in Table 27. Table 28 lists the average growing season in days between those dates. Detroit Dam, at an elevation of 1,220 feet, has an exceptionally long growing season, probably due to the fact that its location above the valley floor prevents significant accumulation of cold air on clear nights, while the presence of nearby Detroit Lake serves to moderate any low temperatures. The growing season at higher elevation sites such as McKenzie Bridge, Marion Forks, and Belknap Springs is only about 50% as long as at Detroit: for example, Marion Forks at 2,480 feet has an average of only 116 days between occurrences of 32°F temperatures compared with 244 days at Detroit Dam.

Table 25. Monthly and annual precipitation (in inches). 1961-1990 means.

Station/Elevation (feet)	Jan	Feb	Mar	Apr	May	Jun	Jul	Aug	Sep	Oct	Nov	Dec	Year
Belknap Springs (2150)	11.18	9.22	8.02	4.97	3.55	2.29	.90	1.19	2.55	5.80	11.89	12.98	73.39
Detroit Dam (1220)	12.79	10.24	9.42	6.39	4.87	3.27	.90	1.61	3.56	6.42	13.21	13.98	87.10
Government Camp (3980)	13.65	10.01	8.92	7.15	4.75	3.42	1.13	1.83	3.90	6.13	11.92	14.01	86.03
Marion Forks (2480)	10.70	8.24	7.30	4.30	3.31	2.14	.91	1.27	2.40	4.91	10.62	11.40	68.06
McKenzie Bridge (1480)	9.88	7.33	7.03	5.02	3.58	2.59	.85	1.36	2.93	5.26	10.01	10.76	67.88
Oakridge (1280)	6.49	4.86	4.84	3.62	2.61	1.68	.53	1.18	1.74	3.33	7.18	7.12	45.18
Santiam Junction (3750)	7.85	5.89	7.23	4.70	3.51	2.23	1.45	1.60	.74	2.74	11.63	7.98	54.32
Three Lynx (1120)	11.37	8.31	7.85	5.36	3.95	2.67	.90	1.33	2.99	5.32	10.58	11.82	72.43

Table 26. Monthly temperatures (°F). 1961-1990 means.

Station	Code	Jan	Feb	Mar	Apr	May	Jun	Jul	Aug	Sep	Oct	Nov	Dec	Year
Belknap Springs	MMXT	39.2	44.4	49.7	56.7	64.6	73.0	80.6	80.7	74.2	62.3	47.1	38.9	59.4
	MMNT	27.1	29.0	30.6	33.5	38.5	45.0	48.4	48.3	43.6	37.5	32.8	28.4	37.0
	MNTM	33.2	36.7	40.2	45.1	51.6	59.0	64.5	64.5	58.9	49.9	39.9	33.6	48.2
Detroit Dam	MMXT	43.2	47.4	51.7	56.4	63.3	70.3	77.3	77.9	72.2	61.9	49.6	43.6	59.5
	MMNT	32.9	34.4	35.8	38.3	43.4	49.4	53.1	53.9	50.3	44.5	38.8	34.2	42.4
	MNTM	38.1	40.9	43.7	47.4	53.4	59.9	65.2	65.9	61.3	53.2	44.2	38.9	51.0
Government Camp	MMXT	35.4	38.5	40.6	45.2	52.2	60.0	67.7	68.1	62.0	53.4	40.8	36.2	50.0
	MMNT	23.5	25.6	27.1	29.9	34.6	40.9	45.8	46.3	41.9	36.2	29.5	24.7	33.8
	MNTM	29.5	32.1	33.9	37.5	43.4	50.5	56.8	57.2	51.9	44.8	35.1	30.5	41.9
Marion Forks Fish Hatchery	MMXT	38.3	43.5	48.2	54.5	62.9	72.1	79.7	79.4	71.6	60.6	45.4	38.1	57.7
	MMNT	25.8	27.5	29.4	32.3	37.0	43.4	46.1	45.3	39.7	34.5	31.0	26.9	34.8
	MNTM	32.0	35.5	38.8	43.4	50.0	57.8	62.9	62.4	55.6	47.5	38.2	32.5	46.2
McKenzie Bridge	MMXT	42.7	50.3	55.4	62.9	71.7	78.8	85.8	86.2	79.0	64.9	50.4	42.5	66.7
	MMNT	28.3	31.0	32.6	35.3	40.0	45.8	47.8	47.4	42.8	37.5	33.8	30.2	38.7
	MNTM	35.5	40.6	44.0	49.1	55.8	62.3	66.8	66.8	60.9	51.2	42.1	36.4	52.8
Oakridge Fish Hatchery	MMXT	46.3	52.0	56.1	61.3	68.0	75.2	82.1	82.9	77.3	66.7	52.3	45.5	63.8
	MMNT	29.7	31.4	33.5	36.8	41.5	47.2	49.7	49.5	44.5	38.8	34.8	30.7	39.0
	MNTM	38.0	41.7	44.8	49.1	54.8	61.2	65.9	66.2	60.9	52.8	43.6	38.1	51.4
Santiam Junction	MMXT	36.9	39.7	43.5	56.4	60.3	70.8	76.4	76.1	73.0	62.8	44.6	41.5	57.2
	MMNT	21.1	19.7	25.3	30.5	33.8	39.4	42.9	41.6	38.6	32.6	28.7	21.3	31.5
	MNTM	29.0	29.7	34.4	43.4	47.1	55.1	59.7	58.8	55.8	47.7	36.6	31.4	44.3
Three Lynx	MMXT	41.7	46.7	51.9	57.5	64.1	70.8	77.4	78.3	72.7	62.0	48.5	42.0	59.5
	MMNT	30.7	32.4	34.3	37.1	41.8	47.4	50.3	50.4	46.4	40.7	36.1	31.6	40.0
	MNTM	36.2	39.6	43.1	47.3	53.0	59.1	63.9	64.3	59.5	51.3	42.3	36.8	49.7

Codes for Table 26
MMXT = mean maximum
MMNT = mean minimum
MNTM = monthly mean

Table 27. Median frost dates. 1961-1990 means.

	Median dates of last occurrence in spring of				Median dates of first occurrence in fall of			
	24°F	28°F	32°F	36°F	24°F	28°F	32°F	36°F
Belknap Springs	1 Mar	20 Apr	12 May	1 Jun	4 Dec	5 Nov	7 Oct	18 Sep
Detroit Dam	25 Jan	5 Feb	30 Mar	5 May	29 Dec	20 Dec	29 Nov	1 Nov
Government Camp	12 Mar	19 Apr	13 May	1 Jun	24 Nov	5 Nov	11 Oct	22 Sep
Marion Forks	16 Mar	29 Apr	25 May	13 Jun	27 Nov	14 Oct	17 Sep	2 Sep
McKenzie Bridge	14 Mar	25 Apr	20 May	8 Jun	23 Nov	19 Oct	23 Sep	6 Sep
Oakridge Fish Hatchery	7 Feb	31 Mar	30 Apr	26 May	11 Dec	11 Nov	13 Oct	27 Sep
Santiam Junction	13 May	25 May	20 Jun	19 Jul	3 Oct	17 Sep	18 Aug	6 Aug
Three Lynx	30 Jan	2 Mar	16 Apr	15 May	25 Dec	6 Dec	24 Oct	9 Oct

Table 28. Growing season. 1961-1990 means.

	Average days between occurrences of			
	24°F	28°F	32° F	36°F
Belknap Springs	278	199	148	109
Detroit Dam	340	319	244	181
Government Camp	256	200	151	113
Marion Forks	256	169	116	81
McKenzie Bridge	255	177	126	90
Oakridge Fish Hatchery	307	226	166	124
Santiam Junction	143	115	59	18
Three Lynx	330	279	191	147

Zone 5. The High Plateau

Oregon's High Plateau, a region bordered by the Cascades on the west and several minor mountain ranges on the south and east, comprises much of Klamath County and parts of Lake and Deschutes counties. Due to generally high elevations, the Plateau has cool temperatures and receives a significant amount of snow. Its distance from the coast, coupled with its location downwind of the Cascades, causes its annual precipitation to be lower than in the mountainous areas surrounding it.

The Cascade crest, running north-south at a longitude of about 122°W, is lower in elevation in the High Plateau than in most parts of Oregon. Only one peak, Mt. Thielsen, exceeds 9,000 feet. As a result, the rain shadow effect produced by the mountains is less dramatic in this zone than in areas to the north. Another notable difference between the High Plateau and surrounding zones is its average elevation east of the Cascades. Whereas the places east of the northern and central Oregon Cascade peaks are typically 2,000-4,000 feet above sea level, the lower elevations of the High Plateau average about 5,500 feet.

As air moves from west to east over the Cascades in Zone 5, it begins to descend; the greater the descent, the drier the air becomes. While air parcels reaching Bend to the north have descended about 4,000 feet from the crest and are usually quite dry, similar air parcels moving into the High Plateau drop only about 2,000 feet. This difference is reflected in the average annual precipitation total for these two areas. Bend receives only about 12 inches per year, while some points in the High Plateau receive more than 20 inches.

The remoteness and ruggedness of the High Plateau has resulted in low population. Only a few small towns, including Chemult, Silver Lake, and Odell Lake, serve as population centers, but none exceeds one thousand residents. Primary economic enterprises in the area include tourism (such as Oregon's only national park, Crater Lake), livestock raising (primarily beef cattle and sheep), and agriculture (including alfalfa hay, grass and legume seed crops, and wheat).

Normal precipitation values in Zone 5 are dependent upon west-east orientation and elevation. Crater Lake, in the west, receives an average of more than 65 inches per year, while Fremont and Summer Lake to the east receive about 12 inches. Crater Lake's elevation is about 2,000 feet higher

Scale of miles
0 10 20 30 40 50

Wickiup Dam

Odell Lake East

Fremont

Crater Lake

Summer Lake

than the latter stations. Table 29 lists normal monthly and annual precipitation totals at the Zone 5 climate stations.

Temperatures in Zone 5 vary considerably during each day and throughout the year. The Crater Lake weather station, highest in elevation, has the coolest temperatures. Average maximum temperatures range from the high 60s in summer to the mid 30s in winter; lows are near 40 in summer and the high teens in winter (see Table 30). Summer Lake and Fremont are the warmest sites during the summer, and the latter has the coldest average low temperatures in winter.

The combination of high elevation and distance from the coast can produce cold temperatures in any month of the year for the High Plateau. Table 31 shows the area's median dates for specific temperature thresholds in spring and fall, while Table 32 lists the growing season (average number of days between these dates). All Zone 5 sites except Summer Lake have very short seasons (less than two months with low temperatures at or above 32°F). With such a short (and highly variable) season, it is little wonder that Zone 5 is not a major Oregon agricultural area.

Table 29. Monthly and annual precipitation (in inches). 1961-1990 means.

Station/Elevation (feet)	Jan	Feb	Mar	Apr	May	Jun	Jul	Aug	Sep	Oct	Nov	Dec	Year
Crater Lake (6480)	9.66	7.78	8.09	4.60	3.01	2.01	.68	1.29	2.38	4.75	10.56	10.84	66.28
Fremont (4510)	1.63	.92	1.17	.62	.78	1.01	.43	.61	.38	.76	1.63	1.81	11.67
Odell Lake E (4800)	4.20	3.54	3.48	1.78	1.37	1.33	.39	1.01	.93	1.50	4.30	5.44	33.35
Summer Lake (4190)	1.43	1.06	1.02	.70	.98	.99	.48	.60	.58	.98	1.65	1.89	12.40
Wickiup Dam (4360)	3.39	2.41	1.95	1.09	.93	1.00	.65	.79	.80	1.38	3.13	3.68	21.23

Table 30. Monthly Temperatures (°F). 1961-1990 means.

Station	Code	Jan	Feb	Mar	Apr	May	Jun	Jul	Aug	Sep	Oct	Nov	Dec	Year
Crater Lake	MMXT	34.5	35.2	36.4	41.8	49.2	58.0	67.9	68.5	61.7	51.7	38.5	34.4	48.1
	MMNT	17.5	18.0	18.1	21.2	27.0	33.8	39.7	40.2	35.6	30.1	22.5	18.3	26.8
	MNTM	26.0	26.6	27.2	31.5	38.1	45.9	53.8	54.4	48.6	40.9	30.5	26.3	37.4
Fremont	MMXT	39.0	44.0	48.5	57.4	66.6	74.9	84.4	83.6	75.4	64.4	47.4	38.9	59.5
	MMNT	15.1	18.1	21.3	23.0	27.9	35.1	36.3	35.5	28.4	22.9	20.0	14.6	24.2
	MNTM	27.2	31.1	35.0	40.2	47.3	55.0	60.4	59.6	51.7	43.5	33.9	26.5	41.7
Odell Lake E	MMXT	36.1	38.8	40.7	45.4	54.0	62.5	73.7	73.1	68.4	57.0	41.5	36.2	51.6
	MMNT	19.9	18.4	22.6	25.5	30.8	37.5	41.1	40.8	36.0	30.8	26.3	20.4	29.1
	MNTM	28.0	29.2	31.7	35.5	42.4	50.0	57.4	57.0	52.2	43.9	33.9	28.3	40.3
Summer Lake	MMXT	41.0	46.2	50.6	58.0	67.3	76.2	85.3	84.3	75.9	64.7	48.8	41.3	61.5
	MMNT	22.9	26.6	29.1	32.4	39.3	46.7	51.4	49.9	42.4	34.4	28.6	23.5	35.6
	MNTM	31.9	36.4	39.9	45.2	53.3	61.4	68.3	67.1	59.1	49.6	38.7	32.4	48.5
Wickiup Dam	MMXT	37.8	41.9	46.0	53.6	62.4	71.3	80.0	79.9	71.9	60.9	44.9	38.1	57.6
	MMNT	17.1	20.1	23.5	27.9	33.6	40.3	43.6	42.1	35.1	29.1	25.5	19.0	29.8
	MNTM	27.5	30.9	34.8	40.8	48.0	55.8	61.9	61.0	53.5	45.0	35.2	28.5	43.7

Table 31. Median frost dates. 1961-1990 means.

	Median dates of last occurrence in spring of				Median dates of first occurrence in fall of			
	24°F	28°F	32°F	36°F	24°F	28°F	32°F	36°F
Crater Lake N.P.	6 Jun	28 Jun	12 Jul	22 Jul	25 Sep	12 Sep	13 Aug	5 Aug
Fremont 5 NW	30 Jun	12 Jul	23 Jul	29 Jul	30 Aug	14 Aug	6 Aug	3 Aug
Silver Lake RS	23 May	21 Jun	1 Jul	16 Jul	23 Sep	11 Sep	1 Sep	14 Aug
Summer Lake 1 S	19 Apr	5 May	27 May	27 Jun	20 Oct	5 Oct	21 Sep	10 Sep
Wickiup Dam	4 May	30 May	30 Jun	15 Jul	3 Oct	14 Sep	7 Sep	13 Aug

Codes for Table 30

MMXT = mean maximum

MMNT = mean minimum

MNTM = monthly mean

Table 32. Growing season. 1961-1990 means.

	Average days between occurrences of			
	24°F	28°F	32°F	36°F
Crater Lake N.P.	112	76	32	15
Fremont 5 NW	61	33	14	5
Silver Lake RS	123	82	62	29
Summer Lake 1 S	184	153	118	75
Wickiup Dam	152	107	70	29

Zone 6. The North Central Area

North central Oregon, climatic Zone 6, is east of the Cascade Mountains, which serve as an effective moisture barrier, causing storms to dump much of their moisture west of the peaks and leaving areas to the east in a rain shadow. As a result, Zone 6 is generally rather dry. The region extends from the Columbia River southward over hill country to the forested mountain areas that border climate Zone 7. The Columbia is used in irrigation, transportation, and hydroelectric power, and therefore dominates the area.

This region is Oregon's major wheat-producing area. Grain production on dryland farms is the main source of agricultural income except for the Hood River Valley, which produces mostly tree fruits and, despite its relatively small dimensions, is one of the most important production areas in the Northwest, deriving an annual income of approximately $60 million mostly from pears, apples, and cherries. Other important commodities produced in Zone 6 include green peas, irrigated truck crops, beef cattle, sheep, alfalfa, and poultry.

Like most of Oregon, this region has a definite winter rainfall climate. The months of November through February generally receive the most precipitation due to winter storms which bring rain to lower elevations and snow to higher ridges and peaks. Occasional summer thunderstorms bring localized, occasionally heavy showers.

Table 33 lists normal monthly and annual precipitation for stations in Zone 6. Locations at the lowest elevations (adjacent to the Columbia) such as Arlington and Hermiston receive less than 10 inches per year. Precipitation increases steadily with elevation. Highest annual totals are found in the Blue Mountains along the extreme east border of the region, where totals exceeding 50 inches occur.

The Columbia Gorge is a major east-west passageway connecting Zone 6 with the Willamette Valley and Oregon coast. Vigorous winds are common in and around the Gorge. During summer, wind direction is predominantly from the west, causing strong, steady winds within the Gorge and along the

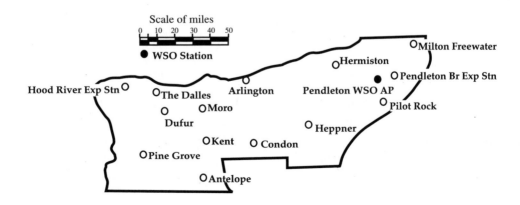

northern edge of Zone 6 and making Hood River a world-renowned wind-surfing location. Winter winds can blow from the west or the east and can reach speeds sufficient to cause widespread damage.

A major effect of the Gorge is to moderate air temperatures near the Columbia by allowing maritime air to reach the area from the west; this can occur both in summer and winter. Occasionally, however, a large-scale easterly flow brings very cold continental air to the region. During such periods, the cold air passes westward through the Gorge, creating extreme conditions in the western valleys as well.

Table 34 lists normal monthly and annual temperatures in the region. Highest summer temperatures are observed at the low-lying points near the Columbia (i.e. Arlington, Hermiston, and Milton-Freewater), and mean temperatures decrease with increasing elevation. Winter temperatures follow the same pattern, with mildest temperatures at the lower elevation sites.

Median frost dates and length of the growing season are listed in Tables 35 and 36, respectively. These also follow the same elevation relationship evident in the temperature data: the longest growing seasons are at the mild and low elevation sites, while increasing elevation generally causes a shortening of the season. Antelope and Condon, at nearly 3,000 feet above sea level, have much shorter growing seasons than lower sites like The Dalles and Arlington.

Codes for Table 34

MMXT = mean maximum
MMNT = mean minimum
MNTM = monthly mean

Table 33. Monthly and annual precipitation (in inches). 1961-1990 means.

Station/Elevation (feet)	Jan	Feb	Mar	Apr	May	Jun	Jul	Aug	Sep	Oct	Nov	Dec	Year
Antelope (2841)	1.58	1.10	1.16	.95	1.11	1.02	.40	.70	.81	.89	1.86	1.74	13.41
Arlington (285)	1.31	.88	.75	.64	.56	.38	.22	.32	.38	.56	1.29	1.62	8.83
Condon (2861)	1.54	1.24	1.22	1.23	1.20	1.04	.44	.71	.75	1.00	1.90	1.85	14.10
Dufur (1330)	1.92	1.28	1.21	.77	.71	.59	.27	.50	.55	.81	1.76	2.18	12.50
Heppner (1883)	1.53	1.12	1.49	1.32	1.42	.92	.35	.69	.80	1.04	1.73	1.56	14.04
Hermiston (620)	1.21	.84	.78	.71	.67	.46	.22	.40	.44	.62	1.28	1.37	9.06
Hood River Exp. Stn. (500)	5.36	3.91	2.93	1.63	.95	.69	.25	.59	1.14	2.20	5.11	6.00	31.05
Kent (2723)	1.34	1.00	1.02	.96	.92	.72	.46	.58	.61	.78	1.65	1.72	11.77
Milton-Freewater (971)	1.71	1.17	1.52	1.20	1.27	.94	.46	.65	.77	1.08	1.84	1.71	14.43
Moro (1870)	1.60	.89	.98	.80	.75	.56	.27	.54	.42	.69	1.60	1.71	10.81
Pendleton Br Exp. Stn. (1440)	1.96	1.49	1.74	1.47	1.38	.98	.40	.67	.81	1.23	2.06	2.01	16.50
Pendleton WSO (1482)	1.51	1.14	1.16	1.04	.99	.64	.35	.53	.59	.86	1.58	1.63	12.02
Pilot Rock (1723)	1.53	.99	1.38	1.32	1.22	1.20	.42	.76	.76	.91	1.61	1.52	13.64
Pine Grove (2220)	3.29	2.33	1.55	.92	.68	.69	.25	.47	.68	1.15	2.78	3.24	18.34
The Dalles (102)	2.24	1.81	1.22	.77	.48	.43	.20	.49	.50	.88	2.07	2.90	13.97

Table 34. Monthly temperatures (°F). 1961-1990 means.

Station	Code	Jan	Feb	Mar	Apr	May	Jun	Jul	Aug	Sep	Oct	Nov	Dec	Year
Antelope	MMXT	40.2	46.1	52.1	58.5	67.0	76.1	84.6	84.2	75.3	63.6	48.6	40.1	61.4
	MMNT	24.5	27.8	30.1	32.9	38.6	45.7	50.6	50.6	43.8	36.6	30.6	25.0	36.3
	MNTM	32.4	36.9	41.1	45.7	52.9	60.9	67.6	67.4	59.6	50.1	39.4	32.6	48.8
Arlington	MMXT	40.8	48.0	56.9	65.5	75.3	83.9	91.6	90.1	80.1	65.5	50.0	41.0	65.4
	MMNT	28.8	32.0	36.1	41.4	48.2	55.8	60.9	60.5	51.6	41.9	35.6	29.5	43.3
	MNTM	34.8	40.0	46.5	53.5	61.8	69.8	76.2	75.3	65.9	53.7	42.8	35.2	54.4
Condon	MMXT	38.4	44.1	50.4	56.8	65.6	74.4	82.3	81.5	72.4	61.3	46.3	39.2	59.1
	MMNT	23.6	27.5	30.1	33.2	38.9	45.2	50.0	50.3	43.5	36.2	29.9	24.2	35.8
	MNTM	31.0	35.8	40.3	45.0	52.2	59.8	66.1	65.9	58.0	48.8	38.1	31.7	47.4
Dufur	MMXT	40.7	47.6	55.1	62.0	70.3	78.0	85.1	84.5	76.6	64.2	48.8	40.6	62.9
	MMNT	24.4	27.8	30.4	33.4	38.4	44.6	48.2	48.3	42.7	35.3	30.4	25.0	35.8
	MNTM	32.5	37.7	42.8	47.7	54.4	61.3	66.6	66.4	59.6	49.8	39.6	32.8	49.4
Heppner	MMXT	41.6	47.6	53.7	60.3	68.9	77.8	85.7	84.6	75.4	64.1	50.1	42.2	62.7
	MMNT	25.9	29.8	33.1	36.0	42.0	48.6	52.4	52.7	45.9	38.4	32.4	26.6	38.7
	MNTM	33.7	38.7	43.4	48.1	55.4	63.2	69.0	68.7	60.7	51.3	41.2	34.4	50.7
Hermiston	MMXT	40.6	48.2	57.3	64.5	72.9	81.0	88.4	87.2	78.3	65.7	50.6	41.1	64.7
	MMNT	25.7	29.3	33.8	38.7	45.7	53.0	57.4	56.3	47.5	37.4	32.3	26.3	40.2
	MNTM	33.1	38.8	45.6	51.6	59.3	67.0	72.9	71.8	62.9	51.4	41.5	33.7	52.5
Hood River Exp Stn.	MMXT	40.6	46.8	53.7	60.0	67.5	74.2	80.1	80.5	74.0	63.4	49.3	41.3	61.0
	MMNT	28.2	31.2	34.4	38.4	43.8	50.0	53.4	52.8	45.8	38.1	34.4	29.4	40.0
	MNTM	34.4	39.0	44.1	49.2	55.6	62.1	66.8	66.6	59.9	50.8	41.9	35.3	50.5
Kent	MMXT	38.0	43.9	50.5	56.9	65.6	74.6	83.4	83.1	73.9	62.4	46.9	39.2	59.4
	MMNT	23.1	27.0	30.2	33.1	38.7	46.2	51.5	52.1	44.6	36.9	29.6	24.0	36.1
	MNTM	30.5	35.5	40.3	45.1	52.2	60.4	67.5	67.6	59.3	49.6	38.2	31.6	47.7
Milton-Freewater	MMXT	41.7	48.3	56.4	63.7	72.0	80.7	88.6	87.5	77.5	65.3	51.0	42.3	64.4
	MMNT	27.8	32.5	37.3	41.8	47.8	54.6	59.2	58.0	50.0	41.4	34.5	28.3	42.7
	MNTM	34.7	40.4	46.9	52.8	59.9	67.6	73.9	72.9	63.7	53.3	42.8	35.3	53.5
Moro	MMXT	37.7	44.0	50.6	57.5	65.2	74.0	82.0	81.0	73.9	62.1	47.3	39.6	59.6
	MMNT	23.7	28.6	31.5	35.8	41.5	48.7	53.9	53.1	45.8	37.0	31.3	26.0	38.1
	MNTM	30.7	36.3	41.1	46.6	53.4	61.4	67.9	67.0	59.8	49.5	39.3	32.8	48.8
Pendleton Br Exp. Sn.	MMXT	40.1	47.1	54.2	61.6	69.6	78.9	88.5	87.3	77.2	65.3	49.8	41.2	63.3
	MMNT	24.9	29.3	32.5	35.7	41.5	47.5	51.5	51.0	42.7	34.5	31.5	25.6	37.3
	MNTM	32.5	38.2	43.4	48.7	55.5	63.2	70.0	69.1	59.9	49.9	40.6	33.4	50.3
Pendleton WSO	MMXT	39.7	46.9	54.2	61.3	70.0	79.5	87.8	86.2	76.3	63.8	48.9	40.5	62.9
	MMNT	27.3	31.6	35.4	39.4	45.8	52.9	57.9	57.7	49.9	41.0	34.1	27.9	41.7
	MNTM	33.5	39.2	44.8	50.3	57.9	66.2	72.9	72.0	63.1	52.4	41.5	34.2	52.3
Pilot Rock	MMXT	42.1	48.0	55.0	61.8	70.3	79.6	88.9	87.5	77.7	65.9	51.3	42.7	64.2
	MMNT	25.4	28.5	32.2	35.6	41.4	48.0	51.4	51.6	44.2	36.5	31.5	25.7	37.6
	MNTM	33.8	38.3	43.6	48.7	55.9	63.8	70.1	69.5	61.0	51.2	41.4	34.2	50.9
Pine Grove	MMXT	39.3	44.5	52.2	58.7	67.6	75.0	83.1	82.2	72.4	61.9	46.9	39.8	60.2
	MMNT	24.4	27.5	31.3	34.2	41.0	47.6	52.9	52.7	44.3	36.8	30.2	25.0	37.2
	MNTM	31.9	36.0	41.8	46.5	54.4	61.3	68.0	67.4	58.3	49.4	38.6	32.5	48.7
The Dalles	MMXT	43.1	49.6	58.3	66.0	73.2	81.0	87.8	87.8	80.7	68.5	52.2	43.1	66.1
	MMNT	29.9	32.7	36.9	42.4	48.5	55.6	60.0	59.2	51.2	42.4	36.1	30.6	43.9
	MNTM	36.5	41.2	47.6	54.2	60.9	68.3	73.9	73.5	66.0	55.5	44.2	36.8	55.0

Table 35. Median frost dates. 1961-1990 means.

	Median dates of last occurrence in spring of				Median dates of first occurrence in fall of			
	24°F	28°F	32°F	36°F	24°F	28°F	32°F	36°F
Antelope	19 Apr	10 May	29 May	25 Jun	8 Nov	12 Oct	22 Sep	11 Sep
Arlington	7 Mar	28 Mar	18 Apr	30 Apr	19 Nov	31 Oct	17 Oct	6 Oct
Condon	12 Apr	6 May	28 May	29 Jun	28 Oct	14 Oct	2 Oct	10 Sep
Dufur	12 Apr	7 May	29 May	18 Jun	29 Oct	11 Oct	29 Sep	11 Sep
Heppner	19 Mar	19 Apr	6 May	30 May	15 Nov	20 Oct	4 Oct	20 Sep
Hermiston 2 S	19 Mar	8 Apr	24 Apr	15 May	3 Nov	16 Oct	5 Oct	26 Sep
Hood River Exp. Stn.	17 Feb	1 Apr	4 May	21 May	27 Nov	22 Oct	8 Oct	23 Sep
Kent	1 Apr	7 May	25 May	9 Jun	8 Nov	19 Oct	4 Oct	10 Sep
Milton-Freewater	26 Feb	20 Mar	7 Apr	27 Apr	17 Nov	30 Oct	10 Oct	4 Oct
Moro	27 Mar	19 Apr	18 May	29 May	2 Nov	16 Oct	5 Oct	16 Sep
Pendleton Br. Exp. Stn.	3 Apr	1 May	17 May	4 Jun	16 Oct	5 Oct	22 Sep	10 Sep
Pendleton WSO	18 Feb	16 Mar	15 Apr	4 May	26 Nov	9 Nov	19 Oct	5 Oct
Pilot Rock	2 Apr	21 Apr	16 May	30 May	30 Oct	14 Oct	3 Oct	13 Sep
Pine Grove	8 Apr	28 Apr	14 May	30 May	28 Oct	12 Oct	2 Oct	13 Sep
The Dalles	10 Feb	25 Feb	2 Apr	17 Apr	16 Dec	28 Nov	5 Nov	15 Oct

Table 36. Growing season. 1961-1990 means.

	Average days between occurrences of			
	24°F	28°F	32°F	36°F
Antelope	203	155	116	78
Arlington	257	217	182	159
Condon	199	161	127	74
Dufur	200	157	123	86
Heppner	241	184	151	113
Hermiston 2 S	229	191	164	134
Hood River Exp. Stn.	285	204	157	125
Kent	221	166	132	93
Milton-Freewater	266	224	186	161
Moro	221	180	141	111
Pendleton Br. Exp. Stn.	196	158	128	99
Pendleton WSO	282	239	187	154
Pilot Rock	211	176	141	106
Pine Grove	204	167	141	107
The Dalles	310	277	218	181

Zone 7. The South Central Area

South central Oregon, the largest of the Oregon climatic zones, is a vast area of high desert prairie punctuated by a number of mountain ranges and isolated peaks. This region is predominantly livestock country; in addition to beef cattle, there are large numbers of sheep, dairy herds, horses, and swine. There are large amounts of land under irrigation as well, particularly in Deschutes, Crook, Jefferson, and Klamath counties. Among the major field crops grown are potatoes, alfalfa and other hay crops, mint, wheat, oats, barley, and onions. In the remaining counties comprising this zone (Grant, Harney, and Lake), irrigated acreage is much smaller; grazing lands and dryland farming predominate.

Most of this region receives relatively low amounts of precipitation. As can be seen in Table 37, most stations receive less than 15 inches per year, though some higher mountain sites receive significantly more. For example, Steens Mountain in Harney County, the summit of which is more than 9,000 feet above sea level, receives more than 40 inches per year at its higher elevations. High elevation points can easily be spotted on precipitation maps, since they correspond to high annual precipitation amounts.

Most of the stations in Zone 7 receive their highest monthly precipitation in the winter months with a secondary maximum during late spring and early summer. Stations near the Cascades (such as Sisters, Bend,

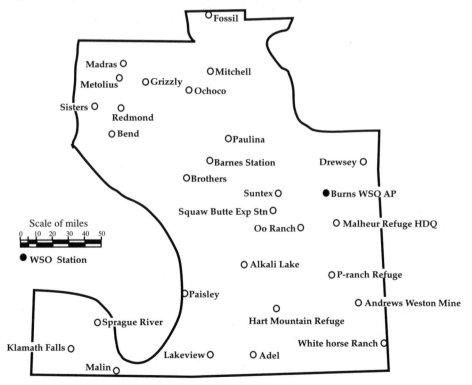

Chiloquin, Klamath Falls, and Madras) tend to have annual distributions very similar to those in western Oregon: winter maxima are followed by a steady decrease, with lowest monthly averages in midsummer. For other locations farther east, the precipitation is greatest during spring and summer. At Hart Mountain, for example, the four wettest months are March through June. The months of July through September are generally the driest of the year throughout the region, but these months are characterized by isolated local thunderstorms that can produce a relatively high monthly total.

Table 38 lists normal monthly temperatures for Zone 7 measurement stations. Summers are generally quite warm, although the relatively high elevations tend to moderate the temperatures somewhat. Pelton Dam and Dayville, with mean maximum temperatures in the 90s during the warmest summer months, are the hottest stations in this region. The coldest sites listed are Brothers, Hart Mountain, Sprague River, and Ochoco Ranger Station, but it is certain that some of the higher elevations are colder than the areas listed here.

Median dates of low temperature thresholds in spring and fall are listed in Table 39, and Table 40 gives the length of the growing season at each station.

Table 37. Monthly and annual precipitation (in inches). 1961-1990 means.

Station/Elevation (feet)	Jan	Feb	Mar	Apr	May	Jun	Jul	Aug	Sep	Oct	Nov	Dec	Year
Adel (4580)	1.11	.98	.93	.87	.82	1.01	.42	.59	.58	.46	1.13	1.09	9.79
Alkali Lake (4330)	.64	.52	.73	.79	1.10	1.14	.57	.75	.57	.70	.78	.70	9.11
Andrews Weston Mine (4780)	2.13	1.79	2.14	1.52	1.12	.90	.53	.79	.96	1.00	2.38	2.55	17.86
Barnes Station (3970)	1.22	.88	.97	.79	1.11	1.06	.71	.89	.60	.79	1.62	1.52	12.19
Bend (650)	1.83	.97	.92	.60	.77	.86	.49	.58	.47	.65	1.57	1.99	11.70
Brothers (4640)	1.06	.49	.64	.64	1.05	.95	.52	.72	.49	.67	1.21	1.10	9.31
Burns WSO AP (4140)	.99	.76	1.01	.65	.98	.83	.40	.66	.56	.72	1.25	1.15	9.96
Drewsey (3520)	1.09	.94	1.12	.69	.84	.51	.31	.52	.51	.54	1.29	1.28	9.53
Fossil (2650)	1.66	1.23	1.34	1.41	1.27	1.03	.49	.80	.84	1.16	1.92	1.80	15.11
Grizzly (3640)	1.54	1.00	1.09	.97	1.23	1.04	.42	.77	.71	.88	1.79	1.36	12.40
Hart Mountain Refuge (5620)	.87	.74	1.22	1.33	1.43	1.34	.43	.61	.82	.97	1.16	1.13	12.21
Klamath Falls (4100)	1.81	1.28	1.35	.75	.85	.69	.35	.62	.55	1.07	1.97	2.23	13.47
Lakeview (4770)	2.01	1.43	1.52	1.22	1.43	1.15	.36	.54	.63	1.20	2.13	2.09	15.78
Madras (2440)	1.33	.88	.84	.71	.79	.78	.44	.54	.54	.70	1.49	1.48	10.90
Malheur Refuge HDQ (2230)	.89	.57	1.00	.71	1.06	.91	.40	.74	.51	.79	1.18	1.04	10.47
Malin (4630)	1.50	1.18	1.60	1.02	1.14	.85	.38	.75	.79	1.15	1.60	1.50	13.59
Metolius (2500)	1.32	.86	.86	.68	.76	.76	.38	.60	.47	.66	1.54	1.41	9.96
Mitchell (2650)	.86	.65	1.04	1.13	1.55	1.25	.57	.78	.74	.75	1.23	.99	11.57
Ochoco (3980)	2.13	1.55	1.37	1.13	1.24	1.29	.70	.88	.94	1.25	2.49	2.38	17.10
OO Ranch (4140)	1.03	.69	.84	.68	1.17	.98	.39	.84	.56	.78	1.09	1.10	10.98
P-Ranch Refuge (4200)	1.05	.84	1.18	1.08	1.27	1.18	.39	.74	.76	.90	1.36	1.14	11.69
Paisley (4360)	1.40	.84	.97	.75	.96	1.08	.39	.64	.50	.79	1.18	1.52	11.05
Paulina (3680)	1.33	.88	1.03	.81	1.08	1.08	.61	.67	.53	.83	1.44	1.39	12.49
Prineville (2840)	1.01	1.15	.99	.90	.98	.83	.76	.33	.62	.76	1.20	1.35	10.74
Redmond (3060)	1.06	.60	.69	.58	.71	.73	.45	.54	.41	.54	1.16	1.09	8.62
Sisters (3180)	2.55	1.66	1.23	.74	.55	.53	.41	.45	.49	.90	2.20	2.45	14.18
Sprague River (4360)	2.45	1.52	1.81	.90	.99	.84	.34	.69	.68	1.33	2.24	2.34	16.97
Squaw Butte Exp Stn (4660)	1.27	.72	.86	.73	1.13	.94	.36	.73	.52	.71	1.23	1.22	10.55
Whitehorse Ranch (4200)	.59	.63	.83	.97	.77	.61	.24	.84	.59	.55	.82	.63	8.61

Table 38. Monthly temperatures (°F). 1961-1990 means.

Station	Code	Jan	Feb	Mar	Apr	May	Jun	Jul	Aug	Sep	Oct	Nov	Dec	Year
Adel	MMXT	41.9	46.6	52.3	59.3	69.9	78.4	87.9	86.2	77.8	67.1	50.2	42.1	63.7
	MMNT	21.8	24.3	27.8	31.7	39.1	46.6	52.1	50.1	42.0	34.0	27.7	21.5	35.4
	MNTM	31.8	35.4	40.1	45.5	54.5	62.5	70.0	68.1	59.9	50.6	39.0	31.8	49.5
Alkali Lake	MMXT	19.1	23.4	25.4	28.6	34.8	42.5	46.9	45.4	37.0	29.7	25.1	19.1	31.4
	MMNT	41.7	46.6	51.3	59.4	69.3	78.5	88.1	86.5	77.9	65.9	50.2	42.1	63.1
	MNTM	30.5	35.0	38.4	44.0	52.1	60.4	67.5	66.0	57.5	47.8	37.9	30.6	47.3
Andrews Weston Mine	MMXT	37.0	42.6	48.7	56.7	65.7	76.6	85.7	84.3	73.5	61.8	46.4	38.3	59.7
	MMNT	22.4	26.8	30.9	36.0	42.7	51.6	59.3	58.7	49.5	40.7	30.7	23.6	39.3
	MNTM	29.7	34.7	39.8	46.3	54.2	64.1	72.5	71.5	61.6	51.3	38.5	30.9	49.5
Barnes Station	MMXT	38.4	44.3	49.7	57.3	66.0	74.9	84.1	82.9	74.8	63.7	47.2	39.2	60.1
	MMNT	17.8	22.8	25.5	28.1	34.1	41.0	45.3	44.2	36.8	30.1	25.3	18.8	30.8
	MNTM	28.1	33.5	37.6	42.7	50.1	58.0	64.7	63.6	55.7	46.9	36.2	29.0	45.4
Bend	MMXT	41.6	46.3	51.1	57.5	65.1	73.6	81.5	80.9	73.1	63.1	48.5	41.7	60.3
	MMNT	21.9	24.5	25.9	29.1	34.5	41.1	45.0	44.6	37.4	31.2	27.1	22.4	32.1
	MNTM	31.7	35.4	38.5	43.3	49.8	57.3	63.2	62.7	55.2	47.2	37.8	32.1	46.2
Brothers	MMXT	37.6	42.8	48.1	56.0	64.4	73.0	81.9	80.9	73.0	62.6	45.9	38.3	58.7
	MMNT	16.8	21.0	22.4	24.8	30.6	37.7	41.8	41.0	33.8	27.9	22.8	17.3	28.2
	MNTM	27.2	31.9	35.3	40.4	47.5	55.4	61.9	60.9	53.4	45.2	34.4	27.8	43.4
Burns WSO AP	MMXT	33.3	38.4	48.7	57.8	64.9	74.5	84.2	83.6	73.3	61.1	44.1	33.1	57.0
	MMNT	12.7	17.1	26.2	30.1	36.3	42.0	47.2	45.3	36.5	28.1	21.3	12.2	29.4
	MNTM	23.0	27.8	37.4	43.9	50.6	58.3	65.7	64.5	54.9	44.6	32.7	22.7	43.2
Drewsey	MMXT	34.3	42.7	52.7	62.5	71.1	81.0	89.4	87.9	78.0	66.0	47.0	36.2	62.9
	MMNT	12.8	19.9	25.5	29.7	36.6	43.9	48.9	45.6	35.4	26.9	21.7	14.5	30.5
	MNTM	23.5	31.3	39.1	46.1	53.8	62.4	69.1	66.7	56.7	46.4	34.4	25.3	46.7
Fossil	MMXT	41.1	46.9	51.9	58.6	66.9	75.0	83.5	83.2	74.8	65.8	48.7	41.5	61.2
	MMNT	23.8	26.8	28.6	31.0	35.5	42.3	45.1	45.9	39.8	34.1	29.8	25.3	33.8
	MNTM	32.5	36.7	40.3	44.8	51.4	58.6	64.3	64.5	57.3	50.0	39.2	33.4	47.3
Grizzly	MMXT	40.4	45.0	49.5	55.6	63.6	73.2	81.9	81.8	72.6	62.6	47.4	40.8	59.6
	MMNT	21.6	24.5	25.4	27.4	32.4	39.2	42.1	42.4	36.9	31.4	27.3	22.0	31.2
	MNTM	31.0	34.7	37.5	41.5	48.0	56.2	62.0	62.1	54.7	46.9	37.3	31.4	45.1
Hart Mountain Refuge	MMXT	39.3	41.9	45.0	52.9	62.4	71.5	81.2	80.2	71.2	60.9	46.0	39.5	57.9
	MMNT	18.2	21.1	22.2	26.0	32.2	39.1	43.9	43.6	37.0	30.6	24.3	18.0	29.9
	MNTM	28.9	31.6	33.5	39.4	47.3	55.3	62.5	61.9	54.1	45.8	35.2	28.9	44.1
Klamath Falls	MMXT	39.2	45.2	50.6	58.3	67.6	76.5	84.9	83.8	76.2	64.1	47.4	39.2	61.0
	MMNT	20.5	24.9	27.8	31.1	38.3	45.6	50.9	49.7	42.8	34.6	27.6	21.8	34.6
	MNTM	29.8	35.0	39.2	44.7	52.9	61.0	67.9	66.8	59.5	49.4	37.5	30.5	47.8
Lakeview	MMXT	37.9	42.2	47.6	55.7	65.0	73.9	83.7	82.1	74.1	62.9	46.3	38.9	59.0
	MMNT	19.0	23.0	26.4	30.6	37.3	44.4	50.3	48.4	41.3	33.4	26.5	20.8	33.5
	MNTM	28.5	32.6	37.0	43.1	51.2	59.2	67.0	65.2	57.8	48.1	36.4	29.9	46.3
Madras	MMXT	42.6	49.5	55.7	62.8	70.8	79.4	87.0	86.6	78.0	66.2	50.7	42.8	64.5
	MMNT	23.2	26.4	28.2	31.4	36.7	43.2	46.3	45.8	39.3	32.2	28.8	23.9	33.7
	MNTM	32.9	38.0	41.9	47.3	53.8	61.3	66.7	66.2	58.5	49.0	39.7	33.4	49.0
Malheur Refuge HDQ	MMXT	37.4	44.3	49.8	58.4	67.4	75.1	84.8	83.2	74.5	63.1	47.3	37.5	60.3
	MMNT	17.6	22.9	25.5	29.9	37.5	44.8	49.2	47.4	38.5	29.9	24.6	17.2	32.1
	MNTM	27.5	33.8	37.6	44.2	52.5	60.1	66.9	65.3	56.5	46.5	35.9	27.4	46.3
Malin	MMXT	40.3	44.4	48.7	56.3	65.9	74.8	83.0	82.1	73.9	62.4	47.2	40.2	59.9
	MMNT	21.7	25.0	27.0	30.5	36.7	43.8	48.9	48.0	41.7	34.9	27.7	22.2	34.0
	MNTM	31.0	34.7	37.8	43.4	51.3	59.3	65.9	65.0	57.8	48.7	37.4	31.2	47.0

Station	Code	Jan	Feb	Mar	Apr	May	Jun	Jul	Aug	Sep	Oct	Nov	Dec	Year
Metolius	MMXT	40.8	47.1	53.5	59.8	67.9	76.5	84.3	84.0	75.5	63.7	48.6	40.8	61.8
	MMNT	23.3	26.4	27.8	30.5	36.0	42.2	45.4	45.1	39.3	33.2	28.9	23.7	33.4
	MNTM	32.1	36.7	40.6	45.2	52.0	59.4	64.9	64.5	57.4	48.4	38.8	32.2	47.6
Mitchell	MMXT	41.3	47.1	52.9	59.8	68.0	77.5	85.8	85.3	75.8	64.6	48.9	41.5	62.7
	MMNT	23.6	27.1	30.4	33.4	39.4	46.8	51.0	50.7	42.7	35.3	29.2	24.4	36.5
	MNTM	32.4	37.0	41.7	46.6	53.7	62.1	68.4	68.0	59.3	49.9	39.0	33.0	49.6
Ochoco	MMXT	35.3	41.1	47.9	55.7	63.7	72.6	81.1	81.7	73.4	61.4	43.3	35.6	58.2
	MMNT	15.3	18.8	22.9	26.3	31.5	37.6	40.1	39.6	33.8	28.4	23.9	17.7	28.4
	MNTM	25.2	30.0	35.4	41.0	47.6	55.1	60.6	60.6	53.6	44.9	33.6	26.6	43.4
OO Ranch	MMXT	38.8	44.6	50.6	59.2	69.0	76.8	86.3	84.8	75.8	63.2	49.0	38.5	61.8
	MMNT	19.1	23.3	26.5	30.5	36.7	44.0	48.3	46.1	37.6	29.2	25.3	18.2	32.5
	MNTM	28.9	33.9	38.6	44.9	52.9	60.3	67.3	65.4	56.6	46.2	37.2	28.3	47.2
Paisley	MMXT	41.5	46.9	51.2	58.8	67.5	75.9	84.6	83.7	76.1	65.2	49.0	41.7	62.1
	MMNT	21.6	25.2	27.3	31.4	38.2	45.3	49.2	48.3	40.6	33.4	26.9	22.0	34.3
	MNTM	31.5	36.1	39.3	45.1	52.9	60.7	66.9	66.0	58.3	49.3	37.9	32.0	48.2
Paulina	MMXT	38.0	45.1	51.5	59.7	68.5	77.3	86.9	85.9	78.0	66.3	48.4	39.0	62.0
	MMNT	16.6	22.3	25.3	27.5	33.7	40.6	43.4	41.8	33.7	27.0	24.5	17.7	29.5
	MNTM	27.3	33.7	38.4	43.6	51.1	58.9	65.1	63.8	55.9	46.6	36.4	28.3	45.8
P-Ranch Refuge	MMXT	42.0	48.0	53.5	60.7	68.5	77.0	85.6	85.0	77.1	66.9	51.1	42.3	62.4
	MMNT	20.4	24.2	26.8	30.6	37.3	43.8	46.6	44.4	36.4	30.0	27.1	21.5	32.1
	MNTM	31.2	36.2	40.1	45.7	52.9	60.4	66.2	64.7	56.7	48.5	39.1	32.0	47.2
Prineville	MMXT	43.5	48.5	55.6	63.3	69.4	77.5	85.6	86.1	76.0	65.7	50.0	41.6	63.5
	MMNT	23.2	24.4	27.1	29.5	35.2	41.1	43.3	41.8	35.5	30.4	26.6	20.1	31.5
	MNTM	33.4	36.4	41.4	46.4	52.3	59.3	64.5	63.9	55.8	48.0	38.3	30.8	47.5
Redmond	MMXT	41.2	47.1	52.7	59.2	67.2	76.7	85.1	84.1	75.0	64.3	49.0	41.7	61.7
	MMNT	21.5	24.9	26.2	28.9	34.8	42.1	46.3	46.1	38.6	32.2	27.3	21.8	32.4
	MNTM	31.3	36.0	39.5	44.1	51.0	59.4	65.7	65.1	56.8	48.3	38.1	31.8	47.1
Sisters	MMXT	41.4	46.2	51.3	57.0	65.6	75.1	83.6	83.0	74.7	63.3	47.7	41.0	61.4
	MMNT	20.8	23.7	25.5	27.7	32.7	38.9	41.3	41.2	34.5	28.9	25.6	20.3	30.5
	MNTM	31.1	34.9	38.4	42.3	49.1	57.0	62.5	62.0	54.5	46.0	36.6	30.7	45.9
Sprague River	MMXT	39.0	44.7	49.6	57.5	67.1	75.9	84.5	84.1	76.5	65.4	47.9	39.5	60.5
	MMNT	15.7	20.6	23.6	25.3	31.2	38.1	41.5	40.4	32.8	26.9	22.9	17.3	27.7
	MNTM	27.4	32.7	36.6	41.4	49.1	57.1	63.0	62.2	54.6	46.2	35.4	28.4	44.1
Squaw Butte Exp Stn	MMXT	35.4	41.5	46.5	55.5	63.9	74.1	83.4	82.4	73.8	62.1	45.7	37.3	59.1
	MMNT	17.5	22.7	25.2	29.5	35.6	43.8	50.2	49.5	42.5	34.4	26.3	20.7	33.9
	MNTM	26.3	32.2	35.8	42.5	49.7	59.0	66.7	66.0	58.2	48.1	36.0	28.7	46.7
Whitehorse Ranch	MMXT	40.7	47.1	52.9	60.4	69.0	77.7	86.7	84.6	76.0	64.7	51.0	42.0	62.3
	MMNT	18.8	23.2	26.3	30.1	37.1	44.7	50.6	49.7	41.3	33.0	26.0	19.1	33.5
	MNTM	29.8	35.1	39.6	45.2	53.0	61.1	68.7	67.1	58.7	48.9	38.5	30.3	47.9

Codes for Table 38

MMXT = mean maximum

MMNT = mean minimum

MNTM = monthly mean

Table 39. Median frost dates. 1961-1990 means.

	Median dates of last occurrence in spring of				Median dates of first occurrence in fall of			
	24°F	28°F	32°F	36°F	24°F	28°F	32°F	36°F
Adel	22 Apr	6 May	1 Jun	7 Jun	17 Oct	4 Oct	17 Sep	10 Sep
Alkali Lake	12 May	25 May	18 Jun	8 Jul	2 Oct	12 Sep	3 Sep	19 Aug
Andrews Weston Mine	13 Apr	6 May	16 May	6 Jun	8 Nov	28 Oct	7 Oct	26 Sep
Barnes Station	14 May	4 Jun	28 Jun	16 Jul	30 Sep	11 Sep	2 Sep	15 Aug
Bend	13 May	1 Jun	6 Jul	16 Jul	4 Oct	15 Sep	4 Sep	20 Aug
Brothers	25 Jun	11 Jul	21 Jul	25 Jul	8 Sep	16 Aug	8 Aug	4 Aug
Burns WSO AP	1 May	21 May	6 Jun	29 Jun	7 Oct	22 Sep	16 Sep	27 Aug
Drewsey	10 May	22 May	22 Jun	2 Jul	26 Sep	14 Sep	3 Sep	20 Aug
Fossil	5 May	24 May	8 Jun	10 Jul	9 Oct	2 Oct	11 Sep	26 Aug
Grizzly	20 May	8 Jun	9 Jul	22 Jul	4 Oct	15 Sep	28 Aug	6 Aug
Hart Mountain Refuge	31 May	21 Jun	7 Jul	19 Jul	21 Sep	11 Sep	23 Aug	14 Aug
Klamath Falls	29 Apr	19 May	6 Jun	29 Jun	22 Oct	6 Oct	20 Sep	9 Sep
Lakeview	29 Apr	17 May	3 Jun	29 Jun	14 Oct	4 Oct	20 Sep	29 Aug
Madras	2 May	22 May	7 Jun	2 Jul	6 Oct	1 Oct	10 Sep	1 Sep
Malheur Refuge HDQ	30 Apr	14 May	1 Jun	28 Jun	2 Oct	19 Sep	5 Sep	27 Aug
Malin	2 May	20 May	11 Jun	30 Jun	27 Oct	3 Oct	21 Sep	3 Sep
Metolius	4 May	23 May	8 Jun	7 Jul	14 Oct	28 Sep	11 Sep	24 Aug
Mitchell	10 Apr	4 May	24 May	3 Jun	28 Oct	16 Oct	30 Sep	16 Sep
Ochoco	20 May	20 Jun	11 Jul	26 Jul	2 Oct	8 Sep	15 Aug	2 Aug
OO Ranch	30 Apr	21 May	10 Jun	28 Jun	4 Oct	21 Sep	10 Sep	29 Aug
Paisley	21 May	8 Jun	3 Jul	22 Jul	17 Sep	8 Sep	23 Aug	9 Aug
Paulina	28 Apr	16 May	3 Jun	1 Jul	25 Sep	12 Sep	3 Sep	19 Aug
P Ranch Refuge	1 May	15 May	6 Jun	30 Jun	14 Oct	23 Sep	9 Sep	31 Aug
Prineville	7 May	28 May	3 Jul	16 Jul	3 Oct	12 Sep	29 Aug	8 Aug
Redmond	8 May	29 May	28 Jun	10 Jul	13 Oct	24 Sep	9 Sep	19 Aug
Sisters	23 May	29 Jun	14 Jul	26 Jul	18 Sep	8 Sep	17 Aug	4 Aug
Sprague River	28 May	25 Jun	12 Jul	22 Jul	17 Sep	30 Aug	18 Aug	3 Aug
Squaw Butte Exp Stn	6 May	25 May	27 Jun	2 Jul	17 Oct	6 Oct	12 Sep	2 Sep
Whitehorse Ranch	4 May	19 May	8 Jun	28 Jun	9 Oct	25 Sep	16 Sep	8 Sep

Table 40. Growing season. 1961-1990 means.

| | Average days between occurrences of | | | |
	24°F	28°F	32°F	36°F
Adel	182	147	117	90
Alkali Lake	140	116	79	45
Andrews Weston Mine	209	171	140	106
Barnes Station	136	96	65	34
Bend	147	103	59	34
Brothers	83	46	23	13
Burns WSO AP	156	127	99	63
Drewsey	146	115	77	56
Fossil	158	131	90	46
Grizzly	141	105	58	32
Hart Mountain Refuge	115	79	46	27
Klamath Falls	179	141	104	69
Lakeview	167	138	107	64
Madras	160	133	93	60
Malheur Refuge HDQ	157	125	95	61
Malin	171	135	98	60
Metolius	163	129	93	48
Mitchell	204	165	131	97
Ochoco	133	79	41	15
OO Ranch	155	120	88	63
Paisley	163	132	91	58
Paulina	122	89	51	23
P Ranch Refuge	157	121	91	51
Prineville	149	107	57	23
Redmond	155	117	77	45
Sisters	128	75	37	14
Sprague River	108	74	46	27
Squaw Butte Exp Stn	163	134	85	58
Whitehorse Ranch	161	132	105	79

Zone 8. The Northeast Area

Climate Zone 8 occupies the northeastern corner of Oregon, including all of Wallowa, Baker, and Union counties as well as portions of Umatilla and Grant. The area includes several sizable mountain ranges with large valleys between them. Among the larger cities are La Grande, Baker City, John Day, and Enterprise, although La Grande, the biggest of these, has a population of only slightly above ten thousand residents.

Livestock raising is the major industry in this region; several million acres of federal land are being utilized by ranchers for livestock. Beef cattle raising predominates, but sheep, dairy herds, poultry, and hogs are significant income sources as well. Field crops are also an important farm commodity; important crops include wheat, potatoes, barley, oats, and grass seed. Lumber is also produced in significant quantities from the forested areas in the region.

Annual precipitation totals in Zone 8 valley areas are generally below 20 inches. Some locations surrounded by high mountains, such as Baker City and Unity, barely exceed 10 inches per year. High-elevation sites, on the other hand, receive much larger annual totals. Locations near the top of the Wallowa Mountains, for example, may exceed 100 inches of precipitation per year, much of it in the form of snow. Table 41 lists monthly and annual normal precipitation at Zone 8 sites. Unlike most of Oregon, Zone 8's monthly distribution of precipitation is remarkably uniform throughout the year.

Zone 8's distance from the ocean causes its annual temperature variations to be rather large. Table 42 lists normal monthly precipitation at stations in the area. Mean maximum temperatures are mostly in the 80s in summer months and in the 30s in winter. The dry, clear summer days are usually followed by cool nights; nighttime lows generally average in the 40s. The coldest temperatures in the region (and probably in the state) are observed in Seneca, located in a deep valley surrounded by mountain ridges. January low temperatures in Seneca average a cold 8.4°F. Annually, Seneca experiences an average of 22 days with below-zero temperatures. Seneca is in a tie for the coldest temperature ever recorded in Oregon, -54°F, set in February 1933.

Tables 43 and 44 list median frost dates and mean growing seasons, respectively, for four different temperature thresholds. While some of the lower valley sites have fairly long growing seasons, a few of the colder locations have a very short season—at Seneca, Austin, and Ukiah, the mean length of time between freezing temperatures is less than six weeks.

Table 41. Monthly and annual precipitation (in inches). 1961-1990 means.

Station/Elevation (feet)	Jan	Feb	Mar	Apr	May	Jun	Jul	Aug	Sep	Oct	Nov	Dec	Year
Austin (4200)	2.78	1.94	1.98	1.44	1.47	1.62	.72	1.01	1.06	1.32	2.55	3.08	20.49
Baker (3471)	1.03	.62	.84	.82	1.26	1.38	.58	.94	.74	.63	.96	1.07	10.87
Cove (3120)	2.53	1.22	2.59	2.61	3.24	2.17	.42	1.52	.69	1.23	2.49	1.27	22.47
Elgin (2660)	2.98	2.46	2.27	1.68	1.72	1.46	.65	.86	1.05	1.72	3.13	3.52	23.73
Enterprise (3880)	1.44	.76	1.89	1.56	2.09	1.59	1.01	1.76	.52	.55	1.51	.84	15.53
Halfway (2670)	3.28	2.31	1.92	1.40	1.37	1.31	.47	.76	.92	1.31	3.02	3.50	21.58
Huntington (2130)	1.78	1.36	1.27	.81	.91	.94	.38	.67	.60	.79	1.81	2.06	13.57
John Day (3060)	1.15	.82	1.12	1.18	1.56	1.40	.53	.95	.84	.92	1.47	1.40	13.38
La Grande (2760)	1.96	1.47	1.48	1.42	1.61	1.43	.63	.92	.97	1.24	1.86	1.86	17.18
Long Creek (3720)	1.46	.93	1.42	1.33	1.46	1.24	.61	.86	.84	1.20	1.67	1.58	14.34
Monument (2000)	1.48	1.03	1.33	1.31	1.38	1.08	.46	.74	.68	.92	1.51	1.53	13.73
Richland (2220)	1.53	.91	.91	.96	1.22	1.02	.63	.85	.57	.71	1.54	1.39	12.59
Rock Creek (7250)	2.67	1.89	1.87	1.37	1.65	1.78	.92	.98	.92	1.20	2.54	2.91	20.66
Seneca (4660)	1.29	1.03	1.17	.99	1.34	1.11	.55	.87	.66	.88	1.49	1.67	13.12
Ukiah (3360)	1.93	1.30	1.42	1.32	1.63	1.21	.63	.85	.88	1.22	2.08	1.99	16.19
Union (2770)	1.16	.90	1.18	1.24	1.64	1.56	.61	.94	1.04	1.00	1.32	1.19	13.79
Unity (4030)	1.23	.67	.76	.68	1.08	1.14	.44	.92	.54	.57	1.16	1.28	10.91
Walla Walla (2400)	6.22	4.20	4.71	3.53	2.70	2.10	.69	1.17	1.86	3.19	5.69	5.26	41.09
Wallowa (2920)	1.94	1.34	1.40	1.25	1.69	1.41	.85	.90	1.25	1.43	1.88	2.00	17.15

Table 42. Monthly temperatures (°F). 1961-1990 means.

Station	Code	Jan	Feb	Mar	Apr	May	Jun	Jul	Aug	Sep	Oct	Nov	Dec	Year
Austin	MMXT	34.6	40.5	45.9	54.3	62.6	72.0	81.6	81.6	71.2	60.2	43.1	34.7	56.1
	MMNT	10.5	14.6	19.5	25.6	30.7	37.1	39.2	38.1	30.5	24.9	20.9	12.1	24.8
	MNTM	22.5	27.6	32.7	40.0	46.5	54.5	60.4	59.9	50.9	42.6	31.9	23.4	40.3
Baker	MMXT	33.7	41.1	50.0	58.8	67.2	75.8	84.9	84.3	74.7	62.5	45.7	35.3	59.5
	MMNT	16.8	22.4	26.9	31.1	38.1	45.0	48.5	47.4	38.9	30.5	25.1	17.7	32.4
	MNTM	25.3	31.8	38.5	45.0	52.6	60.4	66.7	65.8	56.8	46.5	35.4	26.5	45.9
Cove	MMXT	38.0	37.1	51.4	61.2	63.6	74.2	85.2	81.1	77.5	63.6	48.3	36.9	59.6
	MMNT	23.6	16.6	28.1	35.0	37.2	43.9	48.7	46.9	41.0	35.9	30.1	18.8	33.9
	MNTM	30.8	26.9	39.7	48.1	50.4	59.0	67.0	64.0	59.3	49.8	39.2	27.8	46.7
Elgin	MMXT	37.9	44.8	52.0	60.8	69.3	78.3	87.6	87.8	78.1	65.2	47.8	38.6	62.4
	MMNT	21.6	25.4	28.5	32.0	37.5	43.6	46.0	45.1	37.7	31.3	28.3	22.8	33.3
	MNTM	29.7	35.1	40.3	46.4	53.4	61.0	66.8	66.4	57.9	48.3	38.1	30.7	47.9
Enterprise	MMXT	33.2	37.5	47.7	60.0	61.6	70.8	78.3	76.9	73.7	62.1	44.8	33.9	56.7
	MMNT	12.2	13.3	23.4	29.4	33.4	39.8	41.4	39.3	33.3	26.9	22.3	11.9	27.2
	MNTM	22.7	25.4	35.5	44.7	47.5	55.3	59.9	58.1	53.5	44.5	33.5	22.9	42.0
Halfway	MMXT	32.7	40.3	51.0	61.9	70.8	79.2	88.1	87.1	77.3	64.6	46.4	34.5	61.2
	MMNT	14.4	19.0	25.8	30.9	37.0	43.7	47.6	46.5	38.6	30.5	25.3	16.8	31.3
	MNTM	23.6	29.7	38.4	46.4	53.9	61.5	67.8	66.8	58.0	47.6	35.9	25.7	46.3
Huntington	MMXT	35.6	44.1	55.1	64.7	74.2	84.1	93.6	92.0	80.1	66.5	48.8	37.6	64.7
	MMNT	19.8	25.3	31.6	38.3	46.8	55.9	63.8	61.4	49.8	38.0	29.2	21.6	40.1
	MNTM	27.7	34.7	43.3	51.5	60.5	70.0	78.7	76.7	65.0	52.2	39.0	29.6	52.4
John Day	MMXT	40.4	47.0	52.7	59.8	68.8	78.2	87.9	87.2	77.6	66.1	50.1	41.8	63.0
	MMNT	21.0	25.0	28.4	32.2	38.6	45.2	48.6	47.9	40.4	33.2	28.2	22.1	34.2
	MNTM	30.7	36.0	40.6	46.0	53.7	61.7	68.3	67.5	59.0	49.6	39.1	32.0	48.6
La Grande	MMXT	37.6	43.3	51.1	58.7	67.7	76.8	86.2	86.1	76.0	63.0	46.8	38.5	60.9
	MMNT	23.6	27.0	30.4	34.6	41.3	48.4	52.5	51.4	43.2	35.1	30.3	24.4	36.6
	MNTM	30.6	35.1	40.8	46.6	54.5	62.6	69.3	68.7	59.6	49.0	38.6	31.5	48.5
Long Creek	MMXT	38.8	45.0	50.2	56.7	64.7	74.2	82.7	82.2	73.1	62.6	47.8	39.8	59.5
	MMNT	20.8	24.2	26.3	29.3	35.0	40.7	44.4	43.8	37.7	32.6	27.1	21.2	31.7
	MNTM	29.8	34.7	38.2	43.0	49.8	57.5	63.5	63.0	55.6	47.6	37.4	30.6	45.6
Monument	MMXT	41.6	49.4	56.2	63.4	71.7	81.5	90.1	89.7	79.9	67.9	52.0	43.0	65.4
	MMNT	21.4	25.9	29.4	33.4	39.7	46.6	49.5	48.5	40.7	32.2	28.4	22.6	34.8
	MNTM	31.5	37.7	42.8	48.4	55.7	64.1	69.7	69.1	60.3	50.1	40.2	32.8	50.1
Richland	MMXT	39.1	46.7	56.5	67.7	75.9	84.2	91.9	91.1	81.8	69.4	52.2	40.5	67.3
	MMNT	20.8	24.7	29.6	34.9	41.8	49.7	54.9	54.8	43.7	33.9	27.4	21.9	37.2
	MNTM	29.9	35.7	43.1	51.3	58.8	67.1	73.4	72.9	62.8	51.7	39.8	31.2	52.2
Seneca	MMXT	33.2	38.8	44.3	53.1	61.2	70.6	80.4	80.2	70.1	59.6	43.6	34.3	55.8
	MMNT	8.4	13.4	19.8	25.0	30.9	36.5	37.6	35.6	27.8	21.3	19.5	11.5	23.8
	MNTM	20.8	26.1	32.0	39.0	46.0	53.5	59.0	57.9	48.9	40.4	31.5	22.9	39.9
Ukiah	MMXT	36.1	43.0	49.0	56.3	64.1	73.4	82.6	82.5	73.8	62.9	46.5	37.1	58.8
	MMNT	14.5	19.4	23.4	27.7	32.7	38.1	39.9	39.2	31.9	26.0	23.5	16.4	27.6
	MNTM	25.3	31.2	36.2	42.0	48.4	55.8	61.3	60.9	52.8	44.5	35.0	26.7	43.2
Union	MMXT	36.5	43.0	50.4	57.9	65.6	74.1	83.4	83.7	73.8	62.4	47.3	38.1	59.7
	MMNT	23.5	27.4	29.9	33.8	39.4	45.9	49.5	48.7	41.0	34.0	30.6	24.8	35.7
	MNTM	30.0	35.2	40.2	45.9	52.5	60.0	66.5	66.2	57.4	48.2	39.0	31.5	47.7
Unity	MMXT	33.8	40.9	49.0	57.6	67.8	76.3	86.0	85.0	74.8	62.8	44.2	33.7	61.9
	MMNT	13.5	18.4	23.4	27.2	34.1	39.7	43.4	42.9	34.9	27.3	22.0	13.5	29.7
	MNTM	23.6	29.6	36.2	42.1	50.9	58.0	64.7	63.9	54.9	45.3	33.0	23.5	45.8

Station	Code	Jan	Feb	Mar	Apr	May	Jun	Jul	Aug	Sep	Oct	Nov	Dec	Year
Walla Walla	MMXT	35.5	41.6	49.8	58.4	67.0	75.4	83.5	82.6	72.7	58.9	42.9	36.3	59.3
	MMNT	24.5	27.7	30.5	34.0	38.8	44.6	46.7	46.7	41.7	36.0	30.9	25.8	35.9
	MNTM	30.0	34.6	40.1	46.2	52.9	60.0	65.1	64.7	57.2	47.4	37.1	31.1	47.6
Wallowa	MMXT	34.5	41.9	50.4	59.2	67.3	76.0	84.5	84.1	74.9	62.3	45.2	35.3	59.4
	MMNT	18.3	22.5	26.4	30.9	36.8	42.8	45.1	44.2	37.2	30.1	26.0	19.0	31.5
	MNTM	26.4	32.2	38.4	45.0	52.0	59.4	64.8	64.2	56.1	46.2	35.6	27.1	45.4

Codes for Table 42

MMXT = mean maximum

MMNT = mean minimum

MNTM = monthly mean

Table 43. Median frost dates. 1961-1990 means.

	Median dates of last occurrence in spring of				Median dates of first occurrence in fall of			
	24°F	28°F	32°F	36°F	24°F	28°F	32°F	36°F
Austin	17 May	30 Jun	19 Jul	28 Jul	14 Sep	31 Aug	13 Aug	2 Aug
Baker	20 Apr	9 May	29 May	26 Jun	5 Oct	23 Sep	13 Sep	4 Sep
Cove	11 Apr	9 May	25 May	1 Jun	14 Oct	3 Oct	10 Sep	4 Sep
Elgin	20 Apr	14 May	5 Jun	8 Jul	3 Oct	19 Sep	3 Sep	23 Aug
Enterprise	13 May	1 Jun	8 Jul	22 Jul	20 Sep	12 Sep	6 Sep	2 Aug
Halfway	4 May	17 May	8 Jun	30 Jun	7 Oct	25 Sep	12 Sep	1 Sep
Huntington	24 Mar	12 Apr	1 May	12 May	1 Nov	22 Oct	9 Oct	29 Sep
John Day	20 Apr	4 May	20 May	4 Jun	20 Oct	6 Oct	17 Sep	8 Sep
La Grande	13 Apr	28 Apr	16 May	2 Jun	22 Oct	6 Oct	22 Sep	14 Sep
Long Creek	27 Apr	19 May	14 Jun	10 Jul	17 Oct	22 Sep	11 Sep	21 Aug
Monument	13 Apr	1 May	21 May	3 Jun	16 Oct	5 Oct	20 Sep	11 Sep
Richland	18 Apr	4 May	16 May	2 Jun	17 Oct	11 Oct	30 Sep	14 Sep
Seneca	27 May	7 Jul	24 Jul	29 Jul	1 Sep	19 Aug	4 Aug	1 Aug
Ukiah	14 May	25 Jun	19 Jul	28 Jul	11 Sep	30 Aug	15 Aug	3 Aug
Union	12 Apr	5 May	21 May	24 Jun	17 Oct	4 Oct	17 Sep	8 Sep
Unity	18 May	3 Jun	2 Jul	20 Jul	21 Sep	13 Sep	31 Aug	15 Aug
Walla Walla	19 Mar	19 Apr	19 May	8 Jun	16 Nov	17 Oct	2 Oct	12 Sep
Wallowa	1 May	20 May	17 Jun	7 Jul	2 Oct	13 Sep	3 Sep	19 Aug

Table 44. Growing season. 1961-1990 means.

	Average days between occurrences of			
	24°F	28°F	32°F	36° F
Austin	120	62	26	5
Baker	169	137	107	70
Cove	186	147	108	95
Elgin	167	128	91	46
Enterprise	130	103	60	11
Halfway	157	132	96	63
Huntington	222	193	161	141
John Day	183	155	120	96
La Grande	192	162	130	104
Long Creek	173	126	89	42
Monument	186	157	123	10
Richland	182	160	137	104
Seneca	97	43	11	4
Ukiah	120	66	27	6
Union	188	153	119	76
Unity	126	102	60	26
Walla Walla	242	181	136	96
Wallowa	155	116	78	43

Zone 9. The Southeast Area

Oregon climate Zone 9 occupies the southeast corner of the state, and encompasses only Malheur County, the state's second largest county. This is a region of high desert, mountain ranges, plateaus, and river valleys, with elevations ranging from slightly above 2,000 feet to nearly 8,000 feet above sea level. Less than thirty thousand people occupy the nearly 10,000 square miles which comprise Malheur County. Most reside in the Ontario - Nyssa - Vale areas near the northeast border. More than 90% of the county is rangeland, two-thirds of which is controlled by the Bureau of Land Management.

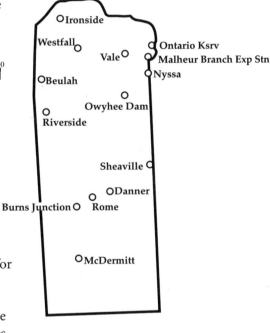

Principal industries in Zone 9 are agriculture, livestock, food processing, and recreation. Agriculture has played the dominant role in the economy, especially as irrigated acreage has increased. Extensive irrigation in the northeastern valleys is the center of very productive and diversified farming. Oregon State University's Malheur Experiment Station, west of Ontario, has been an active agricultural research center for many years, specializing in new farming practices and testing of alternative crops. Among the chief crops grown in the area are potatoes, sugar beets, onions, peas, tomatoes, berries, and sweet corn. Experiments with exotic melons, squash, and other cash crops (much of them for export to the Orient) are also continuing.

With the exception of a few of the higher mountain areas, Zone 9 receives low amounts of precipitation; most of the region averages less than 15 inches of total precipitation per year. The driest portions are in valleys near Rome and Burns Junction, which average 7.62 and 8.04 inches per year, respectively. On the other hand, locations in the Trout Creek Mountains in the southeast corner receive up to 30 inches per year. In even the wettest locations, however, annual precipitation is much lower than evaporation. Average annual evaporation at Malheur Experiment Station is well above 50 inches per year, most of it coming during the months of April through September.

Unlike most of Oregon, annual precipitation in Zone 9 is distributed rather evenly throughout the year. Table 45 shows normal monthly and annual precipitation at various locations in the region. Although winter months tend to have the highest total precipitation, the relative contribution of those months to the annual total is much lower than in areas further west. Some locations, such as McDermitt and Rome, report their highest precipitation during the late spring. Others, such as Danner and Sheaville, have nearly uniform monthly normals for the entire period of October through June. The driest month throughout the region is July.

Due to its distance from the Pacific Ocean, Zone 9 is characterized by large annual temperature variations. Table 46 lists normal monthly temperatures for Zone 9 measurement stations. Summers are quite warm with daytime highs averaging in the high 80s or low 90s from June through September. Malheur Experiment Station (MES) averages about fifty days per year with temperatures of 90°F or above, mostly during July and August. Summer nights in the zone are cool, however, due to the generally clear skies and dry air: even in the warmest months, nighttime lows average in the low to mid 50s.

During winter, average highs are mostly in the 30s and lows in the teens. MES averages about 140 days per year with minimum temperatures of 32°F or below; on 26 of those days, maximum temperatures remain below freezing as well. Occasionally, very cold air reaches the area from the north, causing lows to drop below 0°F. MES averages about six sub-zero days per year.

Table 47 lists median dates of several low temperature thresholds at Zone 9 stations; Table 48 lists average days between those thresholds. While stations in the northeast (MES and Nyssa) have an average of 140-160 days between 32°F temperatures, some of the higher stations have much shorter growing seasons. Examples would be Sheaville (4,620 feet) with an average of 87 days between frost dates, and Danner (4,230 feet), which averages 92 days.

Table 45. Monthly and annual precipitation (in inches). 1961-1990 means.

Station/Elevation (feet)	Jan	Feb	Mar	Apr	May	Jun	Jul	Aug	Sep	Oct	Nov	Dec	Year
Beulah (3270)	1.42	.96	1.08	.72	.98	.91	.37	.57	.55	.67	1.56	1.64	11.50
Burns Junction (3930)	.71	.83	.97	.91	.84	.59	.57	.57	.54	.48	.81	.63	8.04
Danner (4230)	1.35	.92	1.17	1.17	1.09	1.19	.44	.61	.78	.93	1.26	1.16	12.57
Ironside (3920)	1.33	.98	.93	.74	1.04	.98	.44	.77	.57	.61	1.36	1.70	11.31
Malheur Exp St (2230)	1.27	.94	.98	.73	.82	.79	.24	.52	.54	.64	1.26	1.39	10.13
McDermitt (4460)	.76	.58	.90	.91	1.29	1.08	.39	.57	.56	.62	.96	.87	9.35
Nyssa (2180)	1.25	1.02	.91	.81	.80	.89	.25	.49	.62	.67	1.25	1.42	10.40
Ontario (2150)	1.33	.87	.82	.63	.73	.72	.20	.44	.53	.61	1.30	1.50	9.68
Owyhee Dam (2400)	.98	.75	.83	.85	.91	1.19	.34	.54	.54	.57	.92	1.08	9.48
Riverside (3330)	1.08	.83	1.05	.71	.89	.85	.48	.57	.51	.61	1.06	1.18	9.76
Rome (3380)	.58	.50	.83	.69	1.01	1.05	.36	.46	.58	.55	.82	.63	7.62
Sheaville (4620)	1.64	1.21	1.27	1.22	1.26	1.24	.46	.65	.65	.99	1.62	1.56	12.48
Vale (2220)	1.17	.83	.89	.71	.79	.81	.35	.51	.56	.64	1.16	1.35	9.77
Westfall (3140)	1.31	.83	.81	.78	.97	1.08	.35	.71	.52	.53	1.33	1.35	11.83

Table 46. Monthly temperatures (°F). 1961-1990 means.

	Code	Jan	Feb	Mar	Apr	May	Jun	Jul	Aug	Sep	Oct	Nov	Dec	Year
Beulah	MMXT	36.3	44.5	53.0	61.9	71.5	80.9	90.3	88.6	79.5	67.1	49.5	37.8	64.0
	MMNT	16.4	22.2	27.2	32.3	40.3	47.7	53.5'	51.6	41.6	31.5	24.1	17.7	34.4
	MNTM	26.4	33.3	40.1	47.1	55.9	64.3	71.9	70.1	60.6	49.0	36.9	27.7	49.2
Burns Junction	MMXT	38.5	47.0	54.2	63.6	71.9	83.2	92.1	89.7	80.6	68.4	50.5	41.2	65.2
	MMNT	16.9	23.0	27.6	32.9	40.0	48.6	54.0	51.4	41.8	32.5	24.1	17.6	34.2
	MNTM	27.7	35.0	40.9	48.2	55.9	65.9	73.1	70.6	61.0	50.4	37.3	29.4	49.6
Danner	MMXT	38.3	46.4	52.1	60.1	68.7	79.1	88.1	86.8	76.3	66.7	49.6	39.8	65.3
	MMNT	14.7	21.6	24.3	28.2	34.8	43.2	48.2	46.1	37.1	27.3	21.7	15.1	31.7
	MNTM	26.4	34.2	38.2	44.1	51.9	61.4	68.2	66.6	57.0	47.3	35.5	27.3	48.3
Ironside	MMXT	33.5	38.6	49.3	57.9	65.8	76.2	86.4	86.2	74.3	62.6	45.0	34.0	60.6
	MMNT	14.9	18.9	26.4	31.7	38.4	46.1	52.9	52.6	42.1	32.4	23.1	14.8	34.0
	MNTM	24.2	28.8	37.9	44.5	52.1	61.1	69.6	69.4	58.4	47.5	34.1	24.5	47.6
Malheur Exp Stn	MMXT	33.7	42.8	54.4	63.9	73.4	82.7	91.3	89.7	78.5	65.0	47.8	35.7	63.2
	MMNT	18.5	24.7	31.0	37.1	45.0	52.8	58.1	55.8	45.9	35.8	28.7	20.7	37.8
	MNTM	26.1	33.7	42.7	50.5	59.2	67.8	74.7	72.8	62.2	50.4	38.2	28.2	50.5
McDermitt	MMXT	40.3	46.7	52.6	61.0	70.6	80.7	91.1	88.7	78.9	67.6	50.6	41.2	64.0
	MMNT	18.0	22.8	25.2	29.2	36.6	44.1	49.4	47.8	39.4	32.1	25.5	19.1	32.3
	MNTM	29.2	34.8	38.9	45.1	53.7	62.3	70.3	68.2	59.2	49.8	38.0	30.3	48.1
Nyssa	MMXT	34.0	43.3	54.9	63.9	73.0	81.8	90.9	89.1	78.4	65.5	48.6	36.1	63.3
	MMNT	20.0	25.3	31.4	38.1	45.9	53.9	58.9	56.7	46.7	36.6	29.6	22.0	38.8
	MNTM	27.0	34.3	43.2	51.0	59.4	67.8	74.9	72.9	62.6	51.0	39.1	29.0	51.0
Ontario	MMXT	35.3	44.7	56.4	66.3	76.4	86.2	95.7	93.3	81.7	67.4	49.4	37.0	65.8
	MMNT	19.1	24.8	30.6	36.2	44.0	51.7	57.4	54.5	44.3	34.5	28.3	20.6	37.2
	MNTM	27.2	34.8	43.5	51.3	60.2	68.9	76.5	73.9	63.0	50.9	38.8	28.8	51.5
Owyhee Dam	MMXT	38.5	46.0	55.6	64.3	74.0	83.7	92.7	91.2	79.9	67.2	50.8	39.6	65.3
	MMNT	21.8	27.2	32.4	37.3	43.4	49.9	53.4	52.8	45.8	37.9	30.4	22.8	37.9
	MNTM	30.1	36.6	44.0	50.8	58.7	66.8	73.1	72.0	62.9	52.6	40.6	31.2	51.6
Riverside	MMXT	37.1	45.3	53.9	62.3	71.5	81.2	90.1	87.9	78.2	65.6	49.2	37.8	63.3
	MMNT	19.4	24.4	28.1	31.9	39.1	47.2	52.8	51.1	41.6	32.0	26.4	19.0	34.3
	MNTM	28.2	34.9	41.0	47.1	55.3	64.2	71.5	69.5	59.9	48.8	37.8	28.4	48.8
Rome	MMXT	40.0	47.9	54.6	62.9	73.2	82.4	92.4	90.6	79.9	68.2	51.6	41.0	65.2
	MMNT	17.7	23.4	25.8	29.9	38.5	46.4	51.2	48.5	38.6	30.2	24.1	18.3	32.6
	MNTM	28.8	35.7	40.2	46.4	55.9	64.4	71.9	69.6	59.3	49.2	37.8	29.7	49.0
Sheaville	MMXT	36.4	42.6	48.5	57.2	66.9	76.2	87.2	85.9	75.0	64.0	46.9	37.7	60.1
	MMNT	16.1	21.3	24.7	29.1	35.9	43.2	48.9	47.9	38.5	30.8	23.7	16.8	31.2
	MNTM	26.0	31.9	36.6	43.1	51.4	59.7	68.0	66.9	56.7	47.4	35.4	27.0	45.7
Vale	MMXT	35.9	45.0	56.6	66.3	75.6	85.3	94.2	91.9	80.3	66.7	49.7	37.6	65.4
	MMNT	18.4	24.3	30.2	35.4	43.4	51.4	56.8	54.4	44.3	34.3	27.8	20.1	36.7
	MNTM	27.1	34.6	43.4	50.8	59.5	68.3	75.4	73.2	62.3	50.5	38.8	28.8	51.1
Westfall	MMXT	34.7	42.6	52.4	60.8	71.3	80.0	90.5	89.4	78.9	65.1	47.4	36.2	61.8
	MMNT	17.3	23.9	28.2	33.0	41.8	48.3	54.8	53.5	44.6	35.0	26.9	19.3	35.4
	MNTM	26.0	33.3	40.3	46.8	56.7	64.3	72.5	71.4	61.7	50.1	37.1	27.7	48.8

Codes for Table 46

MMXT = mean maximum

MMNT = mean minimum

MNTM = monthly mean

Table 47. Median frost dates. 1961-1990 means.

	Median dates of last occurrence in spring of				Median dates of first occurrence in fall of			
	24°F	28°F	32°F	36°F	24°F	28°F	32°F	36°F
Beulah	18 Apr	10 May	25 May	12 Jun	12 Oct	2 Oct	20 Sep	10 Sep
Burns Junction	20 Apr	15 May	30 May	11 Jun	16 Oct	29 Sep	18 Sep	11 Sep
Danner	3 May	23 May	8 Jun	27 Jun	26 Sep	17 Sep	9 Sep	23 Aug
Ironside	22 Apr	11 May	30 May	26 Jun	18 Oct	5 Oct	19 Sep	10 Sep
Malheur Exp St	24 Mar	12 Apr	1 May	15 May	25 Oct	15 Oct	4 Oct	22 Sep
McDermitt	12 May	30 May	11 Jun	1 Jul	1 Oct	18 Sep	9 Sep	29 Aug
Nyssa	18 Mar	8 Apr	29 Apr	10 May	10 Nov	19 Oct	7 Oct	30 Sep
Ontario	1 Apr	20 Apr	10 May	24 May	18 Oct	6 Oct	27 Sep	14 Sep
Owyhee Dam	17 Mar	9 Apr	30 Apr	16 May	3 Nov	16 Oct	8 Oct	26 Sep
Riverside	28 Apr	18 May	1 Jun	13 Jun	7 Oct	30 Sep	21 Sep	7 Sep
Rome	29 Apr	12 May	31 May	11 Jun	5 Oct	21 Sep	12 Sep	3 Sep
Sheaville	9 May	26 May	17 Jun	30 Jun	5 Oct	21 Sep	12 Sep	2 Sep
Vale	11 Apr	20 Apr	13 May	27 May	19 Oct	6 Oct	29 Sep	15 Sep
Westfall	5 Apr	20 Apr	20 May	31 May	28 Oct	20 Oct	2 Oct	20 Sep

Table 48. Growing season. 1961-1990 means.

	Average days between occurrences of			
	24°F	28°F	32°F	36°F
Beulah	177	145	118	91
Burns Junction	179	137	111	92
Danner	146	118	93	57
Ironside	179	147	113	76
Malheur Exp St	215	186	156	131
McDermitt	143	111	91	59
Nyssa	238	195	161	144
Ontario	200	169	140	113
Owyhee Dam	231	190	161	134
Riverside	162	135	112	86
Rome	159	132	104	85
Sheaville	149	118	88	64
Vale	192	170	139	111
Westfall	207	183	135	113

PART 4

Measuring and Reporting
Climate Information

Who Does It?

Weather and climate data are collected from hundreds of locations in Oregon. A variety of agencies are involved in data collection, and many kinds of data are collected.

National Weather Service (NWS)

According to its mission statement, NWS "provides weather, hydrologic, and climate forecasts and warnings for the United States, its territories, adjacent waters and ocean areas, for the protection of life and property and the enhancement of the national economy. NWS data and products form a national information database and infrastructure which can be used by other governmental agencies, the private sector, the public, and the global community. " Currently there are three NWS offices in Oregon: Portland (the state headquarters), Medford, and Pendleton.

History of the NWS

The original weather agency operated under the War Department from 1870 to 1891 with headquarters in Washington, D.C., and field offices concentrated mainly east of the Rockies. Little meteorological science was used to make weather forecasts during those early days. Instead, weather that occurred at one location was assumed to move into the next area downstream.

The beginning of the National Weather Service we know today was on February 9, 1870, when President Ulysses S. Grant signed a joint resolution of Congress authorizing the Secretary of War to establish a national weather service. This resolution required the Secretary of War

> to provide for taking meteorological observations at the military stations in the interior of the continent and at other points in the States and Territories . . . and for giving notice on the northern (Great) Lakes and on the seacoast by magnetic telegraph and marine signals, of the approach and force of storms.

After much thought and consideration, it was decided that this agency would be placed under the Secretary of War because military discipline would probably secure the greatest promptness, regularity, and accuracy in the required observations. Within the Department of War, it was assigned to the Signal Service Corps under Brigadier General Albert J. Myer, who gave the National Weather Service its first name: The Division of Telegrams and Reports for the Benefit of Commerce.

From 1891 to 1940, the Weather Bureau was part of the Department of Agriculture. These first two decades of the 20th century had a remarkable effect on the nation's meteorological services. In 1902, Weather Bureau forecasts were sent via wireless telegraphy to ships at sea. In turn, the first wireless weather report was received from a ship at sea in 1905. Two years later, the daily exchange of weather observations with Russia and eastern Asia was inaugurated.

In 1910, the Weather Bureau began issuing weekly outlooks to aid agricultural planning. And in 1913, the first fire-weather forecast was issued. During these times, weather forecasters began using more sophisticated methods including surface weather observations; kite experiments to measure temperature, relative humidity and winds in the upper atmosphere; and, later, airplane stations.

Realizing that the Weather Bureau played an important role for the aviation community, and therefore commerce, in 1940, President Franklin D. Roosevelt transferred the Weather Bureau to the Department of Commerce where it remains today. During the late 1940s, the military gave the Weather Bureau a new and valuable tool—25 surplus radars—thus launching the network of weather surveillance radars still in use today. In 1970, the name was changed to the National Weather Service, and the agency became a component of the Commerce Department's newly created National Oceanic and Atmospheric Administration.

The advent of computer technology in the 1950s paved the way for the formulation of complex mathematical weather models, resulting in a significant increase in forecast accuracy.

Modernization

The National Weather Service is in the midst of a major modernization program that is offering more timely and precise severe weather and flood warnings for the nation. Recent advances in satellites, radar, sophisticated information processing and communication systems, automated weather observing systems, and high speed computers are the foundation of the modernization. The components of the modernization are the new Doppler Weather Surveillance Radar, the Automated Surface Observing System, a new generation of Geostationary Operational Environmental Satellites, National Center Advanced Computer Systems, and the Advanced Weather Interactive Processing System. The modernization also includes a new structure of field offices for the NWS, including Weather Forecast Offices and River Forecast Centers.

National Climatic Data Center (NCDC)

NCDC is the world's largest active archive of weather data.

The Weather Bureau, Air Force, and Navy Tabulation Units in New Orleans, LA, were combined to create the National Weather Records Center in Asheville, NC, in November 1951. The Center was eventually renamed the National Climatic Data Center. The National Archives and Records Administration has designated NCDC as the Commerce Department's only Agency Records Center. NCDC archives weather data obtained by the

National Weather Service, Military Services, Federal Aviation Administration, and the Coast Guard, as well as data from voluntary cooperative observers. NCDC has increased data acquisition capabilities to ingest new data streams such as NEXRAD and ASOS (see Types of Observations section).

Improving quality control and continuity of these new data sets as well as making them available in timely fashion has been paramount. As operator of the World Data Center-A for Meteorology, which provides for international data exchange, NCDC also collects data from around the globe. The Center has more than 150 years of data on hand with 55 gigabytes of new information added each day—that is equivalent to 18 million pages a day.

NCDC archives 99% of all NOAA data, including over 320 million paper records; 2.5 million microfiche records; and over 500,000 tape cartridges/ magnetic tapes; and has satellite weather images back to 1960. NCDC annually publishes over 1.2 million copies of climate publications that are sent to individual users and 33,000 subscribers. NCDC maintains over five hundred digital data sets to respond to over 170,000 requests each year.

Data are received from a wide variety of sources, including satellites, radar, remote sensing systems, NWS cooperative observers, aircraft, ships, radiosonde, wind profiler, rocketsonde, solar radiation networks, and NWS Forecast-Warnings-Analyses Products. NCDC supports many forms of data and information dissemination such as paper copies of original records, publications, atlases, computer printouts, microfiche, microfilm, movie loops, photographs, magnetic tape, floppy disks, CD-ROM, electronic mail, on-line dial-up, telephone, facsimile, and personal visit.

The Center, which produces numerous climate publications and responds to requests from all over the world, provides historical perspectives on climate that are vital to studies on global climate change, the greenhouse effect, and other environmental issues. The Center stores information essential to industry, agriculture, science, hydrology, transportation, recreation, and engineering. This information can mean tens of millions of dollars to concerned parties.

NCDC's mission is to manage the nation's resource of global climatological in-situ and remotely sensed data and information to promote global environmental stewardship; to describe, monitor and assess the climate; and to support efforts to predict changes in the Earth's environment. This effort requires the acquisition, quality control, processing, summarization, dissemination, and preservation of a vast array of climatological data generated by the national and international meteorological services. NCDC's mission is global in nature and provides the U.S. climate representative to the World Meteorological Organization, the World Data Center System, and other international scientific programs. NCDC also operates the World Data Center-A for Meteorology.

Western Regional Climate Center (WRCC)

The mission of the Western Regional Climate Center is to disseminate high-quality climate data and information pertaining to the western United States; to foster better use of this information in decision making; to conduct applied research related to climate issues; and to improve the coordination of climate-related activities at state, regional, and national scales.

The Western Regional Climate Center, inaugurated in 1986, is one of six regional climate centers in the United States. The regional climate center program is administered by NOAA. Specific oversight is provided by the National Climatic Data Center of the National Environmental Satellite, Data, and Information Service (NESDIS).

The WRCC exists to fill several roles:

—Serve as a focal point for coordination of applied climate activities in the West
- Federal resource management agencies
- Western committees and commissions

—Maintain links to other climate programs
- National Climate Data Center, Asheville, NC
- Regional climate centers
- State climatologists and state climate programs
- Climate Analysis Center, Washington D.C.
- National Weather Service

—Conduct applied research on climate issues affecting the West
- Impacts of climate variability in the western United States
- Quality control of western databases
- Relation of El Niño/Southern Oscillation to western climate
- Climatic trends and fluctuations in the West
- GIS and remote sensing

In support of these functions, WRCC maintains a historical climate database for the West.

Oregon Climate Service (OCS)

OCS is located on the Oregon State University campus in Corvallis and is the state repository for weather and climate information. OCS's mission is fourfold:

—To collect, manage, and maintain Oregon weather and climate data.

—To provide weather and climate information to those within and outside the state of Oregon.

—To educate the people of Oregon on current and emerging climate issues.

—To perform independent research related to weather and climate issues.

Linkages

OCS acts as the liaison with:
- —National Climatic Data Center
- —Western Regional Climate Center
- —National Weather Service
- —Natural Resources Conservation Service
- —Climate Prediction Center
- —American Association of State Climatologists
- —Other state climate offices

Climate Data

OCS maintains the most complete set of state weather and climate records in Oregon. A large amount of the data is stored in a computer-accessible format (hard disks and magnetic tapes) for easy retrieval and manipulation. In addition, various studies, reports, summaries, etc. are stored on paper and/or fiche.

Services

On average, OCS handles about six thousand telephone or mail data requests per year. OCS provides a full range of climate-related services to both the public and private sectors. Services/products include, but are not restricted to:
- —Site-specific climate reports/summaries.
- —Various statistical analysis's, such as means, extremes, probabilities, percentiles, threshold exceedances, etc.
- —Climate tables/inventories.
- —Precipitation maps.
- —Customized research.
- —Current climate data and information.

Computing

OCS uses state-of-the-art computers to store and manipulate climate data. A variety of UNIX, IBM-compatible, and Macintosh workstations are utilized. In addition, a comprehensive World Wide Web (WWW) site is maintained.

Research

OCS has been involved in numerous research projects undertaken by governments, universities, and private interests. Among these are:
- —Climate variability studies.
- —Precipitation mapping (PRISM).
- —Quality control of data.
- —El Niño/Southern Oscillation and its influence on western climate.
- —Drought and flood studies.
- —Climate change.
- —Long-term/lead forecasting.
- —Air quality studies.
- —Wind modeling.

USDA Natural Resources Conservation Service (NRCS)

NRCS installs, operates, and maintains an extensive, automated system to collect snowpack and related climatic data in the western United States called SNOTEL (for SNOwpack TELemetry). The system evolved from NRCS's congressional mandate in the mid-1930s "to measure snowpack in the mountains of the West and forecast the water supply." The programs began with manual measurements of snow courses; since 1980, SNOTEL has reliably and efficiently collected the data needed to produce water supply forecasts and to support the resource management activities of NRCS and others.

Climate studies, air and water quality investigations, and resource management concerns are all served by the modern SNOTEL network. The high-elevation watershed locations and the broad coverage of the network provide important data collection opportunities to researchers, water managers, and emergency managers for natural disasters such as floods.

Types of Observations

L isted below are major types of collection platforms operating in Oregon. Federal agencies provide the bulk of weather and climate data collection, archiving, and delivery.

NOAA Cooperative Stations

Cooperative stations are U.S. stations operated by local observers which generally report maximum/minimum temperatures and precipitation. National Weather Service (NWS) data are also included in this dataset. The data receive extensive automated and manual quality control. Over eight thousand stations are currently active across the country, more than three hundred in Oregon.

Despite all of the state-of-the-art technology associated with the modernization of the NWS, the cooperative program has remained virtually unchanged since its inception over a hundred years ago. Many cooperative stations in the United States have been collecting weather data from the same location for over a hundred years.

The first extensive network of cooperative stations was set up in the 1890s as a result of an act of Congress in 1890 that established the Weather Bureau, but many of its stations began operation long before that time. John Companius Holm's weather records, taken without the benefit of instruments in 1644 and 1645, were the earliest known observations in the United States. Subsequently many persons, including George Washington, Thomas Jefferson, and Benjamin Franklin, maintained weather records. Jefferson maintained an almost unbroken record of weather observations between 1776 and 1816, and Washington took his last weather observation just a few days before he died. Two of the most prestigious awards given to cooperative weather observers are named after Holm and Jefferson. Because of its many decades of relatively stable operation, high station density, and high proportion of rural locations, the cooperative network has been recognized as the most definitive source of information on U.S. climate trends for temperature and precipitation. Cooperative stations form the core of the U.S. Historical Climate Network and the U.S. Reference Climate Network.

Equipment to gather these data is provided and maintained by the NWS and data forms are sent monthly to the NCDC in Asheville, NC, where data are digitized, quality controlled, and subsequently archived. Volunteer weather observers regularly and conscientiously contribute their time so that their observations can provide the vital information needed. These data are invaluable in learning more about the floods, droughts, and heat and cold waves which inevitably affect everyone. They are also used in agricultural planning and assessment, engineering, environmental-impact assessment, utilities planning, and litigation and play a critical role in efforts to recognize and evaluate the extent of human impacts on climate from local to global scales. Many cooperative weather observers report daily precipitation to River Forecast Centers in support of the National Weather Service Hydrology Program.

Historical Climatological Network

The 187-station daily dataset for the contiguous United States consists of three elements: maximum temperature, minimum temperature (both in °F), and precipitation (in hundredths of inches).

Stations in the Daily Historical Climatology Network include 138 long-term stations operated by cooperative (non-paid) observers. Additional stations, chosen from the first order NWS station network, were included to increase the spatial resolution. All stations were selected using the following criteria:

—A station's potential for heat island bias over time should be low.

—It should have maintained a relatively constant observation time.

—Reasonably homogeneous spatial distribution over the contiguous U.S.

The only Oregon stations in the 138-station dataset are Dufur and Grants Pass.

Surface Airways Observations

These observations are collected at airport sites. In general, they are collected and administered by the Federal Aviation Administration (FAA) for NWS. Most of the stations are now automated, 24-hour stations which can be accessed via the Internet. Oregon stations are shown in Table 36.

Instruments for Modernization (NWS)

New observing systems are the key to the ongoing modernization program of the NWS. Below are descriptions of three key measurement platforms as well as a software-hardware processing system.

Automated Surface Observing System

The Automated Surface Observing System (ASOS) will relieve staff from the manual collection of surface observations. Over one thousand ASOS systems across the nation will provide data on pressure, temperature, wind direction and speed, runway visibility, cloud ceiling heights, and type and intensity of precipitation on a nearly continuous basis. The implementation status of ASOS is updated regularly.

NEXRAD

NEXRAD is the commonly used acronym for the Next Generation of Weather Radar which began to be tested and implemented by NWS and the FAA during the 1980s. These new Doppler radar systems, now more appropriately known as the WSR-88D (Weather Surveillance Radar - 1988 Doppler), have replaced the aging network of WSR-57 and WSR-74 radar systems which these agencies had been using for the previous several decades. The WSR-88D provides several advantages over the its older predecessors, including:

—Greater sensitivity.
—Higher resolution data.
—The ability to detect the relative motion of echoes within a storm.
—Multiple volumetric views of the atmosphere.
—Algorithms to estimate the amount of liquid in the atmosphere.
—Algorithms to estimate the amount of precipitation that has fallen.

NEXRAD sites in Oregon are associated with the NWS offices at Portland, Medford, and Pendleton.

Geostationary Operational Environmental Satellites

The Geostationary Operational Environmental Satellites (GOES) will continue to be a major data source for severe weather and flood warnings, short range forecasts, cloud imagery, and atmospheric sounding data.

Advanced Weather Interactive Processing System

The Advanced Weather Interactive Processing System (AWIPS) will be the nerve center of the operations at each Weather Forecast Office. AWIPS will be the data integrator receiving the high-resolution data from a multiple of sources. From this information base all warning and forecast products will be prepared.

SNOTEL Data Collection Network

SNOTEL uses meteor burst communications technology to collect and communicate data in near-real-time. VHF radio signals are reflected at a steep angle off the ever-present band of ionized meteorites existing from about 50 to 75 miles above the Earth. Satellites are not involved; NRCS operates and control the entire system.

There are over six hundred SNOTEL sites in eleven western states including Alaska. The sites are generally located in remote high-mountain watersheds where access is often difficult or restricted. Access for maintenance by NRCS includes various modes from hiking and skiing to helicopters.

Sites are designed to operate unattended and without maintenance for a year. They are battery powered with solar cell recharge. The condition of each site is monitored daily when it reports on eight operational functions. Serious problems or deteriorating performance trigger a response from the NRCS electronic technicians located in six data collection offices.

The SNOTEL sites are polled by two master stations operated by NRCS in Boise, Idaho, and Ogden, Utah. A central computer at NRCS's National Water and Climate Center (NWCC) in Portland, Oregon, controls system operations and receives the data collected by the SNOTEL network.

Basic SNOTEL sites have a pressure-sensing snow pillow, storage precipitation gauge, and air temperature sensor. However, they can accommodate 64 channels of data and will accept analog, parallel, or serial digital sensors. On-site microprocessors provide functions such as computing daily maximum, minimum, and average temperature information. Generally, sensor data are recorded every fifteen minutes and reported out in a daily poll of all sites. Special polls are conducted more frequently in response to specific needs.

Table 49 lists current SNOTEL stations in Oregon.

Table 49. Current SNOTEL stations in Oregon.

ID	Station name	Latitude	Longitude	Elevation
		(degrees & minutes)		(feet)
17D02S	Aneroid Lake #2	4513	11712	7300
19D02S	Arbuckle Mountain	4511	11915	5400
18D09S	Beaver Reservoir	4508	11813	5150
22G21S	Big Red Mountain	4203	12251	6250
23G15S	Bigelow Camp	4205	12321	5120
22G13S	Billie Creek Divide	4225	12217	5300
21D33S	Blazed Alder	4525	12152	3650
18E16S	Blue Mountain Spring	4415	11830	5900
18E05S	Bourne	4449	11812	5800
18D20S	Bowman Springs	4522	11827	4580
22F03S	Cascade Summit	4335	12201	4880
21F22S	Chemult Alternate	4313	12148	4760
21D13S	Clackamas Lake	4505	12145	3400
21D12S	Clear Lake	4512	12143	3500
22G24S	Cold Springs Camp	4232	12211	6100
18D08S	County Line	4511	11832	4800
22E08S	Daly Lake	4437	12203	3600
19E03S	Derr.	4427	11956	5670
22F18S	Diamond Lake	4311	12208	5315
18E03S	Eilertson Meadows	4451	11807	5400
18D04S	Emigrant Springs	4533	11827	3925
18G02S	Fish Creek	4242	11838	7900
22G14S	Fish Lake	4223	12225	4665
22G12S	Fourmile Lake	4224	12213	6000
18E08S	Gold Center	4446	11817	5340
21D01S	Greenpoint	4537	12142	3200
18D19S	High Ridge	4541	11806	4980
21E06S	Hogg Pass	4425	12152	4760
22F42S	Holland Meadows	4340	12234	4900
21F21S	Irish Taylor	4349	12157	5500
22E07S	Jump Off Joe	4423	12210	3500
23G09S	King Mountain	4203	12312	4000
18E18S	Lake Creek R.S.	4411	11836	5200
22E09S	Little Meadows	4437	12213	4000
18D06S	Lucky Strike	4517	11851	5050
19D03S	Madison Butte	4506	11930	5250
21E04S	Marion Forks	4435	12158	2600
21E07S	McKenzie	4412	12152	4800

ID	Station name	Latitude	Longitude	Elevation
		(degrees & minutes)		(feet)
17D06S	Moss Springs	4516	11741	5850
21D08S	Mt Hood Test Site	4520	12143	5400
17D18S	Mt. Howard	4516	11710	7910
21D35S	Mud Ridge	4515	12144	3800
21F10S	New Crescent Lake	4329	12158	4800
22D02S	North Fork	4533	12201	3120
20E02S	Ochoco Meadows	4426	12020	5200
21D14S	Peavine Ridge	4503	12156	3500
20G06S	Quartz Mountain	4216	12047	5700
22F05S	Railroad Overpass	4337	12208	2750
21D04S	Red Hill	4528	12142	4400
22F43S	Roaring River	4354	12202	4900
18F01S	Rock Springs	4359	11851	5100
23D01S	Saddle Mountain	4532	12322	3250
22F04S	Salt Creek Falls	4336	12204	4000
21E05S	Santiam Junction	4426	12156	3750
17D08S	Schneider Meadows	4500	11709	5400
23D02S	Seine Creek	4531	12317	2060
22G33S	Sevenmile Marsh	4241	12208	6200
21F12S	Silver Creek	4257	12111	5720
18G01S	Silvies	4245	11841	6900
19F01S	Snow Mountain	4357	11933	6220
19E07S	Starr Ridge	4416	11901	5300
20G09S	Strawberry	4206	12151	5760
20G02S	Summer Rim	4242	12049	7100
22F14S	Summit Lake	4327	12208	5600
21G03S	Taylor Butte	4242	12124	5100
17D07S	Taylor Green	4502	11732	5740
21E13S	Three Creeks Meadow	4409	12138	5650
18E09S	Tipton	4440	11822	5150
18D21S	Wolf Creek	4504	11808	5700

Snow Surveys

Manual snow surveys require two-person teams to measure snow depth and water content at designated snow courses. A snow course is a permanent site that represents snowpack conditions at a given elevation in a given area. A particular snowpack may have several courses. Generally, the courses are about 1,000 feet long and are situated in small meadows protected from the wind.

Measurements generally are taken on or near the first of every month during the snowpack season, though the frequency and timing of these measurements varies considerably with the locality, the nature of the snowpack, difficulty of access, and cost. On occasion, special surveys are scheduled to help evaluate unusual conditions. The manual surveys involve travel and work in remote areas, often in bad weather, but reliable data are obtained. Locations that are too hazardous or costly to measure on the ground can be equipped with depth markers that can be read from aircraft. Snow depth can be measured in this way with a high degree of accuracy. Although the amount of water in the snowpack is not measured, it can be reliably estimated from the observed snow depth.

NRCS conducts intensive training in snow sampling techniques, safety, and mountain survival. On-the-job training and an annual school develop the needed skills; the school has become known throughout the western United States and Canada for its unique training program offered to NRCS employees and others engaged in the cooperative surveys. A critical part of the training is the overnight bivouac in a snow shelter constructed by the student. Many graduates have credited this training with bringing them safely through unforeseen, hazardous situations.

Snow survey team, 1938, in the Oregon Southern Cascades. (Photo by J.G. Jones, USDA Soil Conservation Service. OSU Archives, P98:870)

AgriMet

In 1983, in cooperation with the Bonneville Power Administration, the U.S. Bureau of Reclamation began "piggy-backing" a network of automatic agricultural weather stations onto Reclamation's regional Hydromet satellite telemetry network. The Hydromet network is a series of automated data collection platforms that provide information necessary for near-real-time management of Reclamation's water operations in the Pacific Northwest. As a subset of the overall Hydromet network, this agricultural network, dedicated to crop water use modeling and other agricultural applications, has been identified as AgriMet.

The present AgriMet network consists of 51 agricultural weather stations located throughout the Pacific Northwest (see Figure 31). Forty-nine are full AgriMet stations with two additional frost control stations (with fewer sensors). An additional ten stations east of the divide in Montana are managed by the U.S. Bureau of Reclamation Great Plains Region .

The network is sponsored by the U.S. Bureau of Reclamation with additional support from the Northwest Energy Efficiency Alliance, the USDA Agricultural Resource Service, the USDA Natural Resources Conservation Service, land grant universities, the Cooperative Extension System, electric utilities, power companies, and other public and private agencies and organizations.

Real-time AgriMet data are transmitted from individual stations to Reclamation's receive site in Boise, Idaho, through the GOES-8, GOES-9, and DOMSAT satellites. Each station transmits data at regular intervals of four hours. Data collection intervals within this four-hour period are dependent on the specific sensor equipment at each station. Types of data collected at each station vary. The data are processed on minicomputers running the OpenVMS operating system at the Boise site, then shared with other organizations and individuals participating in the AgriMet program. Access to the system is available by telephone modem, telnet, DECNET, and the World Wide Web.

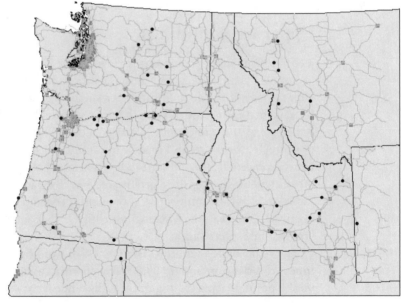

Figure 31. AgriMet stations in the Pacific Northwest.

Remote Automatic Weather Stations

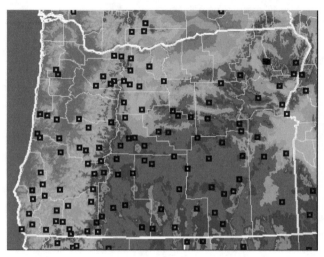

Figure 32. Locations of RAWS stations in Oregon.

Remote Automatic Weather Stations (RAWS) are maintained by federal and state agencies for the purpose of environmental monitoring. They are particularly important for monitoring the influence of the weather on wildland fuels for fire danger calculation. In addition, the RAWS provide a data source for fire weather forecasting in remote areas. The observations presented on the latest Boise Fire Weather Web pages are the latest data received at the National Interagency Fire Center. The NWS, among other federal agencies, maintains a RAWS database, and monitors the weather data collected by this network. Figure 32 shows RAWS station locations in Oregon.

Upper-air Soundings

The following description was provided by the NWS:

For over sixty years, upper-air observations have been made by the NWS with radiosondes. The radiosonde is a small, expendable instrument package that is suspended below a 6 foot-wide balloon filled with hydrogen or helium. As the radiosonde is carried aloft, sensors measure profiles of pressure, temperature, and relative humidity. These sensors are linked to a battery-powered, 300 milliwatt radio transmitter that sends the measurements to a sensitive ground receiver. By tracking the position of the radiosonde in flight, information on wind speed and direction aloft is also obtained. Observations where winds aloft are also obtained are called "rawinsonde" observations.

The radiosonde flight can last in excess of two hours, and during this time it can rise over about 100,000 feet and drift about 125 miles from the release point. During the flight, the radiosonde is exposed to temperatures as cold as -121°F) and air pressures only few hundredths of what is found on the Earth's surface. When the balloon has expanded beyond its elastic limit and bursts (when it is about 20 feet in diameter) , a small parachute slows the descent of the radiosonde, minimizing the danger to lives and property.

Only about 20% of the approximately 75,000 radiosondes released by the NWS each year are found and returned for reconditioning. These rebuilt radiosondes are used again, saving the NWS the cost of a new instrument. If

you find a radiosonde, follow the mailing instructions printed on the side of the instrument.

Although all the data from the flight are used, data from the surface to the 400 mb pressure level (about 23,000 feet) are considered minimally acceptable for NWS operations. Thus, a flight may be deemed a failure and a second radiosonde released if the balloon bursts before reaching the 400 mb pressure level or if more than 6 minutes of pressure and/or temperature data between the surface and 400 mb are missing.

Worldwide, there are nearly nine hundred upper-air observation stations. Most are located in the Northern Hemisphere and all observations are usually taken at the same time each day (00:00 and/or 12:00 UTC), 365 days per year. Observations are made at 92 stations, 69 in the conterminous United States, thirteen in Alaska, nine in the Pacific, and one in Puerto Rico. NWS supports the operation of ten other stations in the Caribbean. Through international agreements, data are exchanged between countries. In Oregon, radiosondes are released from Salem and Medford.

Understanding and accurately predicting changes in the atmosphere requires adequate observations of the upper atmosphere. Radiosonde observations are the primary source of upper-air data and will remain so into the foreseeable future.

Radiosonde launch from Ag Hall, Oregon State University. A rain gauge, anemometer, and instrument shelter are also visible. (OSU Archives)

Radiosonde observations are applied to a broad spectrum of efforts. Data applications include:
- —Input for computer-based weather prediction models.
- —Local severe storm, aviation, and marine forecasts;.
- —Weather and climate change research.
- —Input for air pollution models.
- —Ground truth for satellite data.

Access to Data via the Internet

The Internet has become a widely used tool for obtaining information of various kinds. Weather and climate data and reports are available from a wide variety of public and private organizations. Below we list a few of our favorites. The URL (or Universal Resource Locator) is the Internet address used to access the site, via a Web browser.

Oregon Climate Service
http://www.ocs.orst.edu
Wide variety of Oregon weather and climate information and data sets, including extensive links to other sites.

Western Regional Climate Center
http://www.wrcc.sage.dri.edu
Information for the eleven western states.

National Climatic Data Center
http://www.ncdc.noaa.gov
National and international climate information.

National Weather Service, Portland
http://nimbo.wrh.noaa.gov/Portland
Local NWS headquarters, and a very complete Web site.

Climate Prediction Center
http://nic.fb4.noaa.gov
El Niño information and long-range forecasts (out to 15 months).

The Weather Channel
http://www.weather.com
In case you don't have cable TV.

WeatherNet
http://cirrus.sprl.umich.edu/wxnet
Probably the most complete set of weather-related links available anywhere.

USDA NRCS Water and Climate Center, Portland
http://www.wcc.wrcs.usda.gov
Snow, climate, and natural resources information.

USGS Water Information
http://h2o.usgs.gov
Stream flow data for the U.S.

Oregon Home Page
http://www.state.or.us
Plenty of Oregon info.

Data for Selected Oregon Stations

O n the following pages are climatic summaries for selected stations in Oregon, chosen to represent a wide variety of local Oregon climates. Data from hundreds of additional stations are available from the Oregon Climate Service Web site or on *The Climate of Oregon* CD-Rom (see ad on final page of book).

See the map and table of climate stations on pages x-xi at the front of the book for the location of these stations and other information.

Monthly Means and Extremes, 1961-90

Codes:

MMXT	maximum mean temperature (°F)
MMNT	minimum mean temperature (°F)
MNTM	mean monthly temperature (°F)
EMXT	extreme maximum temperature (°F)
EMNT	extreme minimum temperature (°F)
TPCP	monthly mean precipitation (inches)
EXTP	extreme 24-hour precipitation (inches)
TSNW	monthly mean snowfall (inches)
DX90	average number of days when temperature is 90°F or more
DX32	average number of days when temperature is 32°F or more
DN32	average number of days when temperature is 32°F or less
DN00	average number of days when temperature is 0°F or less
DP00	average number of days with precipitation of .01 inches or more
DP01	average number of days with precipitation of .10 inches or more
DP05	average number of days with precipitation of .50 inches or more
DP10	average number of days with precipitation of 1.00 inches or more
HDD	heating degree days at 65°F
GDD	growing degree days at 50°F

Antelope

	Jan	Feb	Mar	Apr	May	Jun	Jul	Aug	Sep	Oct	Nov	Dec	Year
MMXT	40.2	46.1	52.1	58.6	67.1	76.1	84.6	84.2	75.3	63.6	48.6	40.1	61.3
MMNT	24.5	27.8	30.1	32.9	38.6	45.7	50.6	50.7	43.8	36.6	30.6	24.9	36.4
MNTM	32.3	36.9	41.1	45.7	52.9	60.9	67.6	67.4	59.6	50.1	39.4	32.5	48.8
EMXT	63	69	78	87	98	103	102	109	98	89	73	65	109
EMNT	-18	-13	10	16	18	27	33	31	25	12	-7	-17	-18
TPCP	1.58	1.10	1.16	.95	1.11	1.02	.40	.71	.81	.89	1.86	1.74	13.33
EXTP	1.13	1.00	.64	1.90	1.75	1.48	.66	2.71	1.75	.96	1.26	2.16	2.71
TSNW	6.99	2.97	2.68	1.69	.33	.00	.00	.00	.00	.17	2.94	7.06	25.24
DX90	.0	.0	.0	.0	.3	3.1	9.3	9.2	2.0	.0	.0	.0	23.9
DX32	6.3	2.3	.2	.0	.0	.0	.0	.0	.0	.0	1.1	6.0	15.1
DN32	24.5	20.7	20.2	15.1	6.5	.7	.0	.0	1.7	8.6	16.3	24.4	138.7
DN00	1.0	.4	.0	.0	.0	.0	.0	.0	.0	.0	.1	.9	2.4
DP00	10.4	9.2	10.6	7.9	7.2	6.3	3.0	3.9	4.4	6.1	11.5	11.2	90.9
DP01	5.3	3.5	4.2	2.9	3.3	2.8	1.3	1.8	2.2	3.0	5.8	5.5	41.5
DP05	.6	.3	.2	.4	.4	.4	.1	.2	.2	.2	.7	.8	4.6
DP10	.1	.0	.0	.1	.1	.1	.0	.0	.1	.0	.1	.1	.8
HDD	1014	793	741	579	383	174	58	60	194	464	768	1007	6261
GDD	0	2	8	41	148	334	546	541	301	98	5	1	2022

Arlington

	Jan	Feb	Mar	Apr	May	Jun	Jul	Aug	Sep	Oct	Nov	Dec	Year
MMXT	40.8	48.0	56.9	65.5	75.3	83.9	91.6	90.1	80.1	65.5	50.0	41.0	65.7
MMNT	28.8	32.0	36.1	41.4	48.2	55.8	60.9	60.5	51.6	41.9	35.6	29.5	43.5
MNTM	34.8	40.0	46.5	53.5	61.8	69.8	76.2	75.3	65.9	53.7	42.8	35.2	54.6
EMXT	65	70	79	94	107	110	110	115	102	88	73	65	115
EMNT	-10	-11	16	22	31	37	42	40	31	17	-3	-7	-11
TPCP	1.31	.88	.75	.64	.56	.38	.21	.32	.38	.56	1.29	1.62	8.86
EXTP	1.09	.99	.89	1.49	.86	1.07	.80	1.69	.83	1.03	.92	2.27	2.27
TSNW	3.19	1.05	.10	.00	.00	.00	.00	.00	.00	.00	.83	3.06	8.43
DX90	.0	.0	.0	.1	2.5	9.5	18.7	16.9	4.0	.0	.0	.0	50.2
DX32	5.8	1.4	.0	.0	.0	.0	.0	.0	.0	.0	.8	5.2	13.8
DN32	18.4	14.2	9.5	3.1	.2	.0	.0	.0	.3	3.1	9.0	18.5	76.4
DN00	.5	.1	.0	.0	.0	.0	.0	.0	.0	.0	.0	.6	1.2
DP00	9.1	7.3	7.0	5.0	4.0	2.9	1.8	2.6	3.0	4.6	9.7	10.6	67.6
DP01	4.2	3.1	2.9	1.8	2.1	1.1	.6	1.0	1.2	1.9	4.4	4.9	29.1
DP05	.5	.1	.1	.3	.1	.1	.1	.1	.1	.1	.3	.4	2.3
DP10	.0	.0	.0	.0	.0	.0	.0	.0	.0	.0	.0	.1	.3
HDD	937	706	575	348	149	29	3	3	69	352	667	924	4756
GDD	3	5	25	134	365	594	814	784	476	153	13	2	3383

Ashland

	Jan	Feb	Mar	Apr	May	Jun	Jul	Aug	Sep	Oct	Nov	Dec	Year
MMXT	46.3	52.3	56.2	62.1	70.0	78.7	86.8	85.7	78.6	66.6	52.3	45.4	65.1
MMNT	29.6	31.9	33.7	36.2	41.6	48.0	51.7	51.6	45.7	39.1	34.1	30.0	39.4
MNTM	37.9	42.1	45.0	49.1	55.8	63.4	69.3	68.7	62.1	52.8	43.2	37.7	52.3
EMXT	70	75	76	87	97	104	105	108	103	97	79	70	108
EMNT	4	8	20	21	27	32	32	34	30	19	13	-4	-4
TPCP	2.37	1.72	1.95	1.61	1.29	.91	.32	.58	.95	1.60	2.82	3.06	19.19
EXTP	1.50	1.42	1.02	1.26	1.20	1.46	1.35	.90	2.10	2.61	1.37	3.00	3.00
TSNW	2.73	1.16	1.02	.45	.00	.00	.00	.00	.00	.00	.28	2.39	8.38
DX90	.0	.0	.0	.0	.9	4.7	12.6	11.0	3.7	.3	.0	.0	33.2
DX32	.8	.1	.0	.0	.0	.0	.0	.0	.0	.0	.0	1.2	2.2
DN32	20.7	15.9	13.7	8.7	1.9	.0	.0	.0	.2	4.3	13.3	19.9	98.8
DN00	.0	.0	.0	.0	.0	.0	.0	.0	.0	.0	.0	.1	.1
DP00	12.0	10.9	12.4	10.3	8.1	5.6	2.0	3.2	4.5	7.7	14.4	14.1	105.1
DP01	6.2	5.2	5.9	5.3	4.2	2.8	.9	1.5	2.6	4.3	7.7	7.4	54.0
DP05	1.3	.7	.9	.6	.4	.3	.1	.3	.5	.8	1.5	1.5	8.8
DP10	.3	.1	.0	.1	.0	.0	.0	.0	.2	.2	.2	.4	1.6
HDD	839	646	621	477	296	110	26	28	125	379	654	846	5048
GDD	5	8	17	67	200	402	597	578	365	129	14	4	2387

Astoria (Airport)

	Jan	Feb	Mar	Apr	May	Jun	Jul	Aug	Sep	Oct	Nov	Dec	Year
MMXT	47.9	51.1	53.2	55.9	60.2	64.4	67.8	69.0	67.7	61.2	53.5	48.3	58.4
MMNT	35.9	37.4	37.9	40.1	44.5	49.5	52.5	52.7	49.1	44.1	40.2	36.6	43.4
MNTM	41.9	44.2	45.6	48.0	52.3	56.9	60.2	60.9	58.4	52.7	46.9	42.4	50.9
EMXT	67	72	73	83	87	91	100	96	95	85	71	64	100
EMNT	11	9	22	29	31	37	39	39	33	26	19	6	6
TPCP	10.01	7.59	7.07	4.61	3.02	2.40	1.15	1.33	2.91	5.73	10.05	10.55	66.42
EXTP	4.53	2.80	2.05	2.24	1.74	2.07	1.72	1.50	1.83	3.52	3.10	3.59	4.53
TSNW	2.24	.39	.44	.05	.00	.00	.00	.00	.00	.00	.21	1.43	4.74
DX90	.0	.0	.0	.0	.0	.1	.1	.1	.1	.0	.0	.0	.4
DX32	.7	.1	.0	.0	.0	.0	.0	.0	.0	.0	.1	.9	1.7
DN32	9.5	6.5	5.7	2.1	.1	.0	.0	.0	.0	.5	4.2	8.7	37.3
DN00	.0	.0	.0	.0	.0	.0	.0	.0	.0	.0	.0	.0	.0
DP00	21.5	19.2	20.6	18.0	15.0	12.2	7.6	7.7	10.1	15.1	21.0	22.2	190.0
DP01	16.7	14.3	14.7	11.4	8.0	5.8	2.8	3.3	6.4	10.7	16.5	16.9	127.7
DP05	7.2	5.6	5.3	2.9	1.5	1.5	.6	.8	2.2	3.9	7.2	7.5	46.3
DP10	2.6	1.6	1.3	.5	.3	.3	.1	.1	.4	1.3	2.6	3.3	14.5
HDD	715	586	602	511	393	245	154	134	203	383	545	700	5171
GDD	4	10	11	26	90	208	315	336	253	107	26	7	1391

Austin

	Jan	Feb	Mar	Apr	May	Jun	Jul	Aug	Sep	Oct	Nov	Dec	Year
MMXT	34.6	40.5	45.9	54.3	62.6	72.0	81.6	81.6	71.2	60.2			
MMNT	10.5	14.6	19.5	25.6	30.7	37.1	39.2	38.1	30.5	24.9	20.9	12.1	25.5
MNTM	22.5	27.6	32.7	40.0	46.5	54.5	60.4	59.9	50.9	42.6	31.9	23.4	41.2
EMXT	59	63	72	85	92	95	100	103	95	86	71	56	103
EMNT	-35	-35	-12	4	14	22	25	22	12	-5	-23	-37	-37
TPCP	2.78	1.94	1.98	1.44	1.47	1.62	.72	1.01	1.06	1.32	2.55	3.08	20.59
EXTP	1.78	1.43	1.05	1.62	1.18	1.90	1.43	2.04	.96	1.30	1.29	1.74	2.04
TSNW	22.20	14.68	11.22	5.32	.43	.00	.00	.00	.08	1.13	14.10	23.34	90.00
DX90	.0	.0	.0	.0	.1	1.1	6.4	6.2	.7	.0	.0	.0	14.6
DX32	11.6	3.5	1.1	.0	.0	.0	.0	.0	.0	.2	2.6	11.3	30.5
DN32	30.5	27.4	30.1	26.6	18.8	7.6	3.8	5.5	19.0	27.0	28.1	30.4	253.8
DN00	8.1	3.7	1.2	.0	.0	.0	.0	.0	.0	.1	1.1	5.2	19.5
DP00	13.8	12.1	12.8	9.1	9.6	8.1	3.9	5.5	6.0	7.7	13.6	14.6	115.3
DP01	8.6	7.0	7.1	4.9	5.1	4.6	2.1	2.6	3.3	4.3	7.8	9.5	66.8
DP05	1.4	.5	.4	.5	.2	.8	.3	.4	.4	.4	.9	1.3	7.2
DP10	.1	.0	.0	.1	.0	.1	.1	.1	.0	.0	.1	.2	.8
HDD	1317	1056	1002	752	574	321	165	179	425	696	992	1290	8745
GDD	0	0	0	8	49	171	329	314	106	16	0	0	1012

Baker City

	Jan	Feb	Mar	Apr	May	Jun	Jul	Aug	Sep	Oct	Nov	Dec	Year
MMXT	33.7	41.1	50.0	58.8	67.2	75.8	84.9	84.3	74.7	62.5	45.7	35.3	59.5
MMNT	16.8	22.4	26.9	31.1	38.1	45.0	48.5	47.4	38.9	30.5	25.1	17.7	32.4
MNTM	25.3	31.8	38.5	45.0	52.6	60.4	66.7	65.8	56.8	46.5	35.4	26.5	45.9
EMXT	59	66	78	89	94	102	102	106	98	89	69	58	106
EMNT	-28	-28	1	12	20	26	31	30	17	9	-15	-39	-39
TPCP	1.03	.62	.84	.82	1.26	1.38	.58	.94	.74	.63	.96	1.07	10.87
EXTP	.76	.78	.68	1.34	1.03	1.46	1.59	2.29	1.28	.80	.77	.66	2.29
TSNW	6.31	3.24	2.83	1.26	.47	.01	.00	.00	.00	.41	3.33	7.11	24.96
DX90	.0	.0	.0	.0	.4	2.7	9.6	9.7	1.9	.0	.0	.0	24.4
DX32	12.3	3.9	.3	.0	.0	.0	.0	.0	.0	.0	1.7	9.8	28.1
DN32	28.5	24.6	24.8	18.2	5.9	.5	.1	.2	5.3	19.1	24.0	28.4	179.6
DN00	3.9	1.2	.0	.0	.0	.0	.0	.0	.0	.0	.3	2.7	8.1
DP00	11.9	9.0	9.6	7.7	9.3	8.4	4.4	5.3	5.2	5.8	11.4	11.8	99.8
DP01	2.9	1.9	2.7	2.6	3.9	4.2	1.5	2.7	2.0	2.0	3.2	3.9	33.5
DP05	.2	.0	.1	.3	.5	.7	.2	.5	.4	.2	.1	.1	3.2
DP10	.0	.0	.0	.0	.1	.1	.0	.1	.0	.0	.0	.0	.3
HDD	1232	939	823	601	387	170	50	65	255	574	888	1193	7177
GDD	0	0	3	30	134	318	516	490	226	41	1	0	1761

Bandon

	Jan	Feb	Mar	Apr	May	Jun	Jul	Aug	Sep	Oct	Nov	Dec	Year
MMXT	53.4	55.2	55.7	57.2	60.4	63.7	66.1	67.0	67.4	63.2	57.5	53.6	60.1
MMNT	38.2	39.5	39.8	40.7	43.9	48.1	50.4	50.4	47.6	44.3	41.8	38.7	43.5
MNTM	45.8	47.3	47.7	48.9	52.1	55.9	58.3	58.7	57.5	53.7	49.6	46.1	51.8
EMXT	75	79	78	84	90	85	85	90	100	91	79	77	100
EMNT	16	14	26	29	30	35	38	35	32	27	21	8	8
TPCP	9.29	7.20	7.47	4.36	2.76	1.54	.40	.97	1.69	4.08	9.19	9.83	58.89
EXTP	3.73	4.99	3.87	3.30	2.56	1.80	1.14	3.40	1.30	3.18	4.45	5.61	5.61
TSNW	.80	.22	.03	.00	.00	.00	.00	.00	.00	.00	.00	.07	1.20
DX90	.0	.0	.0	.0	.0	.0	.0	.0	.1	.0	.0	.0	.3
DX32	.0	.0	.0	.0	.0	.0	.0	.0	.0	.0	.0	.1	.1
DN32	7.2	5.0	3.7	1.7	.3	.0	.0	.0	.0	.6	2.8	6.8	28.8
DN00	.0	.0	.0	.0	.0	.0	.0	.0	.0	.0	.0	.0	.0
DP00	19.6	18.2	19.7	15.6	12.1	8.6	4.1	6.1	7.6	12.3	20.3	21.2	166.5
DP01	14.3	12.9	14.5	9.8	6.6	4.0	1.1	2.0	3.9	7.2	14.7	14.9	106.3
DP05	6.8	4.9	5.3	2.6	1.5	.8	.1	.5	1.2	2.7	6.7	6.9	40.2
DP10	2.9	1.8	1.5	.6	.4	.2	.0	.2	.2	.9	2.5	2.7	13.9
HDD	594	499	535	482	399	273	210	195	227	351	461	585	4821
GDD	21	28	25	31	84	177	256	270	225	127	55	25	1324

Bend

	Jan	Feb	Mar	Apr	May	Jun	Jul	Aug	Sep	Oct	Nov	Dec	Year
MMXT	41.6	46.3	51.1	57.5	65.1	73.6	81.5	80.9	73.1	63.1	48.5	41.7	60.3
MMNT	21.9	24.5	25.9	29.1	34.5	41.1	45.0	44.6	37.4	31.2	27.1	22.4	32.1
MNTM	31.8	35.4	38.5	43.3	49.8	57.3	63.2	62.7	55.2	47.2	37.8	32.1	46.2
EMXT	67	70	77	86	92	96	98	102	95	90	74	66	102
EMNT	-24	-17	-5	9	13	23	27	27	16	3	-10	-24	-24
TPCP	1.83	.97	.92	.60	.77	.86	.49	.58	.47	.65	1.57	1.99	11.70
EXTP	1.87	1.53	.91	1.26	.81	1.55	1.28	.82	1.17	.61	1.90	2.26	2.26
TSNW	10.03	3.85	4.13	1.98	.32	.00	.00	.00	.00	.20	5.62	9.47	34.78
DX90	.0	.0	.0	.0	.1	1.4	5.3	5.4	1.1	.0	.0	.0	13.2
DX32	4.6	1.9	.3	.0	.0	.0	.0	.0	.0	.0	1.0	4.2	12.0
DN32	26.2	23.3	25.1	20.8	12.8	3.9	1.0	.8	8.3	17.3	21.6	25.9	187.1
DN00	1.5	.6	.1	.0	.0	.0	.0	.0	.0	.0	.2	1.2	3.5
DP00	9.8	7.3	7.5	5.6	5.2	5.1	3.3	4.1	3.8	5.0	8.7	10.0	75.3
DP01	4.5	3.1	3.0	1.8	2.3	2.5	1.4	1.8	1.5	2.1	3.9	5.2	33.1
DP05	1.1	.4	.3	.2	.5	.4	.2	.2	.1	.1	.9	1.0	5.3
DP10	.2	.1	.0	.0	.0	.1	.0	.0	.0	.0	.2	.3	1.0
HDD	1030	836	821	653	475	251	115	123	302	553	817	1021	6997
GDD	0	0	5	29	99	243	413	396	192	62	4	0	1442

Brothers

	Jan	Feb	Mar	Apr	May	Jun	Jul	Aug	Sep	Oct	Nov	Dec	Year
MMXT	37.6	42.8	48.1	56.0	64.4	73.0	81.9	80.9	73.0	62.6	45.9	38.3	58.8
MMNT	16.8	21.1	22.5	24.8	30.6	37.7	41.8	41.0	33.8	27.9	22.8	17.3	28.2
MNTM	27.2	32.0	35.3	40.4	47.5	55.4	61.9	60.9	53.4	45.2	34.4	27.8	43.5
EMXT	61	65	73	85	92	96	98	103	97	87	72	60	103
EMNT	-30	-19	-10	1	8	12	18	20	10	2	-15	-30	-30
TPCP	1.06	.49	.64	.64	1.05	.95	.52	.72	.49	.67	1.21	1.10	9.38
EXTP	1.32	.55	.44	.85	1.02	1.13	1.96	1.30	1.19	.95	1.03	1.70	1.96
TSNW	7.27	2.53	2.48	2.15	.92	.00	.00	.00	.03	.74	3.99	8.42	28.63
DX90	.0	.0	.0	.0	.2	1.1	5.3	4.9	.7	.0	.0	.0	12.3
DX32	8.0	2.7	.8	.1	.0	.0	.0	.0	.0	.0	2.1	6.8	20.7
DN32	28.5	25.9	28.6	24.8	18.5	8.2	3.8	4.4	12.5	22.5	24.9	28.9	231.4
DN00	3.0	.8	.0	.0	.0	.0	.0	.0	.0	.0	.6	2.5	6.9
DP00	7.2	6.3	7.2	6.1	6.3	6.1	3.5	4.0	4.0	5.4	8.7	8.9	75.0
DP01	3.3	1.6	2.6	2.3	3.1	3.2	1.6	2.0	1.5	2.5	3.7	3.6	30.2
DP05	.4	.0	.0	.1	.4	.3	.2	.4	.2	.1	.6	.2	2.7
DP10	.1	.0	.0	.0	.0	.0	.0	.1	.0	.0	.1	.1	.4
HDD	1172	933	922	739	543	301	143	165	353	614	919	1153	7941
GDD	0	0	0	14	70	200	372	344	157	39	1	0	1198

Burns (Airport)

	Jan	Feb	Mar	Apr	May	Jun	Jul	Aug	Sep	Oct	Nov	Dec	Year
MMXT	33.3	38.4	48.7	57.8	64.9	74.5	84.2	83.6	73.3	61.1	44.1	33.1	57.0
MMNT	12.7	17.1	26.2	30.1	36.3	42.0	47.2	45.3	36.5	28.1	21.3	12.2	29.4
MNTM	23.0	27.8	37.4	43.9	50.6	58.3	65.7	64.5	54.9	44.6	32.7	22.7	43.2
EMXT	57	62	71	84	94	95	100	102	97	86	68	54	102
EMNT	-27	-28	4	14	20	23	25	28	17	7	-13	-28	-28
TPCP	.81	1.17	1.60	.80	1.07	.67	.52	.43	.62	.78	1.41	1.41	12.64
EXTP	.56	.81	.71	.52	.69	.62	.81	.99	.74	.75	.62	.67	.99
TSNW	6.57	6.91	4.60	.99	.26	.05	.00	.00	.00	.56	6.37	10.38	42.26
DX90	.0	.0	.0	.0	.4	1.9	8.5	7.3	1.2	.0	.0	.0	15.7
DX32	12.7	6.8	.3	.0	.0	.0	.0	.0	.0	.0	3.7	12.0	40.3
DN32	30.1	26.3	26.2	19.2	9.7	2.6	.6	.4	8.4	22.5	26.9	30.4	207.0
DN00	5.3	2.2	.0	.0	.0	.0	.0	.0	.0	.0	1.1	5.1	14.6
DP00	9.1	9.1	12.8	8.0	8.5	6.3	2.6	3.7	4.5	5.9	11.5	9.7	98.9
DP01	2.8	3.9	5.5	2.9	3.6	2.2	1.3	1.3	2.0	2.7	4.9	4.5	41.0
DP05	.1	.3	.5	.2	.4	.3	.4	.2	.3	.4	.2	.3	4.6
DP10	.0	.0	.0	.0	.0	.0	.0	.0	.0	.0	.0	.0	.0
HDD	1301	1050	855	632	451	224	69	81	312	632	970	1313	8097
GDD	0	0	1	31	110	267	487	448	193	33	0	0	1483

Cascadia

	Jan	Feb	Mar	Apr	May	Jun	Jul	Aug	Sep	Oct	Nov	Dec	Year
MMXT	45.3	50.7	54.3	59.0	64.6	71.5	78.0	79.6	73.8	64.0	51.6	44.7	61.5
MMNT	30.9	32.8	34.4	36.9	41.3	46.7	48.4	47.9	43.6	38.5	35.8	32.2	39.1
MNTM	38.1	41.8	44.4	47.8	53.0	59.1	63.3	63.8	58.6	51.3	43.8	38.5	50.4
EMXT	73	79	78	86	97	98	102	104	101	93	76	69	104
EMNT	3	2	18	24	28	30	36	31	26	23	11	-2	-2
TPCP	8.48	6.82	6.79	5.28	4.10	2.83	.90	1.40	2.65	4.88	9.29	9.37	61.70
EXTP	3.06	4.00	3.05	2.96	1.52	2.00	1.70	1.87	1.65	2.52	3.60	6.52	4.00
TSNW	3.58	1.80	1.14	.14	.00	.00	.00	.00	.00	.00	.26	2.41	7.45
DX90	.0	.0	.0	.0	.3	1.0	2.4	3.6	1.5	.2	.0	.0	9.5
DX32	.9	.3	.0	.0	.0	.0	.0	.0	.0	.0	.2	1.0	2.6
DN32	18.5	14.3	12.4	6.6	1.5	.2	.0	.0	1.0	5.9	9.9	15.8	86.7
DN00	.0	.0	.0	.0	.0	.0	.0	.0	.0	.0	.0	.1	.2
DP00	18.2	16.8	19.3	17.2	13.5	8.9	4.2	4.6	7.7	12.4	18.4	19.2	160.1
DP01	15.0	13.6	15.1	12.0	9.2	6.2	2.5	3.0	5.7	10.0	15.0	15.8	122.3
DP05	6.1	4.8	4.7	3.6	2.9	1.9	.5	1.0	2.1	3.8	7.4	6.9	44.6
DP10	2.0	1.3	.9	.6	.4	.5	.0	.2	.5	.8	2.6	2.4	11.9
HDD	833	656	639	515	378	194	97	83	204	426	636	823	5453
GDD	1	5	13	49	128	276	411	427	261	88	11	1	1692

Condon

	Jan	Feb	Mar	Apr	May	Jun	Jul	Aug	Sep	Oct	Nov	Dec	Year
MMXT	38.4	44.1	50.4	56.8	65.6	74.4	82.3	81.5	72.4	61.3	46.3	39.2	59.3
MMNT	23.6	27.5	30.1	33.2	38.9	45.2	50.0	50.3	43.5	36.2	29.9	24.2	36.1
MNTM	31.0	35.8	40.3	45.0	52.2	59.8	66.1	65.9	58.0	48.8	38.1	31.7	47.7
EMXT	64	68	74	83	96	97	101	103	94	88	73	63	103
EMNT	-12	-19	11	18	24	28	35	33	23	9	-14	-22	-22
TPCP	1.54	1.24	1.22	1.23	1.20	1.04	.44	.71	.75	1.00	1.90	1.85	14.10
EXTP	.79	1.11	.75	1.23	1.17	1.39	1.01	1.52	1.04	1.09	.72	2.25	2.25
TSNW	5.75	4.24	2.26	1.20	.12	.00	.00	.00	.00	.22	4.80	5.97	28.40
DX90	.0	.0	.0	.0	.1	1.2	6.2	5.5	.6	.0	.0	.0	13.5
DX32	8.3	3.3	.3	.0	.0	.0	.0	.0	.0	.0	2.2	7.4	22.6
DN32	25.3	20.9	20.2	14.4	5.9	.4	.0	.0	1.2	9.2	17.9	24.9	140.0
DN00	1.5	.4	.0	.0	.0	.0	.0	.0	.0	.0	.2	1.2	3.2
DP00	12.5	13.0	11.9	10.6	7.6	6.8	3.1	4.0	5.0	7.4	15.0	13.4	114.0
DP01	5.3	4.2	4.4	3.8	3.4	2.5	1.2	2.0	2.5	3.1	6.6	5.6	45.0
DP05	.3	.2	.2	.4	.6	.6	.2	.4	.3	.3	.5	.6	4.8
DP10	.0	.0	.0	.1	.1	.1	.0	.1	.0	.0	.0	.1	.6
HDD	1055	825	767	600	401	188	69	70	227	504	806	1033	6540
GDD	0	2	4	30	127	300	500	493	257	72	5	1	1773

Corvallis

	Jan	Feb	Mar	Apr	May	Jun	Jul	Aug	Sep	Oct	Nov	Dec	Year
MMXT	45.5	50.4	54.9	59.5	66.1	73.1	80.2	81.1	75.4	64.3	52.3	45.6	62.4
MMNT	33.0	35.1	37.0	39.2	43.1	48.6	51.0	51.3	47.8	41.7	38.0	33.9	41.6
MNTM	39.3	42.7	46.0	49.3	54.6	60.9	65.6	66.2	61.6	53.0	45.1	39.7	52.0
EMXT	64	68	76	83	96	98	103	108	103	92	72	66	108
EMNT	9	7	12	24	28	33	38	37	32	25	15	-7	-7
TPCP	6.82	5.04	4.55	2.56	1.95	1.23	.52	.87	1.51	3.11	6.82	7.72	42.71
EXTP	4.28	2.76	1.90	1.83	1.58	1.33	1.26	1.48	2.18	1.81	2.68	2.87	4.28
TSNW	2.18	1.34	.23	.00	.00	.00	.00	.00	.00	.00	.16	1.64	5.71
DX90	.0	.0	.0	.0	.1	1.1	5.1	4.9	2.0	.1	.0	.0	13.3
DX32	1.2	.2	.0	.0	.0	.0	.0	.0	.0	.0	.2	1.5	3.1
DN32	14.8	9.9	6.6	3.3	.4	.0	.0	.0	.0	1.7	6.1	12.3	55.0
DN00	.0	.0	.0	.0	.0	.0	.0	.0	.0	.0	.0	.2	.2
DP00	19.4	17.3	18.2	15.3	11.9	7.4	3.3	4.2	7.5	12.7	19.7	20.8	157.5
DP01	12.9	11.0	11.8	7.6	5.6	3.6	1.6	2.3	3.7	7.4	13.3	13.2	93.9
DP05	4.6	3.6	2.5	1.1	.8	.5	.2	.4	.8	2.2	5.0	5.3	27.1
DP10	1.5	.8	.5	.1	.1	.1	.0	.1	.1	.3	1.4	1.9	7.0
HDD	798	629	590	471	329	153	57	47	129	373	596	783	4955
GDD	3	6	18	58	162	327	485	501	349	123	16	4	2052

Cottage Grove

	Jan	Feb	Mar	Apr	May	Jun	Jul	Aug	Sep	Oct	Nov	Dec	Year
MMXT	47.9	53.1	56.7	61.4	67.6	74.4	81.3	81.9	76.3	65.4	53.6	47.7	63.9
MMNT	32.6	34.3	35.6	36.8	41.0	45.7	47.5	47.6	43.8	40.2	37.5	33.4	39.6
MNTM	40.3	43.7	46.1	49.1	54.3	60.1	64.4	64.8	60.1	52.8	45.5	40.5	51.7
EMXT	66	75	78	86	93	98	103	105	104	96	76	72	105
EMNT	-1	0	15	21	25	29	34	32	25	18	9	-5	-5
TPCP	6.53	5.20	5.38	3.53	2.53	1.39	.53	.95	1.65	3.60	7.46	7.20	45.19
EXTP	3.06	4.57	1.83	1.52	1.30	1.17	1.84	1.44	1.55	1.90	4.80	3.31	4.80
TSNW	3.03	1.49	.53	.05	.01	.00	.00	.00	.00	.00	.30	1.82	6.70
DX90	.0	.0	.0	.0	.3	1.0	4.6	5.3	1.9	.2	.0	.0	13.1
DX32	.7	.1	.0	.0	.0	.0	.0	.0	.0	.0	.1	.7	1.5
DN32	15.5	11.3	10.7	7.6	3.1	.5	.0	.0	1.5	3.8	6.9	13.1	75.5
DN00	.1	.0	.0	.0	.0	.0	.0	.0	.0	.0	.0	.1	.3
DP00	17.6	16.3	18.2	15.1	11.3	7.0	2.9	3.6	7.0	11.6	18.3	18.8	147.3
DP01	12.2	11.4	12.6	9.6	7.1	3.5	1.7	2.3	4.1	7.4	13.5	13.2	97.5
DP05	4.7	3.3	3.3	1.9	1.3	.8	.3	.6	1.1	2.6	5.3	5.0	29.6
DP10	1.5	.8	.9	.2	.1	.1	.0	.2	.1	.6	1.3	1.6	7.1
HDD	767	602	585	478	335	164	69	62	160	380	585	759	4969
GDD	6	11	20	51	151	302	445	458	303	118	22	7	1886

Crater Lake

	Jan	Feb	Mar	Apr	May	Jun	Jul	Aug	Sep	Oct	Nov	Dec	Year
MMXT	34.5	35.2	36.4	41.8	49.2	58.1	67.9	68.5	61.7	51.7	38.5	34.4	48.3
MMNT	17.5	17.9	18.1	21.2	27.0	33.8	39.7	40.2	35.6	30.1	22.5	18.3	26.8
MNTM	26.0	26.6	27.2	31.5	38.1	46.0	53.8	54.4	48.6	40.9	30.5	26.3	37.6
EMXT	58	60	61	68	75	82	86	90	87	76	68	64	90
EMNT	-21	-13	-7	0	5	13	24	24	11	10	-4	-13	-21
TPCP	9.66	7.78	8.09	4.60	3.01	1.98	.68	1.29	2.38	4.75	10.56	10.84	65.82
EXTP	4.43	2.69	3.65	2.00	1.46	1.28	1.73	2.00	2.00	2.78	3.25	7.13	7.13
TSNW	85.27	73.24	87.48	43.04	19.26	3.95	.54	.24	4.05	21.31	69.10	84.02	495.00
DX90	.0	.0	.0	.0	.0	.0	.0	.1	.0	.0	.0	.0	.1
DX32	13.7	11.8	11.7	6.8	1.2	.0	.0	.0	.0	2.0	8.8	14.1	69.8
DN32	30.5	27.9	30.8	28.3	23.9	12.6	4.0	3.3	9.7	18.8	27.4	30.7	247.3
DN00	1.2	.8	.3	.0	.0	.0	.0	.0	.0	.0	.1	.8	3.0
DP00	16.7	15.6	18.5	14.1	10.0	7.6	3.2	4.6	6.3	10.2	17.3	17.8	141.9
DP01	14.3	12.9	15.6	10.3	7.2	5.0	1.9	3.3	4.7	7.9	14.4	15.5	113.2
DP05	7.2	6.3	6.2	3.1	2.2	1.1	.4	.9	1.5	3.9	8.2	7.9	49.0
DP10	2.8	2.0	1.6	.7	.3	.2	.1	.1	.7	1.3	3.5	3.7	17.0
HDD	1210	1084	1172	1005	834	571	349	335	492	748	1034	1199	10002
GDD	0	0	0	0	5	46	163	176	79	21	0	0	503

Dayville

	Jan	Feb	Mar	Apr	May	Jun	Jul	Aug	Sep	Oct	Nov	Dec	Year
MMXT	43.5	49.8	57.8	65.7	72.4	82.0	90.6	90.1	80.5	68.3	52.3	43.2	70.4
MMNT	28.2	28.2	33.6	37.2	42.6	48.9	52.9	52.4	45.4	39.3	31.1	24.2	41.2
MNTM	36.9	38.8	45.7	51.5	57.5	65.4	71.7	71.3	63.0	53.8	41.4	33.7	56.1
EMXT	67	72	80	95	102	103	110	110	106	95	78	65	110
EMNT	-3	-11	18	21	25	33	39	39	25	14	3	-18	-18
TPCP	.77	.85	1.32	1.24	1.82	1.07	.52	.94	.48	.70	1.11	.83	11.65
EXTP	.55	.63	.67	.88	1.51	.64	1.15	1.83	.62	1.15	.72	.49	1.83
TSNW	2.68	2.08	.39	.04	.00	.00	.00	.00	.00	.00	1.71	4.07	8.27
DX90	.0	.0	.0	.2	2.9	7.8	17.9	17.4	6.6	.7	.0	.0	49.3
DX32	3.4	1.2	.0	.0	.0	.0	.0	.0	.0	.0	.4	4.3	7.6
DN32	22.0	16.4	12.8	7.4	2.3	.0	.0	.0	.8	5.5	16.9	22.0	87.7
DN00	.3	1.0	.0	.0	.0	.0	.0	.0	.0	.0	.0	1.4	2.4
DP00	8.0	7.7	12.2	10.1	10.2	8.6	3.5	4.3	4.8	6.5	9.3	7.1	86.8
DP01	2.7	2.8	4.2	3.6	4.7	3.1	1.4	2.4	1.8	2.4	3.6	3.2	33.9
DP05	.1	.3	.3	.4	.9	.4	.2	.5	.1	.1	.4	.0	3.5
DP10	.0	.0	.0	.0	.2	.0	.1	.2	.0	.1	.0	.0	.5
HDD	865	664	579	405	263	86	17	14	131	356	692	869	5215
GDD	3	7	23	121	249	451	673	658	393	169	17	1	2894

Detroit Dam

	Jan	Feb	Mar	Apr	May	Jun	Jul	Aug	Sep	Oct	Nov	Dec	Year
MMXT	43.2	47.4	51.7	56.6	63.3	70.3	77.3	78.0	72.2	61.9	49.6	43.6	59.6
MMNT	32.9	34.4	35.8	38.4	43.4	49.4	53.1	54.0	50.3	44.5	38.8	34.2	42.5
MNTM	38.1	40.9	43.7	47.5	53.4	59.9	65.2	66.0	61.3	53.2	44.2	38.9	51.0
EMXT	67	75	76	85	104	101	103	105	107	92	72	64	107
EMNT	10	5	19	30	32	38	42	40	35	26	15	5	5
TPCP	12.79	10.24	9.42	6.54	4.87	3.27	.90	1.60	3.56	6.42	13.21	13.98	87.32
EXTP	5.11	4.50	3.62	5.56	1.98	2.68	1.26	1.28	2.80	2.91	3.95	5.41	5.56
TSNW	7.92	3.71	2.18	.37	.00	.00	.00	.00	.00	.00	1.00	3.54	18.16
DX90	.0	.0	.0	.0	.3	1.0	3.0	3.3	1.3	.1	.0	.0	9.3
DX32	1.4	.3	.0	.0	.0	.0	.0	.0	.0	.0	.2	1.4	3.2
DN32	11.7	7.9	5.5	.9	.0	.0	.0	.0	.0	.1	2.7	8.6	37.2
DN00	.0	.0	.0	.0	.0	.0	.0	.0	.0	.0	.0	.0	.0
DP00	19.8	17.6	20.3	18.0	14.9	10.1	4.9	5.4	9.1	13.4	20.5	21.1	175.8
DP01	16.3	14.4	16.4	13.0	10.6	6.6	2.3	3.4	6.1	10.2	16.5	16.9	133.0
DP05	9.0	7.7	7.5	4.8	3.6	2.2	.5	1.0	2.6	5.0	9.3	9.3	62.7
DP10	4.4	3.1	2.4	1.2	.7	.6	.1	.2	1.0	2.0	4.6	5.1	25.8
HDD	836	680	659	525	369	187	77	61	147	368	624	810	5347
GDD	1	2	9	47	145	298	472	495	339	133	11	2	1954

Elgin

	Jan	Feb	Mar	Apr	May	Jun	Jul	Aug	Sep	Oct	Nov	Dec	Year
MMXT	37.9	44.8	52.0	60.8	69.3	78.3	87.6	87.8	78.1	65.2	47.8	38.6	62.2
MMNT	21.6	25.4	28.4	32.0	37.5	43.6	46.0	45.1	37.7	31.3	28.3	22.8	33.2
MNTM	29.7	35.1	40.2	46.4	53.4	61.0	66.8	66.4	57.9	48.3	38.1	30.7	47.7
EMXT	65	67	78	91	98	100	104	110	102	92	73	59	110
EMNT	-23	-20	0	11	21	26	30	25	19	11	-23	-31	-31
TPCP	2.98	2.46	2.27	1.68	1.72	1.46	.65	.86	1.05	1.72	3.13	3.52	23.73
EXTP	1.72	2.07	1.19	1.38	1.53	1.10	1.26	1.18	1.12	1.60	2.10	2.50	1.93
TSNW	14.38	6.80	4.07	.82	.00	.00	.00	.00	.00	.10	5.86	14.21	49.47
DX90	.0	.0	.0	.1	.9	4.3	14.4	14.6	4.3	.2	.0	.0	39.0
DX32	7.5	1.9	.0	.0	.0	.0	.0	.0	.0	.0	1.0	5.8	17.5
DN32	25.2	21.5	21.4	15.9	6.5	1.2	.3	.8	8.0	17.6	19.8	25.0	165.8
DN00	2.8	.9	.0	.0	.0	.0	.0	.0	.0	.0	.2	1.9	6.1
DP00	13.7	12.7	14.0	11.1	10.7	8.8	4.6	5.5	5.9	8.6	14.1	14.9	129.8
DP01	7.8	6.9	7.5	5.5	5.3	4.2	2.0	2.6	3.1	4.9	8.7	8.8	69.2
DP05	1.7	1.0	.6	.4	.9	.6	.2	.4	.6	.8	1.7	2.3	10.9
DP10	.4	.2	.1	.1	.0	.0	.1	.1	.0	.2	.2	.4	1.7
HDD	1094	845	767	559	365	154	46	54	227	519	808	1063	6546
GDD	1	0	4	37	146	332	520	509	251	58	3	0	1857

Enterprise

	Jan	Feb	Mar	Apr	May	Jun	Jul	Aug	Sep	Oct	Nov	Dec	Year
MMXT	32.8	37.2	47.1	56.1	61.6	70.6	77.6	78.2	68.6	59.0	42.6	31.3	55.4
MMNT	12.2	14.3	23.4	27.9	33.4	39.6	41.5	41.1	33.0	26.5	20.8	10.0	26.9
MNTM	22.5	25.7	35.3	42.0	47.5	55.1	59.6	59.7	50.8	42.8	31.7	20.6	41.2
EMXT	60	62	73	83	89	89	95	96	91	85	68	57	96
EMNT	-18	-33	-10	3	16	22	29	29	13	8	-16	-32	-33
TPCP	1.26	1.17	1.65	1.55	2.15	1.72	1.00	1.40	1.19	.84	1.50	1.00	16.21
EXTP	.59	.92	.68	1.11	1.06	.77	1.21	2.39	1.14	.33	.55	.55	2.39
TSNW	12.01	8.19	8.12	5.00	1.44	.00	.00	.00	.22	1.33	7.59	9.42	52.56
DX90	.0	.0	.0	.0	.0	.0	1.2	2.1	.3	.0	.0	.0	4.0
DX32	14.6	7.6	.9	.0	.0	.0	.0	.0	.0	.1	3.6	16.2	42.9
DN32	30.4	27.1	28.4	22.4	14.8	4.1	1.4	2.0	13.6	24.4	27.4	29.9	226.8
DN00	5.1	3.4	.2	.0	.0	.0	.0	.0	.0	.0	1.1	6.7	16.0
DP00	11.4	10.9	13.8	11.9	12.7	10.6	6.8	6.8	7.3	7.3	13.7	10.4	119.8
DP01	4.4	4.8	6.0	5.9	6.7	5.4	3.6	3.8	3.9	3.2	5.7	3.4	55.5
DP05	.3	.1	.2	.3	1.1	.7	.2	.4	.2	.0	.2	.2	4.1
DP10	.0	.0	.0	.1	.1	.0	.1	.2	.1	.0	.0	.0	.8
HDD	1318	1108	921	691	545	303	184	184	429	690	999	1377	8721
GDD	0	0	0	18	73	183	304	303	107	21	1	0	1010

Estacada

	Jan	Feb	Mar	Apr	May	Jun	Jul	Aug	Sep	Oct	Nov	Dec	Year
MMXT	45.3	49.9	54.9	60.0	66.6	72.8	78.8	78.8	72.7	61.0	51.1	45.3	61.4
MMNT	33.6	35.8	37.4	39.7	44.0	49.0	51.9	51.9	48.4	43.1	38.6	34.2	42.4
MNTM	39.4	42.8	46.1	49.8	55.3	60.9	65.4	65.4	60.6	52.1	44.8	39.7	51.9
EMXT	67	71	77	90	105	100	104	105	105	89	69	64	105
EMNT	8	8	22	28	31	35	38	40	32	15	13	6	6
TPCP	8.53	6.40	6.27	4.77	3.73	2.58	1.03	1.49	2.63	4.55	8.44	8.60	58.83
EXTP	3.80	3.22	2.40	2.95	1.47	2.26	1.42	1.53	1.84	2.36	2.68	3.04	3.80
TSNW	1.24	.69	.30	.00	.00	.00	.00	.00	.00	.00	.31	1.25	3.40
DX90	.0	.0	.0	.0	.6	1.3	3.5	3.6	1.4	.0	.0	.0	10.7
DX32	1.5	.2	.0	.0	.0	.0	.0	.0	.0	.0	.1	1.4	3.4
DN32	12.7	7.8	5.2	2.0	.1	.0	.0	.0	.0	.7	4.9	11.3	44.9
DN00	.0	.0	.0	.0	.0	.0	.0	.0	.0	.0	.0	.0	.0
DP00	19.7	17.8	20.0	17.5	15.1	10.8	5.8	6.1	9.4	14.4	20.5	21.4	177.8
DP01	14.0	12.9	14.1	11.2	9.4	6.0	3.0	3.4	5.8	9.3	14.9	15.5	119.3
DP05	6.1	4.4	4.1	2.9	2.2	1.4	.5	.9	1.9	3.2	6.2	5.7	39.6
DP10	2.1	1.3	.9	.7	.3	.4	.0	.2	.5	.8	2.3	2.1	11.5
HDD	793	628	585	455	308	148	56	53	155	403	605	784	4963
GDD	3	8	23	64	176	328	476	476	318	101	15	3	2002

Eugene (Airport)

	Jan	Feb	Mar	Apr	May	Jun	Jul	Aug	Sep	Oct	Nov	Dec	Year
MMXT	46.3	51.3	55.9	60.5	67.1	74.4	82.0	82.0	76.2	64.6	52.5	46.2	63.3
MMNT	33.5	35.4	37.2	39.0	42.9	48.3	51.4	51.9	47.8	42.0	38.2	34.3	41.8
MNTM	39.9	43.4	46.6	49.7	55.0	61.4	66.7	66.9	62.0	53.3	45.3	40.2	52.5
EMXT	67	71	77	83	93	100	105	108	103	94	76	68	108
EMNT	1	4	21	27	29	32	39	38	32	19	12	-12	-12
TPCP	7.91	5.64	5.52	3.11	2.16	1.43	.51	1.08	1.67	3.41	8.32	8.61	49.36
EXTP	4.74	3.87	2.21	2.05	1.94	1.34	2.41	1.88	1.34	2.91	3.20	4.89	4.89
TSNW	3.09	.88	.23	.00	.00	.00	.00	.00	.00	.00	.23	1.69	6.13
DX90	.0	.0	.0	.0	.2	1.3	6.3	5.8	2.2	.1	.0	.0	16.0
DX32	1.5	.2	.0	.0	.0	.0	.0	.0	.0	.0	.2	1.2	3.1
DN32	13.6	9.1	6.3	2.7	.4	.0	.0	.0	.1	2.0	6.6	11.5	52.4
DN00	.0	.0	.0	.0	.0	.0	.0	.0	.0	.0	.0	.2	.2
DP00	16.8	14.8	16.1	12.4	9.7	6.3	2.7	4.0	6.1	10.4	17.1	17.6	133.9
DP01	11.8	10.5	11.4	7.7	5.7	3.8	1.3	2.4	3.8	7.1	12.9	12.7	91.2
DP05	5.3	3.8	3.8	1.8	1.1	.8	.2	.7	1.1	2.3	6.4	5.8	33.1
DP10	2.4	1.2	1.2	.5	.2	.1	.0	.2	.3	.5	2.6	2.4	11.7
HDD	778	611	571	458	316	138	41	32	118	364	590	768	4784
GDD	7	9	21	58	167	340	517	525	361	131	24	6	2166

Forest Grove

	Jan	Feb	Mar	Apr	May	Jun	Jul	Aug	Sep	Oct	Nov	Dec	Year
MMXT	45.8	51.2	56.1	61.4	68.4	75.1	81.6	82.5	76.6	65.1	52.7	45.7	63.5
MMNT	32.6	34.7	36.8	39.2	43.7	49.3	52.7	52.5	48.0	41.4	37.5	33.4	41.8
MNTM	39.2	43.0	46.4	50.3	56.0	62.2	67.2	67.5	62.3	53.3	45.1	39.5	52.6
EMXT	63	72	73	86	96	100	105	108	104	93	72	64	108
EMNT	-1	5	13	25	28	34	39	37	30	23	6	-4	-4
TPCP	7.10	5.26	4.86	2.46	1.70	1.32	.47	.92	1.60	3.41	6.91	7.98	43.88
EXTP	2.92	2.17	1.98	2.04	1.03	1.80	1.06	1.62	1.08	2.33	3.12	2.45	2.92
TSNW	2.62	1.40	.51	.01	.00	.00	.00	.00	.00	.00	.73	2.55	8.46
DX90	.0	.0	.0	.0	.4	2.5	6.3	6.8	2.9	.1	.0	.0	18.8
DX32	1.2	.2	.0	.0	.0	.0	.0	.0	.0	.0	.2	1.3	3.0
DN32	15.2	11.0	7.5	3.8	.5	.0	.0	.0	.1	2.3	7.4	12.5	60.2
DN00	.0	.0	.0	.0	.0	.0	.0	.0	.0	.0	.0	.1	.1
DP00	19.4	16.8	17.4	14.2	11.5	7.9	3.7	4.4	7.4	12.3	19.1	19.7	154.1
DP01	12.9	11.6	11.5	7.1	5.3	3.6	1.5	2.3	4.5	7.8	13.7	14.0	95.8
DP05	5.3	4.0	3.0	1.4	.8	.6	.2	.4	.8	2.2	4.9	6.4	29.9
DP10	1.7	.8	.7	.1	.0	.1	.0	.1	.2	.7	1.2	1.9	7.3
HDD	800	623	575	441	288	131	45	39	121	366	597	790	4824
GDD	2	8	20	72	199	366	532	542	369	132	17	3	2255

Fremont

	Jan	Feb	Mar	Apr	May	Jun	Jul	Aug	Sep	Oct	Nov	Dec	Year
MMXT	39.0	44.0	48.5	57.5	66.6	74.9	84.4	83.6	75.4	64.4	47.4	38.9	60.8
MMNT	15.0	18.1	21.3	23.0	27.9	35.1	36.3	35.6	28.4	23.1	20.0	14.6	23.8
MNTM	27.2	31.1	35.0	40.2	47.3	55.0	60.3	59.7	51.6	43.6	33.9	26.5	42.1
EMXT	58	68	75	84	94	96	101	102	98	88	71	63	102
EMNT	-26	-35	-21	1	7	14	16	16	2	-9	-15	-42	-42
TPCP	1.63	.92	1.17	.62	.78	1.01	.43	.61	.38	.76	1.63	1.81	11.68
EXTP	1.85	1.10	1.69	1.37	1.04	1.25	1.30	1.89	.93	.99	1.23	2.15	2.15
TSNW	9.83	5.00	5.40	2.90	.87	.00	.00	.00	.00	.74	5.08	10.06	43.51
DX90	.0	.0	.0	.0	.2	1.9	8.9	7.3	1.2	.0	.0	.0	15.3
DX32	6.9	2.2	.6	.0	.0	.0	.0	.0	.0	.0	1.1	6.1	18.3
DN32	27.4	26.1	27.7	24.9	21.6	10.4	8.7	9.6	19.9	25.7	25.6	27.8	268.5
DN00	4.5	2.0	.5	.0	.0	.0	.0	.0	.0	.0	1.5	4.6	11.5
DP00	8.4	7.4	8.5	6.0	5.3	5.9	2.4	3.2	3.0	4.9	9.2	9.4	74.4
DP01	4.3	3.1	3.5	2.3	2.6	3.1	1.3	1.6	1.4	2.1	4.7	4.9	36.3
DP05	.8	.3	.3	.1	.3	.4	.2	.2	.2	.3	.9	.7	4.6
DP10	.3	.0	.2	.0	.0	.0	.0	.0	.0	.0	.0	.4	.7
HDD	1173	958	932	743	549	305	166	181	403	664	932	1195	8370
GDD	0	0	0	9	60	186	327	305	118	19	0	0	920

Gold Beach

	Jan	Feb	Mar	Apr	May	Jun	Jul	Aug	Sep	Oct	Nov	Dec	Year
MMXT	54.6	55.8	56.2	58.1	61.2	65.1	67.8	68.4	67.7	63.8	57.7	54.6	60.9
MMNT	40.3	41.4	41.5	42.7	45.4	49.3	51.0	51.8	50.6	47.2	43.9	40.8	45.5
MNTM	47.4	48.6	48.9	50.4	53.3	57.2	59.3	60.1	59.2	55.5	50.8	47.5	53.2
EMXT	73	75	79	82	81	89	83	82	102	91	76	72	102
EMNT	12	21	28	28	31	35	40	41	40	31	29	16	12
TPCP	11.85	10.31	10.65	5.90	3.82	1.65	.47	1.18	2.42	5.77	11.98	13.40	78.17
EXTP	6.07	7.00	6.00	4.52	4.83	3.31	2.00	3.38	5.25	4.46	5.80	7.94	7.94
TSNW	.22	.00	.03	.00	.00	.00	.00	.00	.00	.00	.00	.08	.34
DX90	.0	.0	.0	.0	.0	.0	.0	.0	.0	.0	.0	.0	.0
DX32	.0	.0	.0	.0	.0	.0	.0	.0	.0	.0	.0	.0	.1
DN32	3.3	1.7	.7	.4	.0	.0	.0	.0	.0	.1	.6	2.9	8.1
DN00	.0	.0	.0	.0	.0	.0	.0	.0	.0	.0	.0	.0	.0
DP00	14.7	13.5	15.6	11.4	7.3	4.8	2.0	3.3	5.3	9.2	15.1	14.8	115.6
DP01	12.2	11.1	12.8	8.7	5.6	3.2	1.0	2.0	3.3	6.6	12.1	12.6	90.3
DP05	7.1	6.0	7.1	4.1	2.6	1.0	.3	.7	1.4	3.9	7.5	7.7	48.8
DP10	4.3	3.7	3.8	1.9	1.2	.3	.1	.2	.6	2.2	4.5	4.9	27.3
HDD	544	463	499	438	363	236	176	154	180	297	427	543	4319
GDD	30	35	32	48	110	216	290	312	275	174	65	27	1608

Grants Pass

	Jan	Feb	Mar	Apr	May	Jun	Jul	Aug	Sep	Oct	Nov	Dec	Year
MMXT	47.6	54.9	60.5	67.0	74.7	83.0	90.1	89.8	83.1	70.0	53.8	46.3	68.3
MMNT	32.7	34.4	36.0	38.4	43.6	49.7	53.1	52.7	46.7	41.2	37.9	33.6	41.7
MNTM	40.2	44.6	48.3	52.7	59.1	66.3	71.6	71.3	64.9	55.6	45.9	39.9	55.0
EMXT	69	76	82	93	102	108	109	110	108	98	72	67	110
EMNT	2	12	22	25	29	33	39	40	30	20	12	-1	-1
TPCP	5.17	3.82	3.52	1.80	1.16	.51	.22	.48	.90	2.45	5.31	5.69	31.12
EXTP	3.35	2.17	2.23	1.41	1.47	.98	.81	.75	2.86	2.14	3.20	4.07	4.07
TSNW	2.03	.42	.23	.00	.00	.00	.00	.00	.00	.00	.01	1.62	4.62
DX90	.0	.0	.0	.2	2.8	8.5	17.3	16.9	8.2	.6	.0	.0	54.1
DX32	.2	.0	.0	.0	.0	.0	.0	.0	.0	.0	.0	.6	.8
DN32	15.2	11.2	9.6	5.3	.7	.0	.0	.0	.2	2.9	6.0	12.9	63.9
DN00	.0	.0	.0	.0	.0	.0	.0	.0	.0	.0	.0	.1	.1
DP00	15.2	13.6	15.7	10.7	7.4	4.0	1.5	3.0	4.7	9.3	16.4	16.5	118.2
DP01	8.7	8.0	8.1	4.9	3.3	1.9	.7	1.5	2.2	5.3	9.7	9.8	64.3
DP05	3.8	2.7	2.2	.8	.4	.2	.1	.1	.4	1.7	3.7	4.0	20.1
DP10	1.5	.8	.5	.1	.2	.0	.0	.0	.1	.4	1.2	1.2	6.1
HDD	770	575	519	370	209	62	10	11	72	297	574	778	4259
GDD	3	13	43	124	289	490	670	659	448	190	21	4	2943

Hart Mountain Refuge

	Jan	Feb	Mar	Apr	May	Jun	Jul	Aug	Sep	Oct	Nov	Dec	Year
MMXT	39.3	41.9	45.0	52.9	62.4	71.5	81.2	80.2	71.2	60.9	46.0	39.5	57.7
MMNT	18.3	21.1	22.2	26.0	32.2	39.1	43.9	43.6	37.0	30.6	24.3	18.0	29.8
MNTM	29.0	31.6	33.5	39.4	47.3	55.3	62.5	61.9	54.1	45.8	35.2	28.9	43.8
EMXT	60	67	71	81	88	93	97	98	95	84	72	63	98
EMNT	-28	-26	-11	-4	12	21	23	25	11	4	-9	-32	-32
TPCP	.87	.74	1.22	1.33	1.43	1.34	.43	.61	.82	.97	1.16	1.13	12.04
EXTP	1.20	.72	1.01	2.80	1.53	2.21	.82	1.27	1.36	2.00	1.56	1.30	2.80
TSNW	7.29	6.05	8.37	4.31	1.77	.48	.00	.00	.59	1.97	5.32	8.38	49.47
DX90	.0	.0	.0	.0	.0	.6	3.3	2.7	.3	.0	.0	.0	7.4
DX32	6.3	3.6	2.3	.5	.0	.0	.0	.0	.0	.2	2.3	6.8	23.0
DN32	27.5	25.0	27.4	22.8	16.6	5.7	1.5	2.1	8.2	16.9	23.3	27.1	204.4
DN00	2.5	1.1	.4	.0	.0	.0	.0	.0	.0	.0	.2	1.9	6.3
DP00	7.1	6.8	9.0	8.0	7.8	6.9	3.0	4.0	4.6	5.5	8.6	8.3	79.8
DP01	3.1	2.6	3.9	4.2	4.3	3.7	1.4	1.8	2.0	3.0	4.0	3.9	38.0
DP05	.2	.2	.4	.4	.5	.7	.1	.2	.5	.2	.2	.3	3.7
DP10	.0	.0	.0	.1	.1	.1	.0	.0	.0	.1	.0	.1	.7
HDD	1118	943	975	767	549	301	119	135	332	595	893	1119	7804
GDD	0	0	1	12	63	193	391	373	176	48	1	0	1268

Hermiston

	Jan	Feb	Mar	Apr	May	Jun	Jul	Aug	Sep	Oct	Nov	Dec	Year
MMXT	40.6	48.2	57.3	64.5	72.9	81.0	88.4	87.2	78.3	65.9	50.6	41.1	64.7
MMNT	25.7	29.3	33.8	38.7	45.7	53.0	57.4	56.3	47.5	37.4	32.3	26.3	40.3
MNTM	33.1	38.8	45.6	51.6	59.3	67.0	72.9	71.8	62.9	51.6	41.5	33.7	52.5
EMXT	69	74	78	88	102	108	108	113	101	87	77	67	113
EMNT	-13	-12	10	19	29	34	39	38	25	11	-11	-17	-17
TPCP	1.21	.84	.78	.71	.67	.46	.22	.40	.44	.60	1.30	1.35	9.03
EXTP	.96	.56	.72	1.22	1.00	.84	.86	1.57	.67	.94	.74	.80	1.57
TSNW	3.41	.84	.33	.00	.00	.00	.00	.00	.00	.00	1.35	2.61	8.46
DX90	.0	.0	.0	.0	1.5	6.1	14.6	12.5	2.8	.0	.0	.0	37.9
DX32	7.0	1.8	.1	.0	.0	.0	.0	.0	.0	.0	1.0	6.3	16.0
DN32	23.8	18.3	12.5	5.5	.3	.0	.0	.0	.5	7.9	14.1	23.6	106.7
DN00	1.2	.4	.0	.0	.0	.0	.0	.0	.0	.0	.1	1.1	2.8
DP00	11.0	9.3	8.9	7.0	5.8	5.3	2.7	3.5	4.0	5.6	11.7	12.2	87.4
DP01	4.1	3.0	2.7	1.9	2.1	1.3	.6	1.0	1.5	1.8	4.4	4.9	29.8
DP05	.2	.1	.1	.2	.2	.1	.1	.2	.1	.2	.2	.2	1.8
DP10	.0	.0	.0	.1	.0	.0	.0	.0	.0	.0	.0	.0	.1
HDD	988	740	603	404	205	60	12	14	118	415	707	970	5240
GDD	2	5	22	99	293	510	709	675	390	108	12	2	2824

Honeyman State Park

	Jan	Feb	Mar	Apr	May	Jun	Jul	Aug	Sep	Oct	Nov	Dec	Year
MMXT	50.3	52.9	55.5	58.6	62.7	66.0	68.8	69.1	69.3	63.1	54.1	49.9	60.1
MMNT	37.4	38.6	39.5	40.5	44.0	47.8	50.2	51.0	49.1	45.5	41.6	37.5	43.6
MNTM	43.8	45.8	47.5	49.6	53.4	56.9	59.5	60.0	59.2	54.3	47.8	43.7	51.8
EMXT	65	71	78	83	85	92	95	91	99	88	69	63	99
EMNT	14	13	23	29	33	36	40	39	32	26	20	9	9
TPCP	9.97	9.66	9.32	4.92	3.76	2.43	.94	1.31	2.32	5.27	10.90	11.75	72.09
EXTP	3.70	3.15	3.00	3.48	2.16	2.70	1.65	1.53	1.57	3.62	3.40	3.78	3.78
TSNW	.18	.65	.02	.00	.00	.00	.00	.00	.00	.00	.00	.45	1.32
DX90	.0	.0	.0	.0	.0	.1	.1	.1	.4	.0	.0	.0	.7
DX32	.1	.1	.0	.0	.0	.0	.0	.0	.0	.0	.0	.5	.6
DN32	7.1	5.4	2.9	1.8	.0	.0	.0	.0	.1	.3	2.3	7.2	27.0
DN00	.0	.0	.0	.0	.0	.0	.0	.0	.0	.0	.0	.0	.0
DP00	18.6	19.2	19.7	16.4	13.0	9.5	4.9	5.9	7.6	11.4	19.7	20.3	165.8
DP01	15.0	15.5	16.0	11.1	8.2	5.7	2.4	3.2	5.1	8.4	16.3	16.5	122.6
DP05	7.3	7.4	7.3	3.6	2.6	1.4	.6	.8	1.7	3.9	8.5	8.5	52.8
DP10	2.7	2.8	2.4	.7	.6	.4	.1	.2	.5	1.5	3.3	3.6	18.3
HDD	656	544	543	464	362	245	172	155	181	333	515	660	4819
GDD	8	14	19	43	113	207	295	311	275	145	31	10	1477

Hood River Experiment Station

	Jan	Feb	Mar	Apr	May	Jun	Jul	Aug	Sep	Oct	Nov	Dec	Year
MMXT	40.6	46.8	53.7	60.0	67.5	74.2	80.1	80.5	74.0	63.4	49.3	41.3	61.0
MMNT	28.2	31.2	34.4	38.4	43.8	50.0	53.4	52.8	45.8	38.1	34.4	29.4	40.0
MNTM	34.4	39.0	44.1	49.2	55.6	62.1	66.8	66.7	59.9	50.8	41.9	35.3	50.5
EMXT	62	66	76	88	102	104	104	108	99	88	68	66	108
EMNT	-6	-5	14	25	28	32	37	36	26	19	-5	-10	-10
TPCP	5.36	3.91	2.93	1.63	.95	.69	.25	.59	1.14	2.20	5.11	6.00	31.05
EXTP	2.45	2.59	1.75	1.20	.88	1.74	.87	1.27	1.73	2.67	1.83	3.05	3.05
TSNW	14.04	6.44	1.49	.00	.00	.00	.00	.00	.00	.00	3.44	9.87	36.47
DX90	.0	.0	.0	.0	.6	2.3	5.4	6.0	1.3	.0	.0	.0	16.0
DX32	5.0	1.2	.0	.0	.0	.0	.0	.0	.0	.0	.6	3.9	10.9
DN32	20.5	15.5	11.8	5.1	.8	.1	.0	.0	.7	6.5	11.4	19.9	91.7
DN00	.5	.3	.0	.0	.0	.0	.0	.0	.0	.0	.0	.5	1.2
DP00	16.3	13.9	14.3	11.5	8.4	5.6	2.7	3.8	6.0	10.0	18.0	16.8	128.0
DP01	10.4	9.1	8.1	5.2	3.2	2.0	.7	1.7	2.7	5.5	12.0	11.5	72.6
DP05	3.8	2.3	1.4	.5	.1	.2	.1	.3	.7	1.2	3.4	3.9	18.0
DP10	1.2	.8	.2	.1	.0	.1	.0	.0	.1	.3	.7	1.4	5.0
HDD	949	735	649	475	303	138	55	51	177	442	694	920	5580
GDD	1	1	10	62	194	363	519	516	300	84	6	1	2066

John Day

	Jan	Feb	Mar	Apr	May	Jun	Jul	Aug	Sep	Oct	Nov	Dec	Year
MMXT	40.4	47.0	52.7	60.0	68.8	78.2	87.9	87.2	77.6	66.1	50.1	41.8	63.1
MMNT	21.0	25.0	28.4	32.3	38.6	45.2	48.6	47.9	40.4	33.2	28.2	22.1	34.2
MNTM	30.7	36.0	40.6	46.2	53.7	61.7	68.3	67.5	59.0	49.6	39.1	32.0	48.7
EMXT	66	70	80	91	98	103	105	112	104	95	79	66	112
EMNT	-23	-20	8	13	19	25	35	31	21	5	-8	-23	-23
TPCP	1.15	.82	1.12	1.21	1.56	1.40	.53	.95	.84	.92	1.47	1.40	13.36
EXTP	1.01	.57	1.00	1.00	1.52	1.02	1.32	1.89	.89	.71	.84	1.07	1.89
TSNW	6.19	3.67	3.18	1.15	.13	.00	.00	.00	.00	.32	2.52	7.06	24.30
DX90	.0	.0	.0	.0	1.1	5.5	15.0	14.8	4.8	.5	.0	.0	41.4
DX32	5.9	1.4	.1	.0	.0	.0	.0	.0	.0	.0	1.0	4.4	13.2
DN32	27.3	23.9	22.8	16.2	5.5	.3	.0	.1	3.7	13.8	21.2	26.9	161.9
DN00	1.6	.6	.0	.0	.0	.0	.0	.0	.0	.0	.2	1.3	3.9
DP00	11.1	9.0	10.4	9.5	9.7	8.5	3.3	4.7	5.4	7.2	11.4	11.8	101.1
DP01	4.1	3.0	4.1	3.8	5.0	4.4	1.6	2.5	2.8	3.2	5.3	4.9	44.3
DP05	.3	.1	.2	.3	.5	.7	.2	.4	.2	.3	.4	.4	4.1
DP10	.0	.0	.0	.1	.1	.0	.1	.1	.0	.0	.0	.0	.5
HDD	1063	818	758	565	361	152	41	51	208	478	776	1024	6303
GDD	0	1	8	49	166	355	567	544	286	92	7	1	2078

Klamath Falls

	Jan	Feb	Mar	Apr	May	Jun	Jul	Aug	Sep	Oct	Nov	Dec	Year
MMXT	39.2	45.2	50.6	58.3	67.6	76.5	84.9	83.8	76.2	64.1	47.4	39.2	61.2
MMNT	20.4	24.9	27.8	31.1	38.2	45.6	50.9	49.7	42.8	34.6	27.6	21.8	34.7
MNTM	29.8	35.0	39.2	44.7	52.9	61.0	67.9	66.8	59.5	49.3	37.5	30.5	47.9
EMXT	59	67	73	87	98	99	102	104	100	88	74	59	104
EMNT	-14	-10	4	10	17	24	30	32	20	11	2	-17	-17
TPCP	1.81	1.28	1.35	.75	.85	.69	.35	.62	.55	1.07	1.97	2.23	13.47
EXTP	1.82	.97	1.11	.74	.83	.95	1.14	1.25	.88	1.69	1.18	2.58	2.58
TSNW	9.28	4.71	3.73	.94	.08	.00	.00	.00	.00	.52	4.50	9.98	34.91
DX90	.0	.0	.0	.0	.4	2.8	9.6	8.0	1.7	.0	.0	.0	23.0
DX32	5.3	.9	.2	.0	.0	.0	.0	.0	.0	.0	.9	5.2	11.9
DN32	27.5	23.2	23.2	17.8	7.2	1.0	.0	.1	2.3	12.4	22.0	27.2	164.0
DN00	.9	.2	.0	.0	.0	.0	.0	.0	.0	.0	.0	.8	1.7
DP00	10.6	9.4	10.7	6.8	6.1	5.3	2.1	3.4	3.2	5.9	11.3	11.5	85.8
DP01	4.9	4.0	4.1	2.5	2.7	2.3	.9	1.6	1.6	2.9	6.3	6.3	39.6
DP05	1.1	.4	.4	.2	.3	.2	.2	.4	.3	.4	.8	1.1	5.7
DP10	.2	.0	.0	.0	.0	.0	.0	.1	.0	.1	.1	.2	.8
HDD	1090	846	799	609	384	167	48	60	191	486	825	1070	6555
GDD	0	1	3	33	155	341	555	519	297	81	1	0	1988

Lacomb

	Jan	Feb	Mar	Apr	May	Jun	Jul	Aug	Sep	Oct	Nov	Dec	Year
MMXT	46.1	50.4	55.6	60.4	65.9	72.1	78.0	79.1	74.7	64.3	51.9	46.1	62.0
MMNT	31.9	33.7	36.0	38.5	42.5	47.4	49.9	49.5	45.6	40.5	36.7	33.3	40.3
MNTM	39.0	42.0	45.8	49.4	54.2	59.8	64.0	64.3	60.2	52.4	44.3	39.7	51.2
EMXT	66	73	75	85	95	96	101	104	101	94	73	70	104
EMNT	1	5	21	27	29	32	38	36	31	26	15	2	1
TPCP	6.78	6.39	6.03	4.48	3.72	2.72	1.21	1.54	2.12	4.10	8.93	8.10	53.93
EXTP	2.47	2.00	1.53	1.58	1.32	1.95	1.69	1.72	1.20	2.09	2.15	2.81	2.81
TSNW	.99	1.05	.00	.00	.00	.00	.00	.00	.00	.00	.25	.87	3.34
DX90	.0	.0	.0	.0	.2	.8	2.8	3.5	1.5	.1	.0	.0	9.1
DX32	.9	.2	.0	.0	.0	.0	.0	.0	.0	.0	.3	1.2	3.0
DN32	16.4	12.1	9.7	5.1	.7	.1	.0	.0	.1	2.7	8.4	14.5	72.9
DN00	.0	.0	.0	.0	.0	.0	.0	.0	.0	.0	.0	.0	.0
DP00	17.8	17.5	18.7	16.4	13.9	8.8	5.4	5.2	8.7	12.2	19.2	19.0	159.3
DP01	13.6	13.8	14.7	11.5	9.3	6.1	3.0	3.4	5.3	8.8	15.5	14.3	115.6
DP05	4.9	4.2	4.3	3.3	2.2	1.8	.7	1.0	1.4	3.0	6.9	6.0	38.3
DP10	1.4	1.1	.7	.3	.4	.4	.2	.3	.2	.6	2.4	2.0	8.9
HDD	807	649	596	467	341	175	82	76	161	392	620	784	5175
GDD	4	7	18	63	150	295	433	444	305	107	17	6	1862

LaGrande

	Jan	Feb	Mar	Apr	May	Jun	Jul	Aug	Sep	Oct	Nov	Dec	Year
MMXT	37.6	43.3	51.1	58.7	67.7	76.8	86.2	86.1	76.0	63.0	46.8	38.5	60.8
MMNT	23.6	27.0	30.4	34.6	41.3	48.4	52.5	51.4	43.2	35.1	30.3	24.4	36.7
MNTM	30.6	35.1	40.8	46.6	54.5	62.6	69.3	68.7	59.6	49.0	38.6	31.5	48.7
EMXT	61	66	79	88	95	98	102	104	99	87	71	58	104
EMNT	-14	-10	9	16	25	29	32	32	23	13	-14	-18	-18
TPCP	1.96	1.47	1.48	1.42	1.61	1.43	.63	.92	.97	1.24	1.86	1.86	17.18
EXTP	1.99	1.50	.75	1.64	.94	.92	1.02	1.90	.92	.71	1.08	1.85	1.99
TSNW	9.04	4.74	1.67	.67	.01	.00	.00	.00	.00	.24	3.04	7.37	29.66
DX90	.0	.0	.0	.0	.6	3.4	11.9	12.1	3.0	.0	.0	.0	29.3
DX32	8.0	2.1	.2	.0	.0	.0	.0	.0	.0	.0	1.4	6.1	18.4
DN32	25.4	21.2	19.1	11.4	2.7	.1	.1	.0	1.8	11.5	17.7	24.8	138.0
DN00	1.3	.5	.0	.0	.0	.0	.0	.0	.0	.0	.1	1.0	2.5
DP00	11.5	9.3	11.9	10.5	10.2	8.8	4.2	5.2	6.2	7.5	11.3	10.9	108.2
DP01	6.0	4.7	5.6	4.4	4.9	4.7	2.1	2.8	3.2	4.1	6.2	5.9	55.8
DP05	.8	.5	.2	.4	.6	.6	.2	.2	.4	.4	.7	.6	5.6
DP10	.3	.0	.0	.1	.0	.0	.0	.1	.0	.0	.2	.2	1.0
HDD	1066	844	752	552	336	133	36	40	197	495	793	1039	6349
GDD	0	0	7	45	176	381	597	581	301	76	5	0	2141

Lakeview

	Jan	Feb	Mar	Apr	May	Jun	Jul	Aug	Sep	Oct	Nov	Dec	Year
MMXT	37.9	42.2	47.6	55.7	65.0	73.9	83.7	82.1	74.1	62.9	46.3	38.9	59.0
MMNT	19.0	23.0	26.4	30.6	37.3	44.4	50.3	48.4	41.3	33.4	26.5	20.8	33.5
MNTM	28.5	32.6	37.0	43.1	51.2	59.2	67.0	65.2	57.8	48.1	36.4	29.9	46.3
EMXT	59	69	74	87	96	101	100	101	98	87	73	62	101
EMNT	-15	-9	-4	14	17	26	30	31	20	9	-1	-20	-20
TPCP	2.01	1.43	1.52	1.22	1.43	1.15	.36	.54	.63	1.20	2.13	2.09	15.78
EXTP	1.78	1.08	1.22	1.15	1.12	1.21	.79	1.00	1.17	2.10	2.02	2.27	2.27
TSNW	14.51	7.90	8.46	4.87	1.59	.03	.00	.00	.20	1.55	7.65	12.90	64.80
DX90	.0	.0	.0	.0	.1	1.6	7.1	5.2	1.0	.0	.0	.0	13.7
DX32	7.2	2.8	1.0	.0	.0	.0	.0	.0	.0	.1	1.2	6.7	19.1
DN32	27.9	24.6	25.5	19.0	8.3	1.5	.1	.1	3.2	14.4	23.1	27.9	174.5
DN00	1.9	1.0	.1	.0	.0	.0	.0	.0	.0	.0	.1	1.6	5.1
DP00	10.9	9.5	10.6	9.0	7.8	5.9	2.6	3.1	4.0	6.3	11.4	11.4	92.5
DP01	5.3	4.7	5.1	3.8	4.5	3.3	1.1	1.5	1.9	3.5	6.5	6.4	47.7
DP05	1.0	.4	.5	.4	.6	.5	.2	.3	.2	.4	.8	.8	6.1
DP10	.2	.0	.0	.1	.1	.1	.0	.0	.0	.1	.1	.1	1.0
HDD	1133	914	868	656	432	204	52	79	233	523	858	1088	7055
GDD	0	0	1	24	121	291	526	473	256	71	1	0	1744

Madras

	Jan	Feb	Mar	Apr	May	Jun	Jul	Aug	Sep	Oct	Nov	Dec	Year
MMXT	39.8	44.9	53.0	60.0	67.0	76.2	83.6	83.3	75.0	63.4	48.1	40.5	61.1
MMNT	23.7	26.1	29.5	33.2	38.1	44.9	49.3	49.1	42.4	35.1	28.9	23.7	35.3
MNTM	31.8	35.5	41.2	46.6	52.5	60.5	66.4	66.2	58.7	49.3	38.5	32.1	48.2
EMXT	66	71	75	89	101	101	103	103	99	87	74	65	103
EMNT	-14	-14	11	18	23	29	34	36	26	12	-5	-16	-16
TPCP	1.53	1.17	1.00	.90	.91	.71	.59	.71	.55	.73	1.49	1.46	12.01
EXTP	.95	.93	.70	1.30	.85	1.06	1.37	1.40	1.01	.80	1.55	1.40	1.55
TSNW	3.61	4.01	1.12	.05	.00	.00	.00	.00	.00	.00	3.08	4.44	17.75
DX90	.0	.0	.0	.0	.4	2.8	8.6	8.2	1.7	.0	.0	.0	20.8
DX32	6.6	3.2	.3	.0	.0	.0	.0	.0	.0	.0	1.9	6.9	19.5
DN32	25.9	21.3	21.0	14.6	7.3	.8	.0	.0	1.4	10.8	19.5	25.9	148.9
DN00	1.4	.8	.0	.0	.0	.0	.0	.0	.0	.0	.4	1.0	3.6
DP00	9.1	9.1	9.2	6.6	6.4	4.8	3.2	3.8	4.2	5.1	9.8	9.2	81.2
DP01	4.9	4.0	3.8	2.5	3.1	2.0	1.7	2.3	1.8	2.5	4.6	4.4	38.2
DP05	.7	.3	.2	.4	.3	.4	.4	.3	.2	.2	.4	.6	4.4
DP10	.0	.0	.0	.1	.0	.1	.1	.1	.1	.0	.1	.1	.6
HDD	1030	833	737	552	397	175	66	63	211	489	794	1021	6396
GDD	0	1	7	55	136	323	509	502	274	78	7	2	1881

Malheur Branch Experiment Station

	Jan	Feb	Mar	Apr	May	Jun	Jul	Aug	Sep	Oct	Nov	Dec	Year
MMXT	33.7	42.8	54.4	63.9	73.4	82.7	91.3	89.7	78.5	65.0	47.8	35.7	63.2
MMNT	18.5	24.7	31.0	37.1	45.0	52.8	58.1	55.8	45.9	35.8	28.7	20.7	37.8
MNTM	26.1	33.7	42.7	50.5	59.2	67.8	74.7	72.8	62.2	50.4	38.2	28.2	50.5
EMXT	60	66	79	91	100	104	105	108	98	87	77	62	108
EMNT	-26	-24	5	22	27	34	36	39	25	19	-5	-21	-26
TPCP	1.27	.94	.98	.73	.82	.79	.24	.52	.54	.64	1.26	1.39	10.13
EXTP	.90	.78	1.37	.80	.69	.82	.67	1.22	.81	1.03	.71	.91	1.37
TSNW	7.49	2.93	.68	.08	.00	.00	.00	.00	.00	.10	2.23	6.66	20.27
DX90	.0	.0	.0	.1	1.3	7.4	20.4	18.3	4.0	.0	.0	.0	51.5
DX32	12.7	3.2	.1	.0	.0	.0	.0	.0	.0	.0	.8	9.1	25.9
DN32	28.4	24.0	19.3	8.4	1.1	.0	.0	.0	.9	10.2	21.1	28.1	141.6
DN00	2.7	.9	.0	.0	.0	.0	.0	.0	.0	.0	.1	2.1	5.8
DP00	9.0	7.8	8.3	6.3	6.2	5.5	2.1	3.3	3.7	4.8	9.7	9.5	76.2
DP01	4.1	3.4	3.1	2.3	2.8	2.5	.8	1.5	1.7	2.2	4.4	4.6	33.4
DP05	.4	.2	.3	.2	.2	.3	.1	.2	.3	.3	.3	.4	3.0
DP10	.0	.0	.0	.0	.0	.0	.0	.0	.0	.0	.0	.0	.1
HDD	1206	883	691	438	211	57	7	15	135	454	803	1141	6040
GDD	0	0	12	92	296	533	765	705	372	90	3	0	2868

Malheur Refuge

	Jan	Feb	Mar	Apr	May	Jun	Jul	Aug	Sep	Oct	Nov	Dec	Year
MMXT	37.4	44.4	49.8	58.4	67.4	75.1	84.8	83.2	74.5	63.1	47.3	37.5	60.9
MMNT	17.6	22.9	25.5	29.9	37.5	44.8	49.2	47.4	38.5	29.9	24.6	17.2	32.4
MNTM	27.5	33.8	37.6	44.2	52.5	60.1	66.9	65.3	56.5	46.5	35.9	27.4	46.7
EMXT	60	65	76	86	93	100	102	104	95	88	73	63	104
EMNT	-33	-16	0	7	19	19	29	27	16	3	-9	-30	-33
TPCP	.89	.57	1.00	.71	1.06	.91	.40	.74	.51	.79	1.18	1.04	10.21
EXTP	1.53	.50	1.19	.86	1.23	.86	1.22	1.55	1.05	1.12	1.00	1.14	1.55
TSNW	6.35	3.03	3.01	1.59	.36	.00	.00	.02	.03	.19	2.78	8.21	30.55
DX90	.0	.0	.0	.0	.1	1.9	7.9	7.2	1.2	.0	.0	.0	23.1
DX32	8.6	1.7	.5	.0	.0	.0	.0	.0	.0	.1	1.2	8.1	16.7
DN32	27.6	24.1	25.6	19.6	7.5	1.0	.2	.6	7.0	18.4	23.1	27.6	183.6
DN00	2.4	.6	.0	.0	.0	.0	.0	.0	.0	.0	.5	3.3	4.8
DP00	7.8	6.2	8.3	6.6	7.0	6.1	2.5	3.9	3.5	5.8	8.3	9.1	80.3
DP01	2.5	2.2	3.0	2.2	3.8	2.8	1.3	1.9	1.6	2.5	3.8	3.4	32.9
DP05	.3	.0	.4	.2	.2	.4	.1	.4	.3	.3	.4	.1	3.2
DP10	.0	.0	.1	.0	.1	.0	.0	.1	.1	.1	.0	.0	.5
HDD	1163	879	848	625	392	182	47	71	266	575	873	1167	6928
GDD	0	0	2	33	137	310	523	475	225	48	2	0	1813

Medford (Airport)

	Jan	Feb	Mar	Apr	May	Jun	Jul	Aug	Sep	Oct	Nov	Dec	Year
MMXT	45.7	53.3	58.1	64.1	72.5	82.1	90.5	89.9	82.5	69.1	52.3	44.3	67.0
MMNT	30.1	32.0	34.8	37.5	42.8	49.9	54.3	54.3	47.5	39.8	34.8	31.0	40.7
MNTM	37.9	42.7	46.4	50.8	57.6	66.0	72.4	72.1	65.0	54.4	43.5	37.7	53.9
EMXT	71	77	81	93	103	109	110	114	110	99	75	72	114
EMNT	0	9	21	24	28	33	38	39	31	18	10	-6	-6
TPCP	2.69	1.93	1.82	1.16	1.00	.58	.26	.52	.86	1.49	3.23	3.32	18.85
EXTP	1.77	1.73	1.43	.98	.80	.76	1.07	.71	2.80	1.94	1.97	3.30	3.30
TSNW	3.02	.80	.74	.22	.00	.00	.00	.00	.00	.00	.40	2.34	7.52
DX90	.0	.0	.0	.1	1.8	8.2	18.0	17.3	8.3	.9	.0	.0	54.6
DX32	1.0	.0	.0	.0	.0	.0	.0	.0	.0	.0	.0	2.0	3.0
DN32	19.7	14.9	11.3	6.6	.9	.0	.0	.0	.2	4.1	10.9	17.1	85.7
DN00	.0	.0	.0	.0	.0	.0	.0	.0	.0	.0	.0	.2	.2
DP00	12.6	11.1	11.9	9.7	7.0	4.9	1.7	3.1	4.2	7.4	13.7	13.8	101.1
DP01	6.0	5.0	5.4	3.8	3.3	2.1	.7	1.6	2.2	3.8	7.8	7.1	48.9
DP05	1.6	1.0	.6	.3	.3	.2	.1	.2	.4	.9	1.7	1.9	9.2
DP10	.5	.3	.1	.0	.0	.0	.0	.0	.1	.2	.6	.5	2.4
HDD	839	630	576	428	247	70	10	9	79	333	644	848	4713
GDD	3	7	26	89	247	480	695	684	450	168	13	3	2865

Milton-Freewater

	Jan	Feb	Mar	Apr	May	Jun	Jul	Aug	Sep	Oct	Nov	Dec	Year
MMXT	41.7	48.3	56.4	63.7	72.0	80.7	88.6	87.5	77.5	65.3	51.0	42.3	64.6
MMNT	27.8	32.5	37.3	41.8	47.8	54.6	59.2	58.0	50.0	41.4	34.5	28.3	42.7
MNTM	34.7	40.4	46.9	52.8	59.9	67.6	73.9	72.9	63.7	53.3	42.8	35.3	53.7
EMXT	70	76	78	88	98	105	108	111	99	87	79	71	111
EMNT	-14	-9	13	21	29	39	39	40	28	17	-12	-24	-24
TPCP	1.71	1.17	1.52	1.20	1.28	.94	.46	.65	.77	1.08	1.84	1.71	14.38
EXTP	.91	.82	1.09	1.09	1.30	.92	.87	1.44	.83	1.43	1.05	.93	1.44
TSNW	4.53	1.69	.50	.00	.00	.00	.00	.00	.00	.08	.97	4.35	12.25
DX90	.0	.0	.0	.0	1.1	5.8	15.0	13.2	2.1	.0	.0	.0	37.4
DX32	7.5	2.1	.1	.0	.0	.0	.0	.0	.0	.0	1.5	7.2	18.6
DN32	20.2	13.2	6.8	1.8	.1	.0	.0	.0	.6	4.1	11.4	20.0	78.6
DN00	1.2	.2	.0	.0	.0	.0	.0	.0	.0	.0	.1	1.0	2.7
DP00	12.8	11.4	11.4	9.1	8.4	6.7	3.0	4.3	4.9	7.5	13.0	13.4	105.9
DP01	5.5	4.3	5.0	3.9	3.6	3.3	1.4	2.0	2.3	2.8	5.5	5.7	45.4
DP05	.6	.2	.6	.5	.6	.3	.2	.3	.3	.6	.8	.5	5.5
DP10	.0	.0	.0	.0	.1	.0	.0	.0	.0	.1	.0	.0	.4
HDD	938	695	562	370	190	51	8	8	106	366	667	920	4897
GDD	8	11	36	121	308	529	740	708	415	146	22	6	3051

Moro

	Jan	Feb	Mar	Apr	May	Jun	Jul	Aug	Sep	Oct	Nov	Dec	Year
MMXT	37.7	43.8	50.9	57.2	65.2	74.0	81.6	81.3	72.9	61.6	46.7	38.4	59.3
MMNT	24.2	28.4	31.9	35.7	41.5	48.6	53.7	53.2	45.4	36.8	31.0	25.1	38.0
MNTM	31.0	36.1	41.4	46.5	53.4	61.3	67.7	67.3	59.1	49.2	38.9	31.7	48.7
EMXT	63	66	74	87	100	102	106	105	99	86	71	63	106
EMNT	-14	-15	13	19	25	27	35	31	23	14	-15	-16	-16
TPCP	1.49	.98	1.04	.78	.77	.59	.28	.47	.54	.75	1.66	1.74	11.09
EXTP	1.64	1.14	.63	1.21	1.52	1.14	.59	.69	.85	1.08	.98	1.26	1.64
TSNW	5.95	2.70	1.19	.15	.00	.00	.00	.00	.00	.20	2.51	6.18	19.31
DX90	.0	.0	.0	.0	.2	2.4	7.7	6.8	1.0	.0	.0	.0	18.1
DX32	8.3	3.5	.3	.0	.0	.0	.0	.0	.0	.0	2.0	7.8	22.2
DN32	25.3	20.2	16.9	9.6	2.5	.2	.0	.0	.9	8.5	16.9	24.8	125.3
DN00	1.5	.4	.0	.0	.0	.0	.0	.0	.0	.0	.2	1.1	3.3
DP00	11.0	9.4	10.5	8.2	6.5	4.8	2.8	3.6	4.1	6.7	13.0	11.2	90.8
DP01	4.4	3.4	3.7	2.4	2.5	1.8	1.0	1.5	1.7	2.5	5.5	5.4	35.6
DP05	.6	.1	.2	.1	.2	.2	.1	.1	.2	.2	.5	.8	3.3
DP10	.1	.0	.0	.0	.0	.0	.0	.0	.0	.0	.0	.1	.4
HDD	1055	816	732	557	370	169	66	64	205	491	784	1031	6327
GDD	0	1	6	41	151	342	548	535	285	76	4	1	1998

Newport

	Jan	Feb	Mar	Apr	May	Jun	Jul	Aug	Sep	Oct	Nov	Dec	Year
MMXT	50.3	52.7	53.6	55.2	58.6	62.0	64.6	65.3	65.5	61.1	54.8	50.4	57.8
MMNT	37.3	38.5	38.7	39.7	43.4	47.6	49.6	49.9	48.2	44.6	41.5	37.8	43.0
MNTM	43.8	45.6	46.1	47.5	51.0	54.8	57.1	57.6	56.9	52.8	48.1	44.1	50.4
EMXT	69	77	74	82	89	91	100	91	96	94	79	69	100
EMNT	4	12	26	23	32	34	33	37	32	25	18	1	1
TPCP	10.63	8.11	8.21	4.92	3.49	2.69	.99	1.25	2.62	5.43	10.87	11.78	72.04
EXTP	4.60	3.18	3.07	2.49	2.15	3.51	1.45	1.72	2.52	3.07	5.36	3.49	4.60
TSNW	.64	.21	.00	.00	.00	.00	.00	.00	.00	.00	.00	.62	1.57
DX90	.0	.0	.0	.0	.0	.1	.1	.0	.2	.0	.0	.0	.4
DX32	.3	.1	.0	.0	.0	.0	.0	.0	.0	.0	.0	.6	1.0
DN32	7.6	4.3	4.2	2.5	.1	.0	.0	.0	.0	.3	2.5	6.2	28.7
DN00	.0	.0	.0	.0	.0	.0	.0	.0	.0	.0	.0	.0	.0
DP00	20.1	18.3	20.5	17.3	14.2	11.2	6.8	7.8	9.8	14.6	20.8	21.8	187.1
DP01	16.6	14.2	15.5	11.5	8.7	6.0	2.5	3.2	5.5	10.2	17.0	17.1	130.2
DP05	7.5	6.0	5.9	3.5	1.8	1.6	.5	.7	1.7	4.2	8.1	8.6	50.9
DP10	3.1	2.0	1.8	.7	.5	.4	.1	.1	.4	1.1	3.0	3.5	16.9
HDD	657	547	585	526	435	306	246	230	248	378	506	648	5328
GDD	10	17	13	19	59	146	220	236	207	107	35	10	1070

North Bend

	Jan	Feb	Mar	Apr	May	Jun	Jul	Aug	Sep	Oct	Nov	Dec	Year
MMXT	51.9	54.0	54.8	56.5	60.2	63.8	66.3	67.1	66.9	63.0	56.9	52.6	59.5
MMNT	38.9	40.5	41.1	42.4	46.6	50.7	52.5	53.0	50.5	46.7	43.2	40.1	45.5
MNTM	45.4	47.3	48.0	49.5	53.4	57.3	59.4	60.1	58.7	54.8	50.1	46.3	52.5
EMXT	69	76	78	87	84	86	88	91	95	86	75	70	95
EMNT	17	14	27	28	36	39	41	44	34	28	22	0	0
TPCP	9.73	7.76	7.81	4.65	2.89	1.60	.45	.96	1.80	4.59	10.27	10.97	63.27
EXTP	3.37	4.23	2.86	2.65	2.13	2.72	1.29	1.51	2.05	3.63	3.51	5.60	5.60
TSNW	1.22	.21	.12	.00	.00	.00	.00	.00	.00	.00	.09	.20	1.89
DX90	.0	.0	.0	.0	.0	.0	.0	.0	.1	.0	.0	.0	.1
DX32	.1	.0	.0	.0	.0	.0	.0	.0	.0	.0	.0	.1	.2
DN32	5.6	2.9	1.3	.2	.0	.0	.0	.0	.0	.2	1.4	4.4	16.1
DN00	.0	.0	.0	.0	.0	.0	.0	.0	.0	.0	.0	.0	.0
DP00	18.8	17.1	19.6	16.1	12.3	8.7	4.4	5.5	7.2	12.1	19.7	19.5	160.4
DP01	15.1	12.9	14.5	10.5	6.9	4.1	1.4	2.3	4.1	7.8	16.0	15.6	110.8
DP05	6.7	5.3	5.6	2.9	1.9	.9	.1	.5	1.1	3.3	7.7	7.1	43.0
DP10	2.8	2.2	1.9	.7	.3	.2	.0	.2	.3	1.2	2.9	3.3	15.8
HDD	607	501	527	466	359	232	173	154	192	316	448	579	4566
GDD	19	28	29	37	113	218	292	312	261	158	59	25	1544

Ochoco Ranger Station

	Jan	Feb	Mar	Apr	May	Jun	Jul	Aug	Sep	Oct	Nov	Dec	Year
MMXT	35.3	41.1	47.9	55.8	63.7	72.7	81.2	81.7	73.4	61.4	43.3	35.6	58.0
MMNT	15.3	18.9	23.0	26.3	31.5	37.6	40.1	40.0	33.8	28.4	23.9	17.7	28.2
MNTM	25.2	30.1	35.4	41.1	47.6	55.1	60.6	60.8	53.6	44.9	33.6	26.6	43.2
EMXT	57	64	72	85	95	94	100	101	99	89	68	55	101
EMNT	-22	-26	-4	9	15	21	18	27	17	1	-10	-24	-26
TPCP	2.13	1.55	1.37	1.13	1.24	1.29	.70	.88	.94	1.25	2.49	2.38	17.18
EMNT	1.82	1.44	1.66	1.22	.90	1.30	2.70	1.25	1.30	1.04	1.40	2.42	2.70
TSNW	11.06	6.93	5.16	3.04	.58	.00	.00	.00	.00	.82	6.68	11.58	46.30
DX90	.0	.0	.0	.0	.3	1.1	5.5	6.2	1.4	.0	.0	.0	15.5
DX32	10.0	3.9	1.0	.1	.0	.0	.0	.0	.0	.0	2.7	9.6	27.5
DN32	29.8	27.4	28.6	25.7	18.2	7.0	3.0	2.8	12.9	23.5	26.4	29.5	232.1
DN00	3.2	1.4	.2	.0	.0	.0	.0	.0	.0	.0	.3	1.6	6.2
DP00	8.6	7.5	6.4	6.0	5.8	6.1	2.9	4.5	4.4	5.9	9.0	8.8	75.1
DP01	6.2	5.1	4.6	3.7	3.6	3.6	1.6	2.9	2.8	3.9	6.9	6.6	50.6
DP05	1.0	.6	.5	.5	.7	.5	.4	.4	.5	.6	1.7	1.2	8.3
DP10	.3	.1	.1	.1	.0	.1	.1	.0	.1	.0	.3	.3	1.5
HDD	1233	988	917	718	540	304	162	161	347	623	941	1189	8011
GDD	0	0	0	15	65	184	335	339	155	32	0	0	1177

Otis

	Jan	Feb	Mar	Apr	May	Jun	Jul	Aug	Sep	Oct	Nov	Dec	Year
MMXT	47.0	51.1	53.9	56.7	61.3	65.6	69.3	70.8	69.1	61.4	52.3	46.9	58.8
MMNT	36.0	37.5	38.1	39.4	43.1	47.5	49.5	50.3	48.4	44.5	40.3	36.5	42.5
MNTM	41.5	44.3	46.0	48.0	52.2	56.6	59.4	60.5	58.7	53.0	46.3	41.7	50.6
EMXT	65	72	78	83	88	95	96	98	92	82	76	64	98
EMNT	14	11	23	28	30	35	35	39	34	27	15	4	4
TPCP	14.88	11.11	11.11	6.77	4.84	3.69	1.68	1.92	3.91	7.69	14.25	15.55	96.49
EXTP	7.44	4.33	4.00	2.43	2.56	3.28	3.05	2.93	2.60	3.16	4.95	4.60	5.73
TSNW	1.71	.08	.56	.02	.00	.00	.00	.00	.00	.00	.14	1.09	3.81
DX90	.0	.0	.0	.0	.0	.1	.3	.3	.1	.0	.0	.0	.9
DX32	.3	.1	.0	.0	.0	.0	.0	.0	.0	.0	.0	.8	1.0
DN32	10.5	6.3	5.3	3.0	.3	.0	.0	.0	.0	.5	4.4	9.2	40.5
DN00	.0	.0	.0	.0	.0	.0	.0	.0	.0	.0	.0	.0	.0
DP00	21.5	18.6	19.4	17.4	15.3	11.1	6.7	7.3	10.3	14.5	20.5	22.5	184.1
DP01	17.5	15.6	16.7	13.0	10.4	6.4	3.4	4.1	6.5	10.8	16.8	18.1	138.5
DP05	9.8	7.8	8.2	4.8	3.0	2.7	1.0	1.2	2.9	5.3	9.9	10.3	66.3
DP10	4.8	3.8	3.2	1.5	1.0	.8	.3	.3	1.0	2.5	5.1	5.5	29.5
HDD	729	583	588	510	398	257	178	145	192	371	561	724	5251
GDD	5	10	14	31	94	198	291	326	262	116	22	6	1365

Paisley

	Jan	Feb	Mar	Apr	May	Jun	Jul	Aug	Sep	Oct	Nov	Dec	Year
MMXT	41.5	46.9	51.2	58.8	67.5	75.9	84.6	83.7	76.1	65.2	49.0	41.7	61.9
MMNT	21.6	25.2	27.3	31.4	38.2	45.3	49.1	48.3	40.6	33.4	26.9	22.0	34.3
MNTM	31.5	36.1	39.3	45.1	52.9	60.7	66.9	66.0	58.3	49.3	37.9	32.0	48.1
EMXT	62	70	75	85	92	98	99	101	97	90	74	67	101
EMNT	-27	-25	-6	11	10	22	29	30	18	9	0	-28	-28
TPCP	1.40	.84	.97	.75	.96	1.08	.39	.64	.50	.79	1.18	1.52	11.03
EXTP	2.38	1.04	.94	.65	.86	1.52	1.37	1.85	1.00	1.66	1.40	2.01	2.38
TSNW	4.28	3.07	3.61	1.72	.75	.00	.00	.00	.00	.28	2.91	4.72	20.07
DX90	.0	.0	.0	.0	.1	1.8	7.9	7.4	1.2	.0	.0	.0	19.4
DX32	4.9	1.5	.5	.0	.0	.0	.0	.0	.0	.0	1.0	4.2	12.9
DN32	25.1	22.0	22.6	16.9	8.0	1.2	.1	.3	4.6	13.6	21.4	24.5	159.0
DN00	1.1	.5	.1	.0	.0	.0	.0	.0	.0	.0	.1	1.2	3.0
DP00	7.8	6.7	8.1	6.9	6.8	5.8	2.5	3.6	3.3	4.9	7.8	8.3	72.6
DP01	3.4	2.7	3.3	3.0	3.3	3.2	1.1	1.7	1.4	2.2	3.3	3.9	32.4
DP05	.7	.3	.3	.2	.3	.5	.1	.3	.2	.3	.5	.8	4.6
DP10	.1	.0	.0	.0	.0	.1	.0	.1	.0	.1	.1	.1	.7
HDD	1038	816	798	596	383	168	50	66	219	487	813	1024	6422
GDD	0	1	6	45	152	330	523	496	269	89	4	0	1946

Pendleton (Airport)

	Jan	Feb	Mar	Apr	May	Jun	Jul	Aug	Sep	Oct	Nov	Dec	Year
MMXT	39.7	46.9	54.2	61.3	70.0	79.5	87.8	86.2	76.3	63.8	48.9	40.5	62.9
MMNT	27.3	31.6	35.4	39.4	45.8	52.9	57.9	57.7	49.9	41.0	34.1	27.9	41.7
MNTM	33.5	39.2	44.8	50.3	57.9	66.2	72.9	72.0	63.1	52.4	41.5	34.2	52.3
EMXT	68	72	79	91	100	108	108	113	98	92	77	67	113
EMNT	-12	-13	11	23	30	36	42	40	30	19	-12	-19	-19
TPCP	1.51	1.14	1.16	1.04	.99	.64	.35	.53	.59	.86	1.58	1.63	12.02
EXTP	1.10	.57	1.00	1.24	1.05	.65	.88	1.05	1.10	1.40	1.35	1.25	1.40
TSNW	6.05	2.11	1.04	.15	.00	.00	.00	.00	.00	.17	2.24	5.20	16.96
DX90	.0	.0	.0	.0	.8	5.3	14.4	11.7	2.6	.1	.0	.0	34.9
DX32	8.6	2.7	.2	.0	.0	.0	.0	.0	.0	.0	2.1	8.1	21.6
DN32	20.1	14.6	8.8	3.2	.1	.0	.0	.0	.2	3.1	10.8	19.7	80.5
DN00	1.4	.4	.0	.0	.0	.0	.0	.0	.0	.0	.1	1.2	3.1
DP00	12.0	10.9	10.6	8.7	7.2	5.8	2.9	3.6	4.7	6.1	11.7	12.2	96.3
DP01	5.0	4.0	4.3	3.2	3.1	2.2	1.0	1.4	1.9	3.0	4.9	5.5	39.5
DP05	.4	.1	.2	.3	.3	.1	.1	.3	.1	.2	.6	.5	3.3
DP10	.0	.0	.0	.1	.0	.0	.0	.0	.0	.0	.0	.0	.3
HDD	977	728	626	441	241	71	12	14	119	395	706	954	5283
GDD	4	6	17	78	254	486	709	681	395	126	13	4	2773

Portland (Airport)

	Jan	Feb	Mar	Apr	May	Jun	Jul	Aug	Sep	Oct	Nov	Dec	Year
MMXT	45.4	50.9	56.1	60.5	67.2	73.8	79.7	80.1	74.5	64.1	52.7	45.6	62.5
MMNT	33.8	36.0	38.6	41.4	46.9	52.8	56.4	56.8	51.8	45.0	39.5	34.8	44.5
MNTM	39.6	43.4	47.3	50.9	57.1	63.3	68.1	68.5	63.2	54.5	46.1	40.2	53.5
EMXT	63	71	74	86	100	100	107	107	105	92	73	64	107
EMNT	9	9	19	30	32	39	44	44	34	26	13	6	6
TPCP	5.35	3.68	3.54	2.39	2.06	1.48	.63	1.09	1.75	2.66	5.34	6.13	36.12
EXTP	2.33	1.72	1.54	1.25	1.47	1.46	.89	1.47	2.23	1.62	2.42	2.08	2.42
TSNW	1.83	.89	.10	.00	.00	.00	.00	.00	.00	.00	.47	2.03	5.44
DX90	.0	.0	.0	.0	.4	1.4	4.0	4.5	1.6	.1	.0	.0	12.0
DX32	1.7	.1	.0	.0	.0	.0	.0	.0	.0	.0	.2	1.4	3.6
DN32	12.4	8.0	4.2	1.1	.1	.0	.0	.0	.0	.6	4.6	10.4	41.3
DN00	.0	.0	.0	.0	.0	.0	.0	.0	.0	.0	.0	.0	.0
DP00	17.5	15.3	17.0	14.3	11.8	8.5	4.2	5.3	8.0	12.0	18.5	18.7	150.9
DP01	11.5	9.8	10.0	7.5	6.2	4.3	1.8	2.7	4.3	7.5	12.6	12.5	90.5
DP05	3.4	1.8	1.5	.7	.9	.5	.3	.6	1.0	1.5	3.1	4.2	19.4
DP10	1.1	.3	.2	.2	.1	.1	.0	.1	.2	.2	.8	1.1	4.5
HDD	787	609	549	423	257	98	26	20	94	327	567	770	4526
GDD	3	9	24	76	224	399	560	572	396	157	25	4	2451

Riddle

	Jan	Feb	Mar	Apr	May	Jun	Jul	Aug	Sep	Oct	Nov	Dec	Year
MMXT	49.0	54.8	58.7	63.4	69.6	76.8	83.4	83.7	78.7	68.6	54.7	48.3	65.7
MMNT	33.9	35.7	37.1	39.1	43.7	49.5	52.6	52.5	47.0	42.3	39.3	34.9	42.3
MNTM	41.4	45.2	47.9	51.3	56.6	63.1	68.0	68.1	62.9	55.4	47.0	41.6	54.0
EMXT	69	78	81	94	99	103	104	110	108	102	77	74	110
EMNT	-3	8	23	26	31	35	37	40	30	22	13	3	-3
TPCP	4.78	3.42	3.46	1.99	1.24	.64	.29	.63	1.10	2.14	5.36	5.56	30.74
EXTP	2.85	3.26	1.82	1.26	1.94	.69	.65	1.36	1.85	2.02	2.39	3.41	3.41
TSNW	2.69	.97	.50	.00	.00	.00	.00	.00	.00	.00	.46	1.56	6.29
DX90	.0	.0	.0	.1	.8	2.6	7.0	7.5	3.9	.5	.0	.0	22.0
DX32	.2	.1	.0	.0	.0	.0	.0	.0	.0	.0	.0	.4	.6
DN32	12.5	7.9	6.3	2.9	.3	.0	.0	.0	.1	1.6	3.5	9.8	45.3
DN00	.0	.0	.0	.0	.0	.0	.0	.0	.0	.0	.0	.0	.0
DP00	16.2	14.6	15.8	12.6	7.9	5.5	1.8	3.1	5.1	9.4	16.6	17.0	126.2
DP01	9.9	8.0	9.0	6.1	4.3	2.3	.8	1.9	2.7	5.0	11.3	11.0	72.4
DP05	3.3	1.8	1.9	.8	.5	.1	.1	.3	.7	1.2	3.6	3.7	18.1
DP10	1.0	.4	.4	.1	.0	.0	.0	.0	.1	.2	1.0	.9	4.2
HDD	731	558	530	413	270	104	26	23	105	301	541	726	4344
GDD	6	16	39	87	214	394	558	561	386	186	32	8	2479

Rome

	Jan	Feb	Mar	Apr	May	Jun	Jul	Aug	Sep	Oct	Nov	Dec	Year
MMXT	40.0	47.9	54.6	62.9	73.2	82.4	92.4	90.6	79.9	68.2	51.6	41.0	65.2
MMNT	17.7	23.4	25.8	29.9	38.5	46.4	51.2	48.5	38.6	30.2	24.1	18.3	32.9
MNTM	28.8	35.7	40.2	46.4	55.9	64.4	71.8	69.6	59.3	49.2	37.9	29.7	49.1
EMXT	67	70	79	91	100	105	107	107	100	96	73	63	107
EMNT	-27	-17	-4	9	14	27	28	30	15	8	-9	-26	-27
TPCP	.58	.50	.83	.69	1.01	1.05	.36	.46	.58	.55	.82	.63	7.75
EXTP	.75	.67	1.10	.71	1.56	1.50	1.43	1.25	.90	.98	1.26	1.50	1.56
TSNW	4.41	.78	1.42	.51	.19	.00	.00	.00	.00	.15	1.66	3.80	13.54
DX90	.0	.0	.0	.0	2.0	7.8	22.0	19.3	5.6	.3	.0	.0	55.8
DX32	6.0	1.3	.2	.0	.0	.0	.0	.0	.0	.0	.7	5.1	14.7
DN32	28.0	24.2	23.4	19.0	6.4	.7	.0	.1	5.9	19.1	23.8	27.6	174.2
DN00	2.7	.7	.1	.0	.0	.0	.0	.0	.0	.0	.2	2.6	6.9
DP00	4.0	3.4	4.3	3.5	4.3	4.4	1.6	1.7	2.6	2.9	5.0	4.3	41.1
DP01	2.1	2.1	2.9	2.4	3.0	2.8	1.0	1.2	1.4	1.9	3.1	2.3	25.4
DP05	.1	.0	.4	.3	.5	.6	.1	.3	.4	.1	.2	.1	3.2
DP10	.0	.0	.1	.0	.1	.1	.1	.1	.0	.0	.0	.0	.5
HDD	1121	828	770	559	295	99	13	24	194	489	814	1095	6276
GDD	0	1	5	47	212	435	676	607	293	79	3	0	2345

Roseburg

	Jan	Feb	Mar	Apr	May	Jun	Jul	Aug	Sep	Oct	Nov	Dec	Year
MMXT	48.8	53.2	57.9	62.9	69.6	76.6	83.5	84.3	77.9	67.1	54.5	47.9	65.3
MMNT	34.6	35.9	37.6	39.2	44.3	50.3	53.6	53.9	49.3	43.5	39.5	34.9	42.9
MNTM	41.8	44.5	47.7	51.0	56.9	63.4	68.5	69.2	63.6	55.3	47.0	41.4	54.1
EMXT	71	72	81	89	98	101	104	108	104	96	78	73	108
EMNT	9	3	24	26	29	36	41	41	34	23	12	3	3
TPCP	5.13	3.70	3.56	2.24	1.43	.83	.43	.73	1.24	2.23	5.36	5.47	32.44
EXTP	2.63	2.51	1.73	1.40	1.21	1.11	1.60	1.30	1.27	2.02	2.33	3.28	3.28
TSNW	2.27	.64	.06	.00	.00	.00	.00	.00	.00	.00	.04	.67	3.97
DX90	.0	.0	.0	.0	.8	2.9	7.0	8.0	3.5	.4	.0	.0	23.0
DX32	.3	.2	.0	.0	.0	.0	.0	.0	.0	.0	.0	.9	1.5
DN32	11.3	7.9	5.9	3.5	.2	.0	.0	.0	.0	.7	3.3	9.6	42.1
DN00	.0	.0	.0	.0	.0	.0	.0	.0	.0	.0	.0	.0	.0
DP00	17.5	15.3	16.6	13.5	9.2	6.0	2.0	3.3	5.8	10.3	17.6	18.3	136.5
DP01	10.7	8.7	10.0	6.7	4.8	2.7	1.0	2.0	3.2	6.5	11.6	11.4	80.0
DP05	3.2	2.1	1.9	.7	.4	.3	.2	.4	.7	1.0	3.5	3.4	17.9
DP10	1.1	.4	.2	.1	.0	.0	.1	.1	.2	.2	1.1	1.0	4.4
HDD	720	578	535	420	263	101	26	17	93	307	540	730	4369
GDD	9	16	39	86	223	403	573	594	409	180	33	9	2553

135

St. Helens

	Jan	Feb	Mar	Apr	May	Jun	Jul	Aug	Sep	Oct	Nov	Dec	Year
MMXT	46.1	50.7	57.6	63.1	68.0	75.0	80.0	81.2	75.3	65.2	52.2	45.3	63.2
MMNT	33.1	35.6	39.2	41.8	46.1	51.9	55.0	55.7	51.2	44.5	38.7	33.7	43.9
MNTM	39.6	43.1	48.4	52.4	57.1	63.4	67.4	68.4	63.3	54.8	45.4	39.5	53.4
EMXT	62	69	77	87	102	100	103	107	106	94	71	62	106
EMNT	9	4	23	28	28	35	42	42	36	31	10	1	1
TPCP	5.23	5.20	4.61	3.05	2.86	1.94	.87	1.43	1.96	2.86	6.06	5.91	40.80
EXTP	2.30	2.00	2.75	.92	1.31	1.14	.80	1.39	1.80	1.80	2.00	2.10	2.10
TSNW	1.99	.83	.00	.00	.00	.00	.00	.00	.00	.00	1.01	.51	5.32
DX90	.0	.0	.0	.0	.7	1.7	4.2	5.0	1.9	.1	.0	.0	12.9
DX32	.8	.4	.0	.0	.0	.0	.0	.0	.0	.0	.4	1.3	2.7
DN32	13.1	8.1	4.1	1.1	.1	.0	.0	.0	.0	.5	5.2	11.6	41.5
DN00	.0	.0	.0	.0	.0	.0	.0	.0	.0	.0	.0	.0	.0
DP00	17.0	17.1	17.1	14.0	12.1	9.4	5.5	5.5	8.5	11.3	18.6	18.6	145.6
DP01	11.2	11.9	12.2	9.5	8.1	5.4	2.4	3.5	4.9	7.3	13.5	11.7	95.5
DP05	3.3	3.8	2.4	1.3	1.4	1.2	.4	.9	1.2	1.9	4.3	4.1	24.6
DP10	1.0	.5	.4	.0	.2	.1	.0	.2	.2	.4	.9	1.2	4.8
HDD	761	603	504	376	258	96	34	21	98	311	566	762	4505
GDD	1	10	37	112	222	395	531	555	395	163	23	2	2565

Salem (Airport)

	Jan	Feb	Mar	Apr	May	Jun	Jul	Aug	Sep	Oct	Nov	Dec	Year
MMXT	46.2	51.3	55.8	60.4	67.0	74.4	81.6	81.9	76.0	64.3	52.5	46.2	63.1
MMNT	32.6	34.2	35.7	37.7	42.3	48.1	50.7	51.2	46.9	41.0	37.3	33.6	40.9
MNTM	39.4	42.7	45.8	49.0	54.6	61.2	66.2	66.6	61.4	52.6	44.9	39.9	52.0
EMXT	65	72	75	85	100	102	104	108	104	93	72	66	108
EMNT	6	-1	12	23	28	32	37	36	26	23	11	-12	-12
TPCP	5.91	4.50	4.17	2.42	1.88	1.34	.56	.76	1.55	2.98	6.28	6.80	39.16
EXTP	3.07	2.35	2.00	1.54	1.47	1.63	1.80	1.14	1.76	1.64	2.13	2.55	3.07
TSNW	2.18	1.50	.20	.00	.00	.00	.00	.00	.00	.00	.34	2.23	6.45
DX90	.0	.0	.0	.0	.3	2.0	5.9	6.1	2.3	.1	.0	.0	16.6
DX32	1.3	.1	.0	.0	.0	.0	.0	.0	.0	.0	.2	1.2	2.9
DN32	14.3	11.3	9.8	5.9	.9	.0	.0	.0	.2	3.1	7.8	12.7	66.0
DN00	.0	.0	.0	.0	.0	.0	.0	.0	.0	.0	.0	.2	.2
DP00	17.3	15.4	16.5	13.4	10.7	7.2	3.2	4.3	7.2	11.4	18.2	18.5	143.3
DP01	12.1	10.9	11.2	7.2	5.8	3.6	1.5	2.1	4.0	7.3	13.2	12.8	91.6
DP05	3.9	2.8	2.3	1.0	.7	.7	.2	.3	.7	1.9	4.5	4.9	24.1
DP10	1.3	.5	.4	.1	.1	.1	.0	.1	.2	.3	1.1	1.4	5.7
HDD	793	629	597	479	326	141	47	40	130	384	603	778	4948
GDD	5	8	16	49	158	338	501	514	344	116	19	6	2075

Sisters Ranger District

	Jan	Feb	Mar	Apr	May	Jun	Jul	Aug	Sep	Oct	Nov	Dec	Year
MMXT	41.0	45.7	51.3	57.6	65.6	75.1	83.6	83.2	74.7	63.4	47.5	41.0	61.7
MMNT	20.7	23.5	25.6	27.9	32.3	38.8	41.3	41.0	34.4	29.0	25.5	20.4	30.4
MNTM	30.9	34.6	38.4	42.7	49.0	56.9	62.4	62.1	54.6	46.2	36.5	30.6	46.2
EMXT	65	70	78	87	98	103	109	106	97	92	73	63	109
EMNT	-28	-22	8	9	11	20	24	26	15	1	-13	-28	-28
TPCP	2.42	1.69	1.21	.74	.55	.53	.41	.43	.49	.81	2.13	2.39	13.85
EXTP	2.02	2.27	.94	1.52	1.11	1.32	1.25	.66	1.36	1.27	2.33	2.80	2.80
TSNW	8.71	5.48	4.50	.31	.04	.00	.00	.00	.00	.15	4.72	6.98	36.82
DX90	.0	.0	.0	.0	.1	2.5	8.4	7.9	1.5	.2	.0	.0	20.4
DX32	4.6	1.4	.1	.0	.0	.0	.0	.0	.0	.0	1.3	4.6	11.6
DN32	26.6	23.0	25.3	21.7	15.8	6.9	3.0	2.9	12.4	20.8	22.6	26.9	198.0
DN00	1.7	1.0	.0	.0	.0	.0	.0	.0	.0	.0	.5	1.6	4.6
DP00	9.1	8.1	8.7	6.5	5.3	4.2	2.7	3.4	3.5	5.7	10.6	10.0	75.5
DP01	5.9	4.5	4.3	2.2	1.7	1.3	1.1	1.7	1.5	2.4	5.5	5.8	37.0
DP05	1.3	.8	.5	.2	.2	.2	.2	.1	.1	.3	1.0	1.1	5.9
DP10	.5	.4	.0	.1	.1	.1	.1	.0	.1	.1	.4	.4	2.1
HDD	1031	811	807	665	483	249	122	129	307	575	837	1023	7043
GDD	0	0	2	18	75	221	383	363	166	36	2	0	1320

Squaw Butte Experiment Station

	Jan	Feb	Mar	Apr	May	Jun	Jul	Aug	Sep	Oct	Nov	Dec	Year
MMXT	35.2	41.4	46.6	55.7	64.0	74.1	83.0	82.5	73.1	61.8	45.8	36.9	58.5
MMNT	17.6	22.6	25.3	29.6	35.9	44.1	50.1	49.8	42.3	34.4	26.6	20.4	33.3
MNTM	26.3	32.0	35.9	42.7	49.9	59.1	66.4	66.1	57.7	48.0	36.1	28.4	45.9
EMXT	55	64	74	86	92	96	99	104	95	87	72	59	104
EMNT	-17	-16	-2	11	16	23	30	30	19	7	-3	-20	-20
TPCP	1.22	.71	.86	.71	1.10	.91	.40	.73	.65	.77	1.25	1.27	10.73
EXTP	1.23	1.31	.78	1.27	1.00	1.36	1.04	2.02	1.07	2.00	.85	2.05	2.05
TSNW	11.48	4.64	4.85	1.64	.52	.02	.00	.00	.00	.84	5.16	11.04	42.25
DX90	.0	.0	.0	.0	.1	1.9	7.1	7.4	.9	.0	.0	.0	18.5
DX32	10.1	3.1	1.3	.0	.0	.0	.0	.0	.0	.1	2.1	8.7	22.4
DN32	28.7	25.5	26.2	19.7	11.4	2.4	.5	.3	3.9	12.5	23.1	27.4	182.3
DN00	1.7	.6	.0	.0	.0	.0	.0	.0	.0	.0	.0	1.0	4.4
DP00	8.0	6.4	7.5	5.3	6.7	5.6	2.7	3.9	3.6	4.9	8.0	6.9	68.6
DP01	4.3	3.2	3.2	2.8	3.8	3.0	1.3	2.0	1.8	2.3	4.5	3.3	36.0
DP05	.4	.1	.2	.3	.5	.3	.1	.3	.4	.2	.5	.7	4.1
DP10	.1	.0	.0	.0	.0	.1	.0	.1	.0	.1	.0	.1	.5
HDD	1201	930	901	671	472	213	71	80	245	529	867	1135	7302
GDD	0	0	2	31	109	293	511	502	265	82	3	0	1826

Stayton

	Jan	Feb	Mar	Apr	May	Jun	Jul	Aug	Sep	Oct	Nov	Dec	Year
MMXT	46.6	51.6	55.7	60.3	66.9	73.6	80.1	80.8	75.0	64.3	52.9	46.5	63.0
MMNT	32.5	35.2	37.4	39.5	43.7	48.9	51.1	51.0	47.6	42.4	38.1	33.7	41.7
MNTM	39.6	43.4	46.6	49.9	55.3	61.2	65.6	65.9	61.3	53.4	45.5	40.1	52.3
EMXT	66	72	74	83	98	98	103	106	101	91	76	66	106
EMNT	3	7	20	25	31	33	34	34	31	23	11	-7	-7
TPCP	7.12	5.72	5.31	3.65	2.91	2.19	.86	1.28	2.22	3.97	8.04	8.23	51.14
EXTP	3.50	3.10	2.10	1.99	1.60	2.10	1.74	1.45	1.70	2.20	2.51	3.50	3.50
TSNW	.75	.60	.00	.02	.00	.00	.00	.00	.00	.00	.02	.99	2.31
DX90	.0	.0	.0	.0	.2	1.3	4.3	4.6	1.6	.0	.0	.0	12.6
DX32	1.0	.2	.0	.0	.0	.0	.0	.0	.0	.0	.2	1.3	2.2
DN32	15.2	10.3	6.7	2.8	.4	.0	.0	.0	.1	1.6	6.4	13.0	57.7
DN00	.0	.0	.0	.0	.0	.0	.0	.0	.0	.0	.0	.1	.1
DP00	20.7	18.5	18.9	15.9	13.4	8.9	4.0	5.2	8.3	13.9	21.4	22.5	171.0
DP01	13.6	12.2	13.2	10.1	7.9	5.3	2.2	2.7	5.2	8.8	14.7	14.3	109.2
DP05	4.8	3.9	3.2	1.9	1.5	1.4	.4	.9	1.5	2.7	6.0	5.9	33.9
DP10	1.7	.9	.6	.3	.2	.3	.1	.3	.4	.6	2.1	1.9	9.4
HDD	787	609	571	454	308	144	55	49	136	361	586	773	4829
GDD	5	9	24	63	176	338	483	493	340	133	21	6	2095

The Dalles

	Jan	Feb	Mar	Apr	May	Jun	Jul	Aug	Sep	Oct	Nov	Dec	Year
MMXT	43.1	49.6	58.3	66.0	73.2	81.0	87.8	87.8	80.7	68.5	52.2	43.1	65.9
MMNT	29.9	32.7	36.9	42.4	48.5	55.6	60.0	59.2	51.2	42.4	36.1	30.6	43.9
MNTM	36.5	41.2	47.6	54.2	60.9	68.3	73.9	73.5	66.0	55.5	44.2	36.8	54.9
EMXT	65	70	79	94	107	110	109	109	104	92	75	68	110
EMNT	-1	-1	22	28	34	40	42	35	32	26	0	-6	-6
TPCP	2.24	1.81	1.22	.77	.48	.43	.20	.49	.50	.88	2.07	2.90	13.97
EXTP	1.50	1.78	1.06	1.03	.52	.87	1.04	.82	.76	1.38	1.30	2.00	2.00
TSNW	5.62	1.17	.49	.00	.00	.00	.00	.00	.00	.00	1.55	2.81	11.56
DX90	.0	.0	.0	.1	2.0	7.0	13.6	13.4	5.2	.1	.0	.0	40.9
DX32	3.4	1.0	.0	.0	.0	.0	.0	.0	.0	.0	.6	3.2	8.4
DN32	17.6	11.8	6.2	1.0	.0	.0	.0	.0	.1	1.2	8.5	17.0	63.0
DN00	.1	.1	.0	.0	.0	.0	.0	.0	.0	.0	.1	.4	.7
DP00	12.2	11.8	11.2	7.1	5.1	4.0	1.9	3.5	4.2	7.1	13.9	13.3	94.4
DP01	5.9	5.3	4.3	2.3	1.7	1.1	.6	1.4	1.7	2.8	6.2	6.8	40.0
DP05	1.1	.7	.2	.2	.0	.1	.0	.2	.2	.3	.8	1.6	5.5
DP10	.1	.1	.0	.0	.0	.0	.0	.0	.0	.1	.1	.5	1.0
HDD	884	673	540	328	169	44	7	6	63	302	625	874	4510
GDD	2	4	29	147	339	549	740	729	479	188	19	2	3239

Tillamook

	Jan	Feb	Mar	Apr	May	Jun	Jul	Aug	Sep	Oct	Nov	Dec	Year
MMXT	49.9	52.9	54.5	56.9	60.8	64.7	67.2	68.5	68.6	62.8	54.6	49.8	59.3
MMNT	35.7	36.9	36.9	38.5	42.4	46.7	49.2	49.5	46.4	42.2	39.1	36.1	41.6
MNTM	42.8	44.9	45.7	47.7	51.6	55.7	58.2	59.0	57.5	52.5	46.8	42.9	50.4
EMXT	69	73	73	84	86	92	102	102	97	92	80	66	102
EMNT	11	8	21	23	27	31	35	34	27	22	14	4	4
TPCP	13.56	9.94	10.16	6.05	4.43	3.20	1.60	1.75	3.76	7.12	13.06	13.93	88.56
EXTP	5.22	2.94	3.75	2.92	1.68	2.50	2.00	1.57	2.65	3.57	4.26	4.92	5.22
TSNW	.68	.45	.61	.04	.00	.00	.00	.00	.00	.00	.16	.62	2.72
DX90	.0	.0	.0	.0	.0	.1	.1	.2	.5	.0	.0	.0	.9
DX32	.3	.1	.0	.0	.0	.0	.0	.0	.0	.0	.0	.6	1.0
DN32	10.7	7.9	8.8	5.7	1.7	.0	.0	.0	.6	3.3	6.5	9.8	55.1
DN00	.0	.0	.0	.0	.0	.0	.0	.0	.0	.0	.0	.0	.0
DP00	21.3	19.2	20.8	17.5	14.8	10.3	6.8	6.6	10.7	14.8	21.3	22.5	186.5
DP01	17.6	16.0	17.2	12.8	10.0	6.9	3.8	4.1	7.4	11.1	17.8	18.5	143.3
DP05	9.5	7.5	8.5	4.0	3.1	2.1	.9	1.2	2.8	5.5	10.1	9.8	65.0
DP10	4.3	2.8	2.5	1.0	.6	.6	.3	.2	.9	2.3	4.0	4.4	23.7
HDD	689	568	599	520	415	281	212	189	228	390	545	685	5322
GDD	8	15	14	26	80	174	255	279	228	107	27	8	1222

Toketee Falls

	Jan	Feb	Mar	Apr	May	Jun	Jul	Aug	Sep	Oct	Nov	Dec	Year
MMXT	42.5	48.5	53.7	61.1	69.9	78.3	86.0	85.7	77.5	63.3	48.1	41.8	63.1
MMNT	29.0	30.8	32.6	35.5	40.6	46.9	49.9	49.3	44.1	38.1	33.7	29.8	38.4
MNTM	35.7	39.6	43.2	48.3	55.2	62.6	68.0	67.5	60.8	50.7	40.9	35.8	50.7
EMXT	64	75	77	90	105	105	108	109	105	93	72	63	109
EMNT	0	4	14	23	27	31	35	34	26	18	12	-5	-5
TPCP	6.71	5.24	5.42	3.58	2.64	1.51	.57	1.16	1.74	3.65	7.77	7.47	48.17
EXTP	3.09	3.30	2.40	1.53	1.39	1.44	1.61	1.31	1.82	2.08	3.22	3.54	3.54
TSNW	13.67	9.20	6.45	.65	.02	.00	.00	.00	.00	.14	4.21	11.48	50.16
DX90	.0	.0	.0	.1	1.7	4.8	11.9	11.7	4.1	.2	.0	.0	34.6
DX32	.7	.2	.0	.0	.0	.0	.0	.0	.0	.0	.0	1.1	2.0
DN32	23.1	18.3	17.3	9.8	2.3	.1	.0	.0	.8	5.5	13.9	22.0	111.8
DN00	.0	.0	.0	.0	.0	.0	.0	.0	.0	.0	.0	.1	.1
DP00	16.9	16.2	18.6	15.8	11.3	7.9	3.1	4.2	6.5	10.9	18.3	17.9	149.2
DP01	12.6	11.3	13.1	9.5	7.1	4.3	1.5	2.9	4.5	7.1	13.8	13.1	101.9
DP05	4.8	3.6	3.3	2.0	1.5	.7	.3	.8	1.0	2.6	5.6	5.4	32.1
DP10	1.7	.9	.8	.3	.0	.1	.1	.1	.3	.8	1.9	2.0	9.2
HDD	908	717	677	502	316	126	36	39	156	445	723	907	5533
GDD	0	1	8	60	193	379	557	544	327	88	4	0	2169

Ukiah

	Jan	Feb	Mar	Apr	May	Jun	Jul	Aug	Sep	Oct	Nov	Dec	Year
MMXT	36.1	43.0	49.0	56.3	64.1	73.4	82.6	82.5	73.8	62.9	46.5	37.1	58.8
MMNT	14.6	19.4	23.4	27.7	32.7	38.1	39.9	39.2	31.9	26.0	23.5	16.3	27.8
MNTM	25.4	31.2	36.2	42.0	48.4	55.8	61.3	60.9	52.8	44.5	35.0	26.7	43.3
EMXT	60	70	75	87	92	100	101	110	102	92	76	65	110
EMNT	-32	-36	-9	10	14	17	21	20	11	-2	-32	-38	-38
TPCP	1.93	1.30	1.42	1.32	1.63	1.21	.63	.85	.85	1.22	2.08	1.99	16.38
EXTP	.89	.85	1.09	.86	1.53	1.20	2.28	1.12	1.06	1.16	.83	1.17	2.28
TSNW	10.08	5.97	4.18	1.25	.17	.00	.00	.00	.00	.34	6.25	9.89	38.50
DX90	.0	.0	.0	.0	.1	1.3	7.0	7.8	1.7	.2	.0	.0	18.4
DX32	8.8	2.6	.7	.0	.0	.0	.0	.0	.0	.1	1.9	7.9	22.9
DN32	29.1	26.2	28.3	23.7	15.9	7.2	3.8	4.6	16.7	25.1	25.5	28.9	233.9
DN00	5.0	1.9	.4	.0	.0	.0	.0	.0	.0	.1	.8	4.1	12.8
DP00	12.7	10.4	10.8	9.8	9.2	7.5	3.4	4.6	5.2	7.3	12.3	11.9	104.3
DP01	7.0	4.9	5.0	4.7	5.0	3.9	1.7	2.8	2.8	3.7	7.0	6.3	54.6
DP05	.5	.3	.3	.3	.6	.5	.3	.2	.3	.4	.9	.7	5.4
DP10	.0	.0	.0	.0	.1	.0	.0	.1	.0	.1	.0	.1	.5
HDD	1229	954	892	690	516	286	147	157	368	637	900	1187	7970
GDD	0	0	1	15	66	196	351	339	138	29	0	0	1137

Whitehorse Ranch

	Jan	Feb	Mar	Apr	May	Jun	Jul	Aug	Sep	Oct	Nov	Dec	Year
MMXT	40.7	47.1	52.9	60.4	69.0	77.7	86.7	84.6	76.0	64.7	51.0	42.0	62.3
MMNT	18.8	23.2	26.3	30.1	37.1	44.7	50.6	49.7	41.3	33.0	26.0	19.1	33.5
MNTM	29.8	35.1	39.6	45.2	53.0	61.1	68.7	67.1	58.7	48.9	38.5	30.3	47.9
EMXT	65	69	83	84	94	97	102	103	95	87	75	65	103
EMNT	-15	-21	-5	8	12	21	29	30	17	5	-5	-26	-26
TPCP	.59	.63	.83	.97	.77	.61	.24	.84	.59	.55	.82	.63	8.37
EXTP	.56	2.14	1.66	2.00	1.66	.75	1.13	2.05	1.31	.58	1.00	2.03	2.14
TSNW	2.78	1.84	2.68	.99	.10	.00	.00	.00	.26	.14	1.87	2.79	16.53
DX90	.0	.0	.0	.0	.4	2.8	11.5	8.6	1.1	.0	.0	.0	21.4
DX32	5.7	1.8	.2	.0	.0	.0	.0	.0	.0	.0	.9	5.5	14.6
DN32	26.5	23.8	23.2	18.4	8.9	1.3	.2	.1	4.1	13.9	22.8	27.3	169.3
DN00	2.2	.9	.1	.0	.0	.0	.0	.0	.0	.0	.2	2.1	6.8
DP00	4.8	4.6	5.9	5.0	4.9	3.4	1.6	3.0	3.1	3.9	6.0	4.7	59.2
DP01	2.2	2.3	2.4	2.8	2.5	2.2	.7	1.9	1.8	2.1	3.0	2.6	29.5
DP05	.1	.1	.2	.3	.2	.2	.1	.5	.2	.1	.3	.1	2.0
DP10	.0	.0	.1	.2	.0	.0	.0	.2	.1	.0	.0	.0	.2
HDD	1093	843	787	594	377	160	34	52	211	501	796	1077	6544
GDD	0	1	6	42	153	339	578	531	277	82	6	1	1984

PART 5

Time Series

lthough long-term averages (which we term "climate") are useful for many purposes, variations in weather and climate have pronounced effects on people and ecosystems, In many cases, the most extreme conditions have a much more significant impact than do average conditions. For example, hydrologists tell us that the vast majority of changes in river and stream beds occur during a small percentage of big flood events. Extreme temperatures tend to be limiting factors in the kinds of plants (both native and introduced species) that grow in an area. And droughts (and often increased fire danger) occur largely following multiple drier-than-average years.

Climate scientists have identified a number of natural cycles in the sun-earth system that affect weather and climate. The long-term variations in climate (termed the "climate signal") are probably a result of an interplay of these cycles, plus others not yet discovered. Table 50 shows a few of the more profound cycles known to affect weather and climate:

The field of atmospheric cycles is still very much in its infancy. Perhaps some day we will have a much better understanding of the roles of these and other cycles in affecting weather and climate. For now, we present, without comment, time series of precipitation and temperature for Oregon climate zones and individual stations. By definition, a time series involves changes in data over time. In this case, we present annual average precipitation and temperature over the last hundred years or so for locations throughout the state.

Table 50. Some common natural cycles that are known to affect weather and climate.

Cycle	Period
Seasonal cycle	1 year
Quasi-biennial oscillation (stratospheric winds in the tropics)	2.2 years
El Niño-Southern Oscillation	3-7 years
Sunspots	11 years
Lunar tides	18.6 years
Sun's magnetic field	20-27 years
Earth's orbital variations	More than 25,000 years

Water Year Precipitation for Oregon Climate Zones, 1896-1998

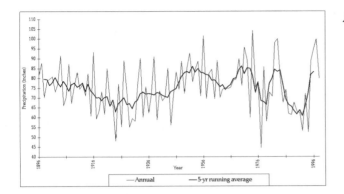

Zone 1. The Coastal Area

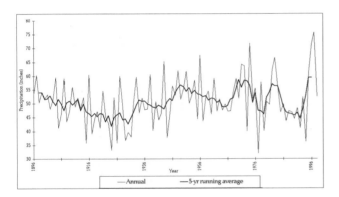

Zone 2. The Willamette Valley

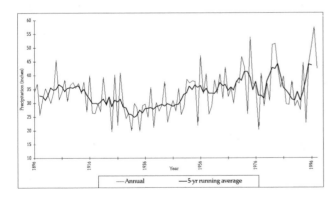

Zone 3. Southwestern Interior

Zone 4. Northern Cascades

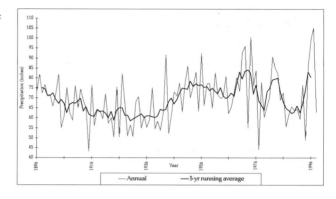

Zone 5. The High Plateau

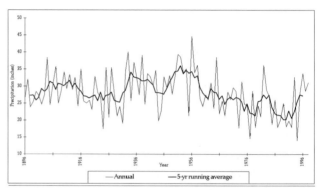

Zone 6. The North Central Area

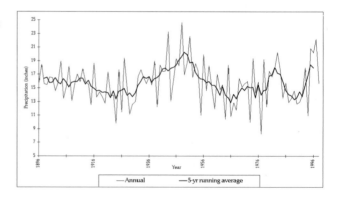

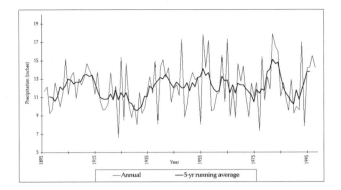

Zone 7. The South Central Area

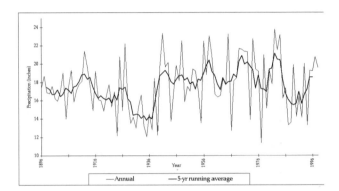

Zone 8. The Northeast Area

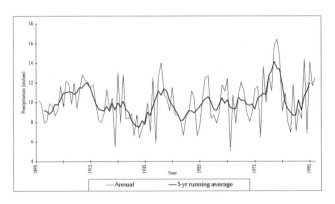

Zone 9. The Southeast Area

Water Year Precipitation for Selected Oregon NOAA Weather Stations

Ashland, precipitation in inches, 1880-1998

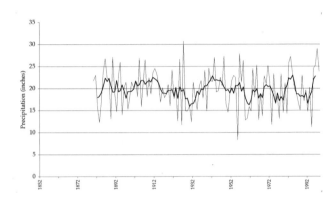

Astoria, precipitation in inches, 1851-1998

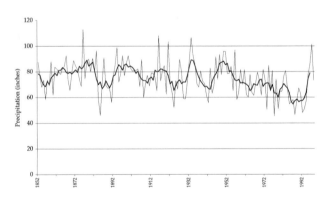

Baker, precipitation in inches, 1890-1998

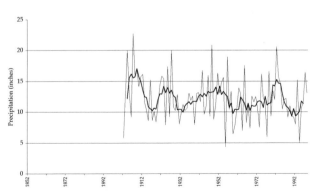

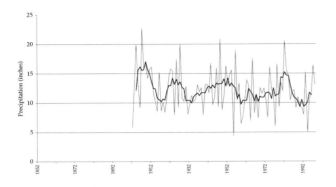

Bend, precipitation in inches, 1902-1998

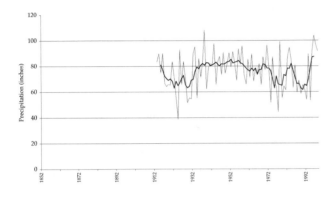

Brookings, precipitation in inches, 1913-1998

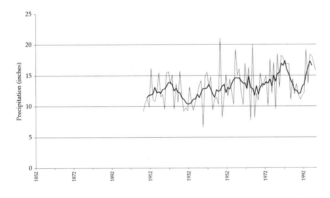

Condon, precipitation in inches, 1908-1998

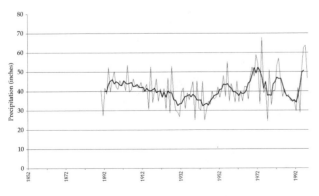

Corvallis, precipitation in inches, 1890-1998

Dufur, precipitation in inches,
1910-1998

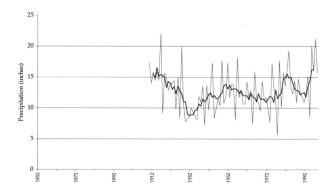

Grants Pass, precipitation in inches,
1890-1998

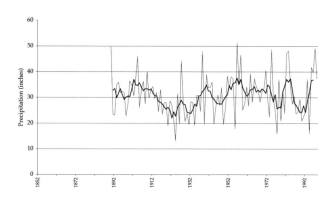

Headworks, precipitation in inches,
1900-1998

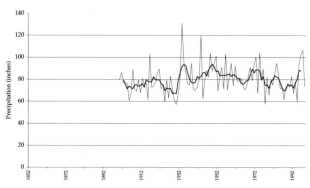

Heppner, precipitation in inches,
1891-1998

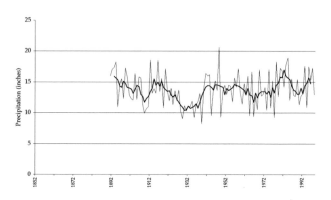

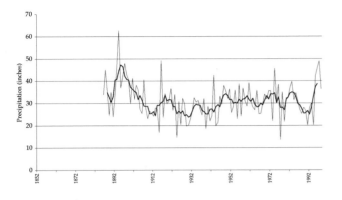

Hood River, precipitation in inches, 1886-1998

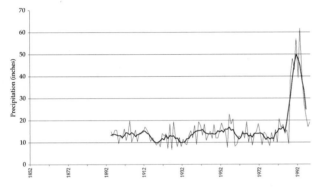

Klamath Falls, precipitation in inches, 1894-1998

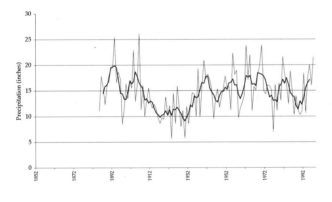

Lakeview, precipitation in inches, 1885-1998

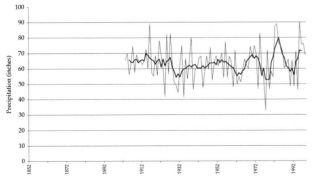

North Bend, precipitation in inches, 1903-1998

Prineville, precipitation in inches, 1898-1998

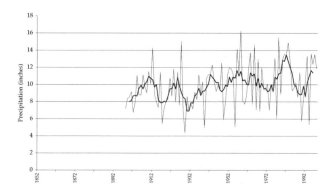

Roseburg, precipitation in inches, 1879-1998

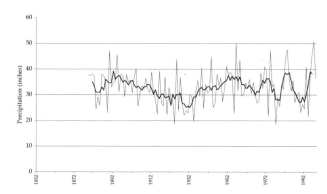

Vale, precipitation in inches, 1892-1998

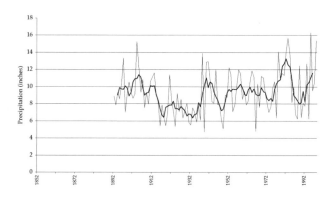

PART 6

Special Topics

Long-term Wet-Dry Cycles in Oregon

Reliable weather and climate information for Oregon extend back about a hundred years. During that time, there have been about an equal number of wet and dry years. We find, however, that during some periods there is a preponderance of wetter than average years while in others there are mostly dry years. These wet and dry cycles generally span 20-25 years. The dry years tend to be warm (due to reduced cloudiness, most likely) and the wet years cool. Figure 33 shows Water Year (October to September) precipitation for Zone 1 since 1896. Notice the dry (and warm) periods from about 1920 to 1945 and 1975 to 1994, and the wet periods before and after. The last four years have been quite wet. Figure 34 shows Portland precipitation since 1920. The wet/dry periods are similar, coinciding almost exactly with those on the coast. Are the recent wet years a harbinger of things to come? Have we reentered a wet cycle?

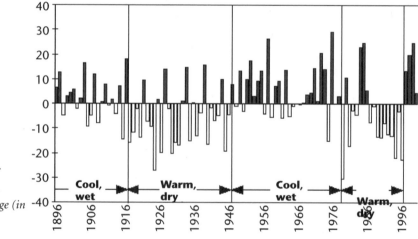

Figure 33. Water year precipitation, Zone 1, departure from average (in inches), 1896-1998

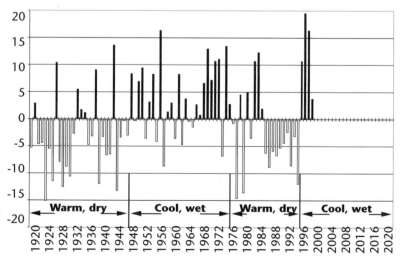

Figure 34. Portland water year precipitation, departure from average (in inches), 1920-2020

152

The Global Conveyor Belt

Several years ago author Taylor heard a talk by Dr. William Gray, who has had significant success in predicting Atlantic hurricanes; he described an exciting new finding based on the work of an oceanographer, Wallace Broeker. Broeker (1991) suggested that there is a global-scale current, operating on a timescale of several decades, that affects worldwide weather patterns. Broeker used data from ice cores to postulate that changes in this current may have been a primary triggering mechanism for the last ice age. Gray and Landsea, however, were more interested in our era (see Gray and Landsea 1993).

The thermohaline current, or conveyor belt, as Gray and Landsea dubbed it, transports warm ocean water from the Pacific through the Indian Ocean and into the Atlantic. In the north Atlantic, this warm water (now very saline due to evaporation during the journey), encounters cold water coming down from farther north. The warm water cools quickly, and sinks (due to its greater density). This sets up a sub-surface countercurrent that transports the cool water back to the Indian and Pacific oceans. Figure 35 illustrates the warm and cold currents associated with an active conveyor cycle.

In looking back over the last hundred years, Gray and Landsea identified four distinct periods, two when the conveyor belt was very active, two when it was quite inactive. They also found several important atmospheric phenomena that correlate quite well with the strength of the conveyor; we have added precipitation in the Northwest to their phenomena (Figure 36). Note also that global temperatures seem to correspond to the active-inactive phases as well. This should not surprise us, since the tropical Pacific is the largest terrestrial heat source to the atmosphere; when the Pacific warms, so does the atmosphere. And during El Niño events, Pacific temperatures (taken overall) warm significantly. Thus the warmup during El Niño-dominated periods when the conveyor belt is inactive.

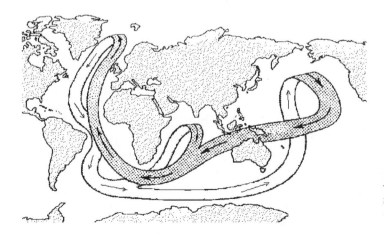

Figure 35. The global thermohaline circulation or "conveyor belt."

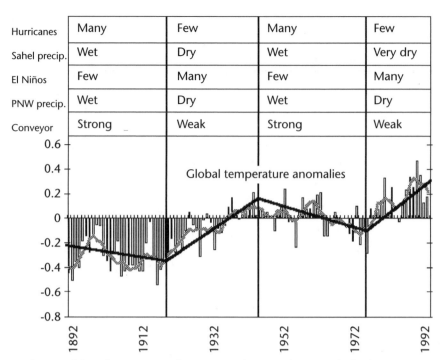

Figure 36. Global climate summary since 1892.

Hurricanes	Many	Few	Many	Few
Sahel precip.	Wet	Dry	Wet	Very dry
El Niños	Few	Many	Few	Many
PNW precip.	Wet	Dry	Wet	Dry
Conveyor	Strong	Weak	Strong	Weak

Gray and Landsea suggest that we may be entering a period of strong conveyor belt activity again. Consider how the four major indicators have changed over the last several years:

—**Atlantic Hurricanes**. After the quietest four-year period of the last fifty years during 1991-1994, 1995 had the largest number of hurricanes since storms were first named in the early 1950s. 1996 and 1998 were active years, and 1997 was about average. The latest four-year period (1995-1998) is the *busiest* on record.

—**Sahel precipitation.** The four years 1995-1998 have seen near-average precipitation after many years of severe drought.

—**El Niños.** Following a twenty-year period with only one La Niña, three of the four years 1995-1998 have seen La Niña conditions in the Pacific.

—**Precipitation in the Northwest.** Following the very dry 1975-1994 period, which saw two significant statewide droughts and ten consecutive dry years, we are now (in 1999) completing the fifth consecutive year of above-average precipitation.

Predictions

The signs are there. All indications are that the conveyor belt has switched back to active again, portending a mostly wet regime for the next twenty years or so. If history repeats itself, we can expect:
  —frequent floods
  —no droughts
  —about 75% of all years wetter than average
  —relatively cool temperatures

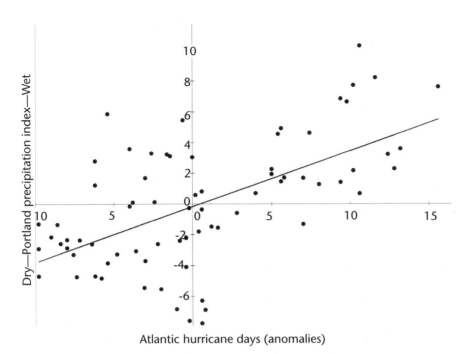

*Figure 37.
Atlantic
hurricane days
plotted against
Portland
precipitation the
following winter.*

Note that the above predictions apply to the cool season only. Summers do not necessarily reflect these trends. Our usual warm, dry, beautiful Northwest summers will still be here.

Technical Note: Atlantic Hurricanes and Portland Precipitation

Since the number of Atlantic hurricanes seems to correspond to precipitation in the Northwest, we decided to plot both types of data together to see how well they correlate. As can be seen in Figure 37, there is a very strong correlation indeed. Active hurricane years are almost always followed by wetter than average winter conditions in Portland, and inactive years by dry winters. This graph not only validates the conveyor belt concept, it suggests that hurricane frequency can be used effectively to predict Portland precipitation the following winter.

References
Broeker, W.S., 1991. The Great Ocean Conveyor. *Oceanography*, 4, 79-89.

Gray, W.M., and C.W. Landsea, 1993. West African rainfall and Atlantic basin hurricane activity as proxy signals for Atlantic conveyor belt circulation strength. Conference on Hydrology, American Meteorological Society, Anaheim, California, January.

Long-term Climate Trends and Salmon Populations

There is increasing evidence that salmon populations in the northeast Pacific are significantly influenced by long-term climate changes. In the Northwest, temperature and precipitation data go back about a hundred years. During that time there have been four relatively distinct climatic periods. These are illustrated in Figure 38, which shows annual precipitation as it varies from the long-term average for the Oregon coast. All stations west of the crest of the Coast Range were averaged together to get a single value each year, and every year's value compared with the long-term average. The Water Year (October through September) was used so that all months from a single winter remained in the same data set.

The four climatic periods were:

1896-1914 Generally wet (and cool)
1915-1946 Generally dry (and warm)
1947-1975 Generally wet (and cool)
1976-1994 Generally dry (and warm)

These were followed by four consecutive wet years: 1995-1998

In any given period, not all the years are dry or wet, but a high percentage follows that pattern. For example, in the 1915-1946 period there were twenty-two dry years and only ten were wet. Consecutive dry years were common (indicating drought periods). The wet period immediately following had twenty-one wet years and only seven dry ones, and there were no consecutive dry years. Droughts were nonexistent during the latter period—there were several major floods.

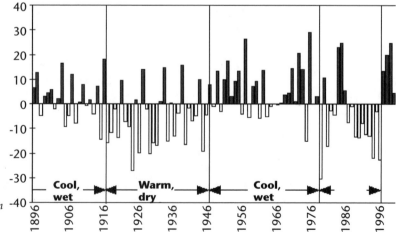

Figure 38. Water year precipitation, Zone 1, departure from average (in inches), 1896-1998

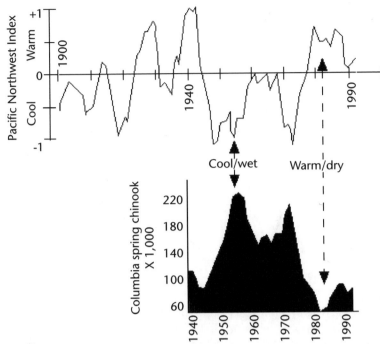

Figure 39. The correlation between the Pacific Northwest Index (PNI) and abundance of Columbia River bright spring chinook salmon (5-year running averages). (Reproduced from Anderson 1995)

Recently, scientists have found that salmon returns in the Northwest show long-term behavior that closely follows these climate cycles. Figure 36 was reproduced from testimony before the U.S. House of Representatives by Anderson (1995), who used the Pacific Northwest Index (PNI) to distinguish cool, wet periods from warm, dry ones; note the similarity of PNI to the graph in Figure 39. Anderson then compared the PNI with Columbia River spring chinook salmon returns going back to 1940 (earlier data are not available). The correlation between returns of spring chinook and the PNI is very strong, and indicates that salmon returns increase during cool, wet periods and decline during warm, dry ones. While humans have undoubtedly affected the fish (by actions including dam construction and habitat destruction), Figure 39 indicates that natural variability may be a very significant influence as well, and should be considered in any salmon restoration plan.

While stocks in the Northwest have shown low numbers in recent decades, Alaska salmon have experienced a tremendous boom period. Climatologists have known for many years that weather patterns in Alaska and the Northwest are out-of-phase: wet periods in the Northwest tend to be dry in Alaska, and vice-versa. The El Niño-Southern Oscillation appears to be the major reason for this. Interestingly (and perhaps not surprisingly), salmon returns in the Northwest and Alaska are similarly out of phase. In Figure 40, also from Anderson (1995), the bottom chart shows that chinook returns in the Rogue and Columbia/Snake rivers behave similarly over time. The upper figure, however, shows that Columbia and Alaska salmon are out of phase, with the abundant 1950-1975 period in the Northwest corresponding with a very poor salmon period in Alaska. When Northwest stocks declined in the 1970s, Alaska's were soaring.

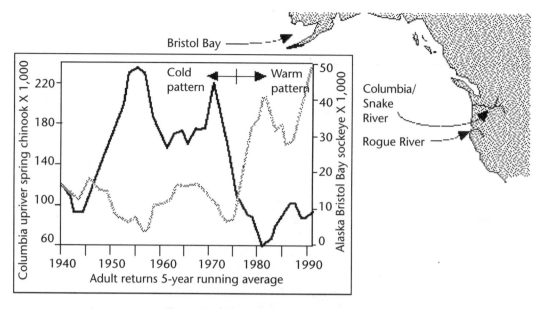

Figure 40. Comparison of Columbia River spring chinook and Bristol Bay, Alaska, sockeye salmon counts since 1940.

An excellent article by Mantua et al (1996) presents a very thorough overview of the differences between Alaska and the Pacific Northwest. It is fascinating to see how trends change, and how Alaskan and Northwest fish fortunes have always been out of phase. The authors quote various issues of *Pacific Fisherman:*

Pacific Fisherman 1915; wet in Northwest

Never before have the Bristol Bay [Alaska] salmon packers returned to port after the season's operations so early.

The spring [chinook salmon] fishing season on the Columbia River [Washington and Oregon] closed at noon on August 25, and proved to be one of the best for some years.

Pacific Fisherman 1939; dry in Northwest

The Bristol Bay [Alaska] Red [sockeye salmon] run was regarded as the greatest in history.

The [May, June and July chinook] catch this year is one of the lowest in the history of the Columbia [Washington and Oregon].

Pacific Fisherman 1972; wet in Northwest

Bristol Bay [Alaska] salmon run a disaster.

Gillnetters in the Lower Columbia [Washington and Oregon] received an unexpected bonus when the largest run of spring chinook since counting began in 1938 entered the river.

Pacific Fishing 1995; dry in Northwest

Alaska set a new record for its salmon harvest in 1994, breaking the record set the year before.

Columbia [Washington and Oregon] spring chinook fishery shut down; west coast troll coho fishing banned.

There are indications that global ocean and atmosphere conditions are the cause of the long-term climate variations shown in Figure 1. There is also evidence that a switch in regimes occurred in late 1994, and that we have returned to the conditions which tend to yield wet, cool winters in the Northwest (see previous section on long-term wet-dry cycles in Oregon). If so, it would appear that environmental conditions may be very favorable for a resurgence of Northwest salmon stocks (and unfavorable in Alaska).

Recent evidence suggests that a rebound may already be occurring. On April 28, 1997, Oregon Department of Fish and Wildlife issued a statement that the number of chinook salmon redds in the Upper John Day River the previous summer were the second highest since 1959. Jim Myron of Oregon Trout said, "It's good news for everybody concerned, whether it's rancher, environmentalist or state employee—and it's especially good news for the fish." Maybe there *is* a silver lining in all those gray rainclouds!

References

Anderson, J. J. (in press). Decadal climate cycles and declining Columbia River salmon. Proceedings of the Sustainable Fisheries Conference Victoria B.C. Canada, 1996. Eric Knudsen Editor. Special publication of the American Fisheries Society.

Anderson, J.J. 1995. Decline and Recovery of Snake River Salmon. Information based on the CriSP research project. Testimony before the U.S. House of Representatives Subcommittee on Power and Water, June 3.

Ebbesmeyer, C.C., and R.M. Strickland. 1995. Oyster Condition and Climate: Evidence from Willapa Bay. Publication WSG-MR 95-02, Washington Sea Grant Program, University of Washington, Seattle, WA. 11p.

Mantua, N.J., S.R. Hare, Y. Zhang, J.M. Wallace, and R.C. Francis, 1996. A Pacific interdecadal climate oscillation with impacts on salmon production. Submitted to the Bulletin of the American Meteorological Society.

The El Niño/Southern Oscillation Phenomenon and its Effects on the Climate of Oregon

The El Niño-Southern Oscillation (ENSO) exerts a profound influence on global weather and climate patterns. A great deal of time and effort have been spent investigating the phenomenon, with good success. Increasingly, ENSO predictions and assessments are being used for decision making, with benefits in terms of economics, public safety, and the environment. Oregon and the Pacific Northwest are strongly influenced by ENSO, and as ENSO information has improved and become more publicized it is being used more frequently in both the public and private sector for everyday and long-term decisions. Below is a brief overview of ENSO's effects in this region, followed by several examples of how such information is influencing decisions.

Average Pacific Conditions

Figure 41 shows typical sea surface temperatures during an "average" winter in the Northern Hemisphere, Off the west coast of South America, the waters are unusually cool, for two reasons: the cool Humboldt current which moves northward along the coast, bringing water from the antarctic regions; and the easterly trade winds, which move surface water away from the coast and cause upwelling, allowing deep, cool water to rise to the surface. The cool water is pushed away from the coast by the trade winds, resulting in a "cool tongue" of water along the equator. Warmest waters are in the western Pacific near Indonesia and the Philippines; average surface temperatures there are about 88°, compared with 68-70° off South America. Figure 42 shows a typical distribution of clouds across the tropical Pacific, as well as storms and jet stream locations in the North Pacific. Since evaporation is a function of water temperature, the water in the western Pacific evaporates the most vigorously, causing extensive cloudiness, abundant rains, and large tropical storms in that area. On the other hand, much cooler water off South America produces less evaporation, fewer clouds, and less rain.

In the North Pacific, the polar jet stream—the area of strongest winds in the upprt atmosphere—moves generally from west to east. The jet stream, which marks the boundary between mild subtropical air and cold polar air, is often called the "storm track," because large cyclonic storms tend to move along its path. In a typical year, the jet stream moves across the Pacific (often veering northward or southward), and generally makes landfall between northern California and southern Alaska—causing this area to be one of the wettest in the world. Peaks in the Oregon Coast Range receive up

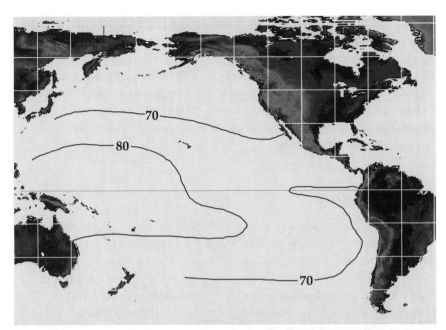

Figure 41. Typical ocean temperatures (°F) in an average year in the tropical Pacific. Lines are isotherms (lines of equal sea surface temperatures).

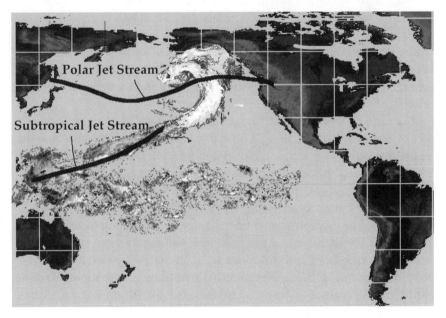

Figure 42. Typical distribution of clouds across the tropical Pacific.

to 200 inches in an average year, the Washington Olympics receive as much as 270 inches, and there is evidence that coastal mountains in southeast Alaska receive over 450 inches, among the highest totals anywhere on earth.

Storms traversing the North Pacific pick up considerable moisture from evaporation, but the biggest surges of moist air come directly from the tropics. Occasionally a large amount of warm, humid air moves northeastward from the tropics (usually from the western Pacific, where water is warmer), carried by upper-level winds. This situation is known as the "subtropical jet stream." The extremely high moisture content of these air masses can cause very high precipitation intensities; in fact, most of the daily rainfall records in western Oregon result at least partially from subtropical moisture. During such events, coastal sites can receive in excess of 6 inches of rain in a single day, while inland valleys can receive more than 3 inches. These surges of warm, humid air, often known as the Pineapple Express because they usually come by way of Hawaii, usually produce the wettest storms in any given year. In an average year, they affect the Northwest one to three times.

El Niño Events

About every three to seven years, the ocean off the South American coast suddenly warms up. At the same time, temperatures in the western Pacific usually decrease. This phenomenon is known as an El Niño, or "warm event." Typical El Niño events begin with a decrease in easterly winds of South America, which reduces upwelling and causes sea surface temperatures to increase. This warms the atmosphere and lowers the pressure over the eastern Pacific, causing the trade winds to be further reduced. Gradually this process continues until an El Niño develops. In strong El Niño situations, warmer than normal waters cover nearly all of the eastern and central tropical Pacific. The area of strong convection (large rain clouds) usually shifts eastward as waters in those areas warm. In the western Pacific, easterly trade winds often reverse and blow from the west, reducing ocean temperatures.

The term El Niño (Spanish for "child," in this case, "the Christ Child") was coined by fishermen along the coasts of Ecuador and Peru, because the unusually warm waters there typically appear around Christmas. December is midsummer in the Southern Hemisphere and the prime fishing season. In an average year, upwelling keeps temperatures cool and brings abundant nutrients to the surface, providing ample food for a thriving fish population. The occasional warm periods see a reduction in or total absence of upwelling, resulting in fewer nutrients and very poor fishing conditions. Fish die in large numbers, sometimes ruining an entire year's harvest. The term "El Niño" has come to apply to these exceptionally strong warm intervals that not only disrupt the normal lives of the fishermen, but also bring heavy rain to the region.

Figure 43 shows sea surface temperatures during the strong El Niño event of 1997. In the eastern Pacific, there was no evidence of the usual "cool tongue," as sea surface temperatures had risen by more than 8°F compared to the average. The warmest temperatures were in the central Pacific, south of Hawaii. Figure 44 shows typical atmospheric response to the shifts in ocean temperature that characterize El Niño. Warmer temperatures in the central and eastern Pacific cause much greater cloudiness in those regions, while cooler than average temperatures in the western Pacific cause that normally very active area to be less cloudy, with

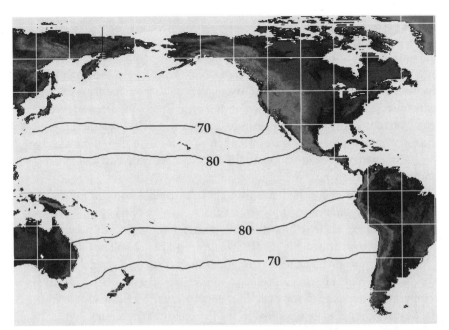

Figure 43. Surface sea temperatures during the El Niño event of 1997.

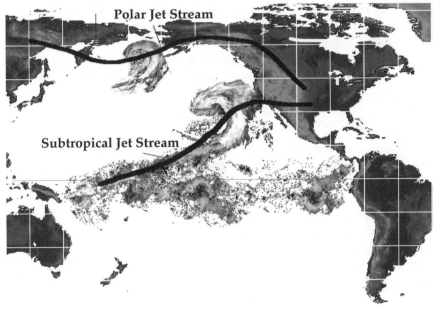

Figure 44. Typical atmospheric response to the shifts in ocean temperature that characterize El Niño.

fewer storms and less rainfall. Both the polar and subtropical jet streams are changed as well. The polar jet often dips southward over the North Pacific, then veers northward into Alaska. Although some storms still reach the Northwest, they tend to be less frequent than during average years. This causes the Northwest to be generally drier than average (and milder, since the cold air stays to the north of us), while Alaska experiences wetter than average winters.

La Niña Events

El Niño has a counterpart that happens approximately as often; it is known as a "La Niña" or "cold event." During La Niña conditions, the water off South America is even cooler than usual, dropping from its usual 68° to only 63-65°. In the western Pacific, on the other hand, temperatures are even warmer than average, sometimes exceeding 90°. This causes an even greater contrast in temperatures between east and west than in an average year, and creates an even stronger and more concentrated area of storms and clouds in the western Pacific.

The sequence of events that is thought to cause El Niño conditions, described avove, may also apply to formation of a La Niña event—but in reverse. Stronger trade winds off South America cause greater upwelling, cooler sea temperatures, higher air pressure, and hence still stronger winds.

Figure 45 shows distribution of temperatures during a typical La Niña. Very warm waters are concentrated in the western Pacific, with a steady temperature decrease to the east. The "cool tongue" is clearly visible from the South American coast almost to the international date line. Figure 46 shows the way La Niñas tend to affect the atmosphere. Cloudiness is concentrated in the western Pacific, and is quite extensive; heavy rains and abundant tropical storms—typhoons—occur. In the North Pacific, the polar jet stream typically takes a path northward toward the Bering Strait and then to the southeast, toward the Pacific Northwest. This brings cold air into our region, resulting in our most severe cold episodes (and most of our low-elevation snowstorms).

In the meantime, a vigorous subtropical jet moves northeastward across the Pacific. The warm, humid air typically makes its landfall in the Northwest, often merging with big North Pacific storms to produce our area's biggest rainstorms and most significant floods. The flood-producing storms of 1996 and 1997 occurred during La Niña conditions, with very warm water in the western tropical Pacific.

Thus, La Niñas produce the Northwest's coldest winter conditions (because of the jet stream path) and wettest events (because of the subtropical jet stream), but not at the same time. Often it seems as if the cold northern and the wet southern air masses are fighting each other to see which can dominate—and we in the Northwest are the victims of that battle.

Identifying El Niños

More than 75 years ago, a British meteorologist working in India first noticed and named the "Southern Oscillation." Sir Gilbert Walker began to study large-scale weather patterns in the tropics hoping that they could explain the occasional disastrous failures of Indian monsoons, leading to widespread famine. He identified the phenomenon by noticing that air pressures in the south Pacific alternated between east and west, ostensibly as

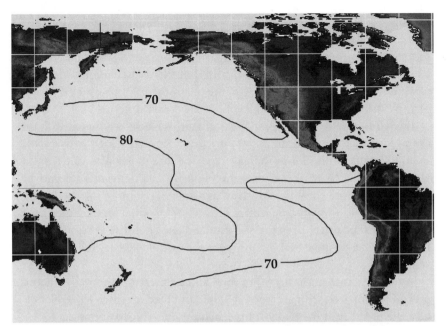

Figure 45. Surface sea temperatures during a typical La Niña.

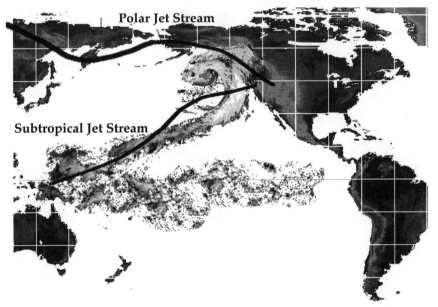

Figure 46. Typical atmospheric response to the shifts in ocean temperature that characterize La Niña events.

a result of changing ocean conditions. When waters are warmer than average, marine air is warmer and more humid, and thus more buoyant. The resultant rising air causes air pressure to be lower than average. Walker found that air pressure in Tahiti, in the eastern Pacific, was exactly opposite to that in Darwin, Australia, in the west. Lower than average pressure at Tahiti coincided with higher than average pressure at Darwin, and vice versa. Walker named this phenomenon the "Southern Oscillation."

Studies since then have proved Walker correct. During an El Niño, warmer than average water in the eastern Pacific and cooler than average in the west cause the pressure at Tahiti to be lower than average and that at Darwin to be higher. A La Niña produces the opposite effect. A very useful index can be obtained by simply comparing Tahiti's and Darwin's pressures, compared with the average. The so-called Southern Oscillation Index (SOI), while not the only such index, is still the one most commonly used to identify the state of the tropical Pacific at any given time.

By definition, the SOI is simply Tahiti's air pressure, compared with the average for that month, minus Darwin's (also compared with its average). In an El Niño, Tahiti's lower than average pressure (a negative value) minus Darwin's higher than average pressure (a positive value) yields a negative number; the more strongly negative this number, the more intense the El Niño; a value of -4 would be a huge El Niño. A La Niña, on the other hand, creates high (positive) pressure at Tahiti and low (negative) pressure at Darwin, and a positive SOI. An average year would yield an SOI close to zero.

Figure 47 shows monthly SOI values and air pressure anomalies (actual pressure compared with average) at Tahiti and Darwin since 1979. Notice how the pressure at the two locations behaves in a directly opposite manner; the oscillation is quite apparent. The big El Niño events of 1982-1983 and 1997 are prominent, as is the 1988-1989 La Niña.

Figure 48 is a plot of SOI values compared with eastern Pacific water temperatures, showing how El Niño years (warm temperatures) are associated with negative SOI values. Figure 49 shows the distribution of air pressures over and near the Pacific during strong El Niño and La Niña events.

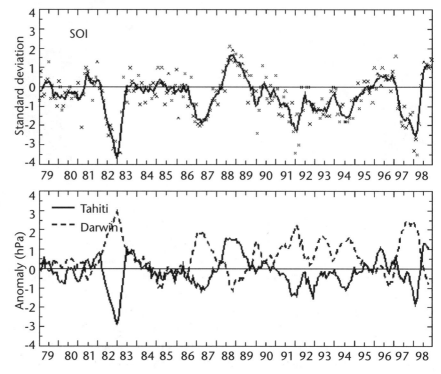

Figure 47. Southern Oscillation Index (top) and air pressure anomalies at Tahiti and Darwin (bottom). From Climate Prediction Center Web site.

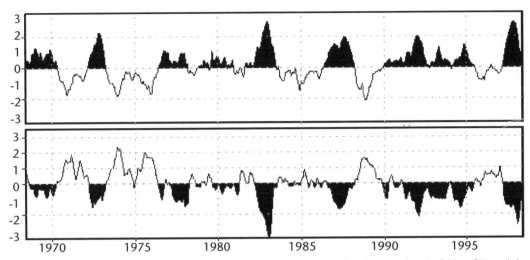

Figure 48. Ocean temperatures (°C) in the eastern Pacific (top) compared with SOI values (Tahiti and Darwin) (below). (From Climate Prediction Center Web site)

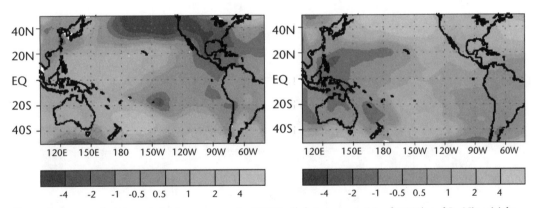

Figure 49. Pressure departure (mb) from average for El Niño (left, January to March 1998) and La Niña (right, January to March 1989) events over and near the Pacific. (From Climate Prediction Center Web site.)

Effects of ENSO on Oregon's Climate

Precipitation

For the most part, El Niño or warm events correlate with average or below-average precipitation during the winter in the Northwest. In southern Oregon, the correlation is fairly low, but north of about Roseburg (and extending into Bristish Columbia) the correlation is rather strong. The winter of 1982-83 was a notable exception (it was a very wet winter throughout the Northwest), but the intensity and timing of that El Niño event was unprecedented, at least in the last 75 years.

Figure 50 shows the summer average SOI conpared with precipitation the following winter at Bonneville Dam on the Columbia River. El Niño

167

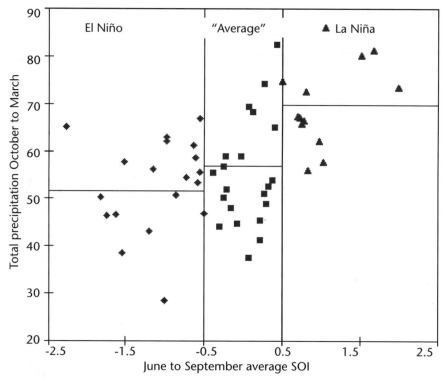

Figure 50. Winter precipitation at Bonneville Dam (in inches) compared with previous summer SOI

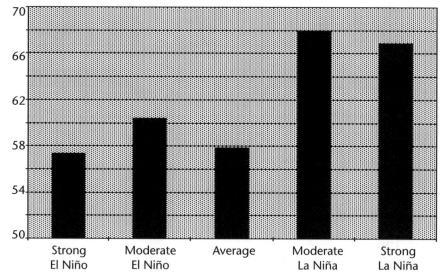

Figure 51. Total water year precipitation, Oregon coast (in inches), compared with previous summer SOI

years (negative SOI values) are associated with average or lower than average winter precipitation, while La Niña conditions (positive SOIs) are likely to produce wetter than average winters. The horizontal lines show the average for each SOI category.

Figure 51 shows Water year (October-September) precipitation for Zone 1, the Oregon coast, compared with the previous summer's SOI (by categories), showing a similar relationship.

Temperature

Winter temperatures correlate well with SOI values. In general, negative SOI (El Niño) conditions are associated with mild winter temperatures, while positive SOI values (La Niñas) correlate with a greater likelihood of colder than average winter temperatures. These correlations apply both long term, over monthly and seasonal averages, and short term, for periods of individual days.

Figure 52 shows mean monthly February temperatures at Astoria, compared with the previous October-December average SOI values. El Niño years (negative values) generally result in mild conditions during late winter, while La Niñas are associated with colder temperatures. Figure 53 shows extreme low temperatures in Salem in February, compared with the same October-December SOI averages. Extreme cold events occur almost exclusively during La Niña years.

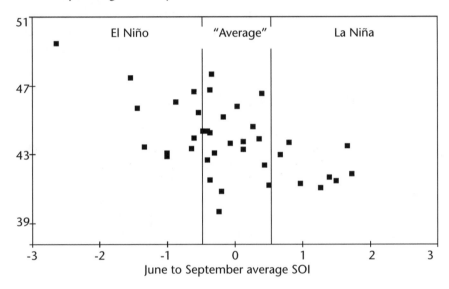

Figure 52. Mean January-March temperature (°F), Astoria, compared with October to December average SOI

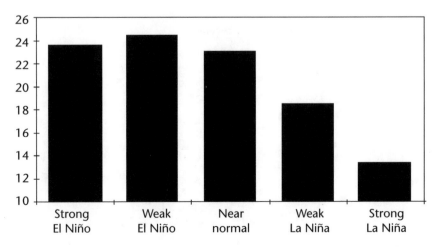

Figure 53. Extreme low temperature (°F), Salem, February, compared with October to December average SOI.

Snowfall

A consistent correlation exists statewide between SOI values and total snowfall. At either end of the SOI distribution (strong El Niños or strong La Niñas), total snowfall in valley locations is relatively low; this is true both east and west of the Cascades. Although years with moderate (near-zero) SOI values may also have low snowfall totals, the years with greatest snowfall occur in conjunction with these moderate values. Figure 54 shows a plot of total snowfall compared with the previous summer SOI values for Hood River, and is typical of low-elevation stations throughout the state.

At high elevations, on the other hand, El Niños tend to have low snowfall (probably because of a combination of high freezing levels and dry conditions), average years tend to have average snowfall, and La Niña years are consistently the biggest snow years. Figure 55 shows plots of total snowfall for five categories of ENSO years at Crater Lake, Government Camp, and Bend; although Bend is in a valley, it is very near the Cascades, its weather is dominated by the mountains, and its elevation is nearly 4,000 feet. Notice the similarity between snow distribution at the three locations.

Effects of ENSO nationwide

ENSO conditions have very different impacts in the northern and southern halves of the U.S. In the southern tier of states, from California on the west to Florida on the east, the wettest winters occur during El Niño years, while La Niñas tend to produce dry winters. The northern states, on the other hand, experience their driest winters during El Niños and the wettest during La Niñas. Figure 56 is a map of precipitation extremes during El Niños during the months of December through February.

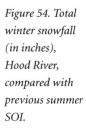

Figure 54. Total winter snowfall (in inches), Hood River, compared with previous summer SOI.

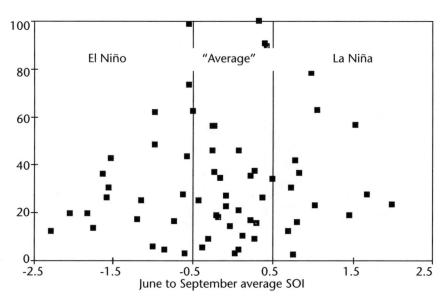

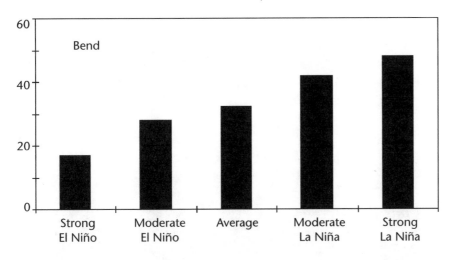

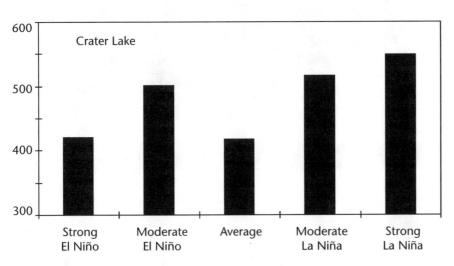

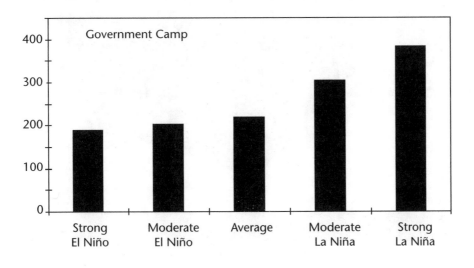

Figure 55. Total snowfall October to March (in inches) compared with ENSO phase at Bend, Crater Lake, and Government Camp.

El Niños generally bring mild winters to the entire West Coast and the northern tier of states as far east as the Great Lakes. Figure 57 shows temperature extremes during El Niños for December through February, and indicates that only in the western Gulf Coast and western Great Plains states are cold winters likely during El Niños.

Figure 56. Precipitation extreme likelihood during El Niño years, Dec-Feb. Green areas receive their wettest winters during El Niños, while orange-red areas receive their driest conditions.

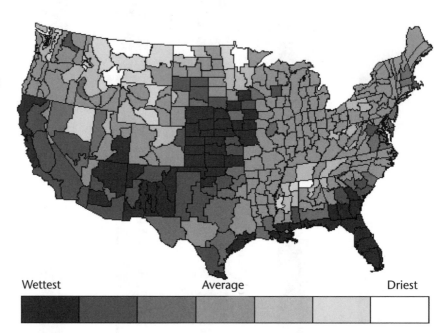

Wettest | Average | Driest

Figure 57. Temperature extreme likelihood during El Niño years, Dec-Feb. Blue-purple areas receive their coldest winters during El Niños, while orange-red areas receive their warmest conditions.

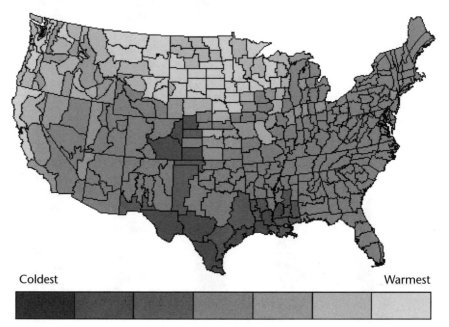

Coldest | Warmest

Implications for Disaster Potential and Emergency Response

As the 1997 El Niño began to unfold, emergency response personnel were warned to take preventive action to mitigate the disasters that were expected to occur. In many cases, these precautions were justified by the very severe weather that affected California and other parts of the U.S. But many areas, including Oregon, were not adversely affected. This should not surprise us, for El Niño winters are generally quite benign here: milder than normal, and with average or below-average precipitation.

Nonetheless, many stern warnings were given to Oregonians. In August 1997, an article appeared in the Los Angeles Times warning of potentially serious weather during the El Niño winter and suggesting that readers prepare their homes and property for heavy rains, mudslides, and flooding. The abundant rains in the area in January and February 1998 are testimonies to accurate forecasts of El Niño's effects. Yet the same article, without modification, ran in the Salem Statesman-Journal, with the headline, "Prepare for a Wild Winter." What's true for California is sometimes completely untrue for Oregon—as it was in this case.

What Oregonians should fear is La Niña. The severe flooding many of us experienced during the winters of 1995-96 and 1996-97 was attributable largely to the effects of La Niña: a combination of heavy snows and warm, intense tropical rain. The tropical moisture arrived in Oregon from the western tropical Pacific, where ocean temperatures were well above normal (La Niña conditions), causing greater evaporation, more extensive clouds, and a greater push of clouds across the Pacific toward the northeast—and during such conditions Oregon is on the receiving end. Severe flooding, the worst in the state since 1964, killed several people and caused widespread property damage. Mudslides and landslides were numerous. The Oregon coast was lashed with strong winds, large surf, and heavy rains. Nearly every river in Oregon reached or exceeded flood stage, some setting all-time records.

Looking back over similar damaging winters in the past, we see that they frequently coincide with La Niñas. There is now evidence that El Niños and La Niñas, which historically occur with about the same frequency, are bunched into periods of 20-25 years, some dominated by El Niños, some by La Niñas. There is also evidence that a regime shift has occurred and that we have moved from an El Niño period (1975-1994) to one with many more La Niñas. This regime will probably resemble that of about 1948 through 1973, a period dominated by cool, wet weather, abundant snows, and floods. Based on what has been observed in such periods in the past, it is likely that about three-quarters of the next twenty years will be wetter than normal.

Watch for La Niña, and be prepared!

Global Climate Change

In this section we answer a number of frequently asked questions on global climate change. Much uncertainty and controversy are associated with the subject of climate change; no one really knows for certain how the climate will change in the future, but we can be certain that it *will* change.

Years ago, author Taylor was involved in the Oregon Task Force on Global Warming, which presented a report to the Legislature outlining ways in which Oregonians could contribute to efforts to reduce the impact of human activities on global climate, mostly through reduction of emissions. We still agree with the basic tenet of that report: we should control and reduce, where feasible, our usage of fossil fuels and the resulting emissions. The report was based on the assumption that human impacts on global climate are and will be very significant. Model predictions from the late 1980s suggested that doubling the CO_2 in the atmosphere would lead to temperature increases of as much as 10°F.

But the more we study the data, rather than trusting the climate models, the less convinced we have become that human-induced global warming is a severe problem. Our attitude on this issue will permeate the answers to questions below, although we have included quotes from others with differing opinions. We cannot pretend to be correct or even objective here; but we can say that our opinions have developed over many years of studying this issue quite thoroughly.

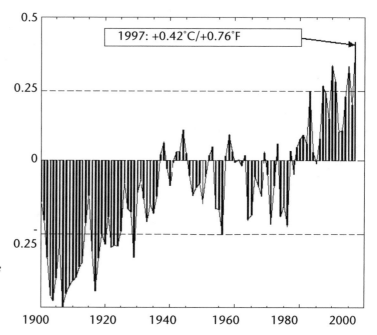

Figure 58. Global temperature change (°C) 1900 to 2000. (National Climatic Data Center/NESDIS/NOAA))

I hear a lot about global warming and the greenhouse effect. Is it really getting warmer?

• What is the greenhouse effect, and is it affecting our climate?

From NCDC: The greenhouse effect is unquestionably real, and is essential for life on Earth. Without it, the temperature of the Earth would be about 0°F (-18°C) instead of its present 57°F (14°C). The greenhouse effect is the result of heat absorption by certain gases in the atmosphere (called greenhouse gases because they trap heat) and re-radiation downward of a part of that heat. Water vapor is the most important greenhouse gas, followed by carbon dioxide and other trace gases.

• How have global temperatures changed in the last century? Over the last twenty years?

Surface temperature data are the only direct measurements we have for the last hundred years. There have been many attempts to quantify the year-to-year changes over that period. One such data set, shown in Figure 58, was published by the U.S. Global Change Research Program. This shows a rise of about 0.5°C from 1880 to 1940, a drop of about 0.2°C from 1940 to the late 1960s, and an increase of about 0.4°C since that time. Much of the increase, especially that for the last thirty years, has been attributed to effects of greenhouse gases.

Some researchers take issue with the trends shown or the conclusions, however. In fact, if one were to ask five researchers, "How have global temperatures changed?" one would probably receive five different answers (see "What is the true temperature of the atmosphere?" below). In particular, the reasons for the observed variations in temperature are being studied and debated within the scientific community.

According to the IPCC, *Global mean surface temperature has increased by between about 0.3 and 0.6°C since the late 19th century, a change that is unlikely to be entirely natural in origin.*

The Earth's surface temperature has warmed about 1°F in the last hundred years, and there is no credible hypothesis for this, other than the net effect of greenhouse gases. —Jerry Mahlman, climate modeler and strong greenhouse warming advocate

Figure 59. U.S. national temperatures, 1895-1997 (°F on left, °C on right). (National Climatic Data Center, NOAA)

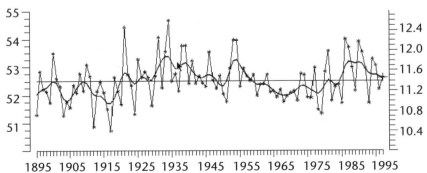

1895 1905 1915 1925 1935 1945 1955 1965 1975 1985 1995

The facts of the present climate change [global cooling] are such that the most optimistic experts would assign near certainty to major crop failures within a decade.—Lowell Ponte, *The Cooling*, 1976

The general economic trend is going to be downhill from now on . . . each decade will be worse than the preceding one for the average American, to say nothing of the average human being.—Paul and Ann Ehrlich, *The End of Affluence*, 1974

. . . a cooling trend has set in—perhaps one akin to the Little Ice Age—and climatic variability can be expected to increase along with the cooling.—Steven Schneider, *The Genesis Strategy*, 1976

There is a finite possibility that a serious worldwide cooling could befall the Earth within the next hundred years—from a U.S. National Academy of Sciences Report, 1975

Interestingly, U.S. temperatures have not seen a significant increase since the late 1930s and early 1940s. Figure 59 shows annual temperatures from the most reliable U.S. stations, as computed by NCDC.

• **When did scientists first start thinking about global warming?**

In the 1970s, following more than two decades of apparent global temperature decreases, many climatologists were predicting a coming Ice Age (see sidebar).

Even if carbon dioxide (CO_2) increases continued, the greenhouse effects on warming atmospheric temperatures were expected to be small.

> *On the short time scale, if CO_2 is augmented by another 10% in the next thirty years, the increase in the global temperature may be as small as +0.1°. An increase by a factor of 8 in the amount of CO_2 (which is highly unlikely in the next several thousand years) will produce an increase in the surface temperature of less than 2°K. However, the effect on surface temperature of an increase in the aerosol content of the atmosphere is found to be quite significant. An increase by a factor of 4 in the equilibrium dust concentration in the global atmosphere, which cannot be ruled out as a possibility within the next century, could decrease the mean surface temperature by as much as 3.5°K. If sustained over a period of several years, such a temperature decrease could be sufficient to trigger an ice age.*—Dr. Stephen Schneider, in 1971 paper on the effect of atmospheric aerosols

Opinions began to change in the 1980s, however, as the multi-decade cooling was replaced by steady warming. One of the first significant statements concerning global warming was made by NASA scientist James Hansen. Speaking to a U.S. Senate Committee in 1988, he said, "With 99% confidence . . . the greenhouse effect has been detected and is changing our climate now."

The prevailing attitude had changed, and predictions of global warming, not cooling, began to dominate.

> *The warming, rapid now, may become even more rapid . . . and it will continue into the indefinite future unless we take deliberate steps to stop it.*
> —R. Houghton and G. Woodell, "Global Climatic Change," *Scientific American*, April 1989

By the year 2000 we are committed to an average global warming of 1.6-4.7° Fahrenheit.—Bill McKibben in *The End of Nature, 1989*, p. 142. [In fact, the net global warming from 1989 to 1997 using either satellite or ground-based temperature measurements is 0.13°F ±0.15°F, or indistinguishable from zero, and less than 10% of McKibben's minimum prediction.—author]

But many scientists questioned the data that were used to derive these conclusions. Some questioned the quality of climate data, especially in developing countries. Others took issue with the way global averages were calculated. Some researchers went through the laborious process of calculating their own averages. U.S. temperature data, arguably the finest such data set in the world, was the most commonly studied. Some statements made by climate experts in 1989 and 1990 appear in the sidebar.

Many scientists who study long-term climate change still think that a coming ice age may be more likely than a long-term warming. Douglas Hoyt, a prominent solar researcher, has published a possible future scenario based on long-term changes in the atmosphere, the sun, and geological records. It is shown in Figure 60.

There appears to have been little or no global warming over the past century.—MIT Technology Review, 1989

There is no statistically significant evidence of an overall increase in annual temperature or change in annual precipitation for the contiguous U.S.A., 1895-1987.—Thomas Karl et al., NOAA, 1989

We looked at a thousand stations in the United States that came from very small towns averaging no more than about 5,800 people. We looked at the temperature patterns over this century and found that most of the United States has cooled this century, not warmed.—Dr. Robert Balling, University of Arizona, 1990

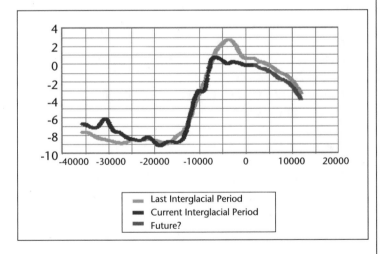

Figure 60. A possible trend in global climate (temperature in °C). (Douglas Hoyt)

There is no reason not to anticipate the onset of the next cycle of ninety thousand years of glaciation beginning at any time. In this context, I find it remarkable that one rarely, if ever, hears the suggestion that increased carbon dioxide in the atmosphere is just what is needed to prevent or delay the onset of the next period of glaciation which, if anything, is apparently already overdue, or already in progress.—Dr. Hugh Ellsaesser, 13 February 1990

If there is global warming, what is causing it?

It is clear that there are a number of reasons for climatic change. Among those suggested as being especially significant are:

- Changes in Earth's orbit or axis
- Changes in solar radiation
- Pacific Ocean temperatures (including ENSO)
- Volcanic activity
- Human activities

While it is almost impossible to quantify the contribution of each to changes in Earth's climate, one can analyze each variable independently and come to some conclusions about the relative contribution of the various factors.

• Changes in Earth's orbit or axis

The theory that changes in Earth's orbit are responsible for variations in temperature is known as the "Milankovitch theory" after Milutin Milankovitch, who first suggested the idea in the 1930s. There are three separate irregularities in Earth's rotation and revolution about the sun that can affect climate:

Changes in the shape of the Earth's orbit (*eccentricity*), from nearly circular to more elliptical, over periods of about a hundred thousand years. The more elliptical the orbit, the greater the variation in annual temperatures. Currently the eccentricity is low (the orbit is nearly circular), causing the seasonal solar difference to be about 7% between winter and summer; at its maximum, solar radiation can change by about 20% as a result of eccentricity.

A slight wobble in the Earth's axis, known as *precession*, occurs in a cycle of about twenty-three thousand years. Currently, the earth is closer to the sun in January than in July, but in eleven thousand years the reverse will be the case. At that time, winters in the northern hemisphere will be colder than at present, and summers warmer.

Changes in the tilt of the Earth's axis, or *obliquity*, operate on a forty-one-thousand-year cycle, and range from 22.5 to 24.5° (currently it is 23.5°). The smaller the tilt, the smaller the seasonal variations between winter and summer.

• **Changes in solar radiation**

Recently there has been a great deal of research on long-term variations in solar radiation and the effects of those variations on climate. Since actual solar data go back only several hundred years, longer-term records are based on various kinds of "proxy" data—ice cores, tree rings, and other records that enable researchers to estimate the actual solar variations.

The two dominant short-term variations involve sunspots and the Sun's magnetic field. Sunspots vary over an eleven-year cycle that is very consistent temporally but that varies considerably in intensity. Figure 61 shows the annual number of sunspots since 1701. The Sun's magnetic field, on the other hand, has an irregular period, varying from about twenty to twenty-seven years. These two changes cause measurable variations in solar irradiance, or radiation received by the Earth's atmosphere.

Past sunspot cycles have correlated strongly with global temperature changes. Active periods in the cycle (with large numbers of sunspots) have coincided with general increases in temperatures. This makes sense from an energy standpoint, since large numbers of sunspots indicate increased solar radiation. Figure 62 shows global temperatures plotted against sunspot numbers since 1600.

The magnetic field has shown similar effects on global temperatures, with longer magnetic field length corresponding to periods of generally rising temperatures. Figure 63 shows global temperatures since 1865 plotted with magnetic field half-length. Figure 64 shows Northern Hemisphere temperatures and solar irradiance; again, the correspondence is striking.

As solar research continues, we will learn more about the variation of the Sun's energy output over time and better understand the nature of its effects on temperature. For now, we will be content to quote Dr. Judith Lean, a prominent solar researcher at the Naval Research Laboratory:

> *We figure half the climate change from 1850 to now can be accounted for by the Sun.*

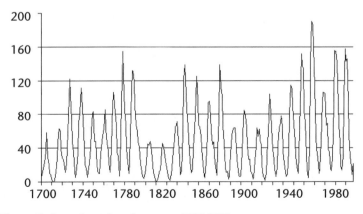

Figure 61. Annual number of sunspots, 1700-1980

179

Figure 62. A comparison of global temperature anomalies (˚C) with sunspot numbers, 1600 to present.

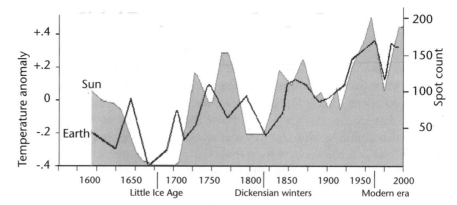

Figure 63. A comparison of global temperatures (˚C) with magnetic field length, 1865 to present. (Meteorologiske Institut, Denmark)

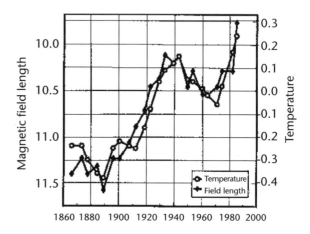

Figure 64. A comparison of Northern Hemisphere temperature anomalies (˚C) and solar irradiance, 1750 to present.

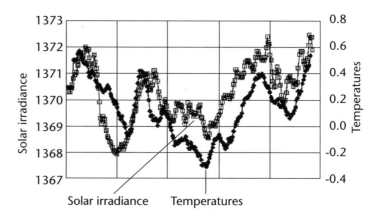

180

• Pacific Ocean temperatures

The Pacific Ocean has been called "the largest terrestrial source of heat to the atmosphere." The Pacific occupies nearly half the Earth's surface, and has a huge area of very warm water (in the tropics and subtropics, mostly in the eastern half of the basin) that supplies tremendous amounts of heat and moisture to the atmosphere. It has been found that significant variations in Pacific temperatures occur, mostly in association with the El Niño-Southern Oscillation. In general, basin-wide temperatures in the Pacific are higher than average during El Niño events and lower than average during La Niñas. El Niños, then, would tend to have a net warming effect on the atmosphere, and La Niñas a cooling effect.

Figure 65 shows variations in tropical Pacific temperatures and air temperatures from 1874 to 1984. Notice how periods of increased ocean temperatures have corresponded to increases in air temperatures, both in the short-term and long-term. Warm years (and decades) in ocean temperatures have seen warming in the atmosphere as well.

The discovery that the frequency of El Niños changes over periods of several decades suggests that much of the variation in global air temperatures over the last century may have resulted from cyclical variations in ocean currents (see Long-term Wet-Dry Cycles in Oregon).

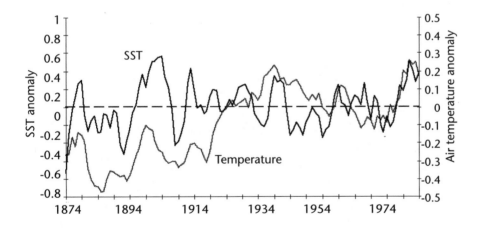

Figure 65. Variations in tropical Pacific temperatures (SST = sea surface temperature) and global air temperatures (°C), 1874-1984.

• Volcanic activity

The effects of volcanoes on global climate have been studied for some time. The general effect is to reduce global temperatures; the large amounts of dust and ash in the atmosphere following a major eruption cause a significant increase in the reflectivity of the atmosphere. In effect, volcanic dust acts just the way increased cloudiness would: by reflecting a greater percentage of the Sun's radiation than would occur during clear sky conditions, thereby reducing heating in the lower atmosphere.

Figure 66 shows the combined effects of sea surface temperature and volcanic activity on global air temperatures since 1979 (from NASA satellites). The plot uses the inverse of the SOI (see El Niño chapter) and global temperature anomalies. In nearly every case, increases in the SOI value coincide with increases in air temperatures; actually, changes in SOI *precede* air temperature changes, suggesting a cause-effect relationship. But notice the hatched areas, coinciding with the big El Chichon and Pinatubo volcanic eruptions. Despite a concurrent El Niño, both periods saw little or no increase in atmospheric temperatures (in fact, global temperatures decreased following the Pinatubo eruption). During the 1997 El Niño, no such eruption occurred, and temperatures were the highest of the entire record. Were it not for the eruptions, the 1982-83 and 1991-93 periods would probably have been as warm as or warmer than in 1997, but the effects of the eruptions suppressed the air temperatures.

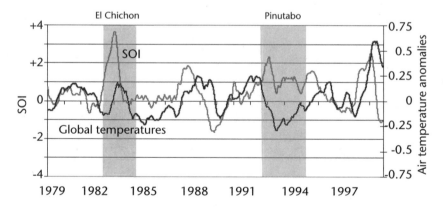

Figure 66. The combined effects of sea surface temperature and volcanic activity on global air temperatures (°C).

• Human activities

Are human activities affecting global air temperatures? To what degree? That's the main question in this entire chapter, and one that you will have to decide for yourself.

The data, so far, can be explained by natural climate variations. It would be better to tell people the truth instead of keeping them upset with false arguments. This whole affair stems from the European mentality: everything that changes is dangerous.—Reinhard Bohm, Austrian Central Institute for Meteorology and Geodynamics.

If the wind trends [i.e., the equatorial Pacific trade winds are weakening] reflect greenhouse warming, it must be concluded that the anomalous 1990s are not caused by greenhouse warming.—M. Latif et al., *Journal of Climate*, September 1997

Isotopic records indicate that solar activity today is similar to that of the Medieval Warm Period of about a thousand years ago. In the interim, during the Maunder Minimum about three hundred years ago, solar irradiance is estimated to have been approximately 0.1-0.7% lower than today. Much of the decrease in irradiance appears to have been in the UVb range, and hence could have caused a cooling force through a total atmospheric ozone concentration decrease of about 4%. Values at the upper end of estimates for reduced irradiance could be enough to fully explain temperature trends over the past century.—Climate Change Newsletter, July 1997

Are human activities influencing climate? Yes, of course. The rise of agriculture and the growth of cities have changed the local climate significantly. With increasing populations and rising industrial activity there have also been some worldwide changes: temperature extremes have softened, the stratosphere is cooling, the frequency of hurricanes has been diminishing—all of these are thought to be human influences on the atmosphere. But this does not mean there will be a catastrophic or even a substantial warming of the climate in the next century.—Dr. Fred Singer, the Science and Environmental Policy Project

How is the global climate changing? How can we measure and predict change?

• Is weather becoming more extreme?

The IPCC report (1995) suggests that if the climate is changing noticeably due to anthropogenic causes, then extreme weather events, particularly heavy precipitation events and drought, would be expected to increase. A study* performed at the National Climatic Data Center indicates that heavier precipitation events are increasing in the United States.

> *All these escalating climate extremes share a common source, according to the overwhelming consensus of scientific thought: they are nature's expressions of the early stages of the heating of the atmosphere.*—Ross Gelbspan, *The Heat is On, p. 3*

According to the IPCC,

> *Potentially serious changes have been identified, including an increase in some regions in the incidence of extreme high temperature events, floods, and droughts, with resultant consequences for fires, pest outbreaks, and ecosystem composition, structure, and functioning, including primary productivity.*—IPCC Second Assessment Synthesis of Scientific-Technical Information relevant to interpreting Article 2 of the UN Framework Convention on Climate Change

Yet IPCC also says, "Overall, there is no evidence that extreme weather events, or climate variability, have increased in a global sense, through the 20th century" (*Climate Change 1995: The Science of Climate Change.* Cambridge, England: Cambridge University Press).

According to Accu-Weather, one of the nation's largest private weather consulting firms,

> *No convincing observational evidence has been found to show that hurricanes, violent tornadoes, and other extreme events are more common now than they were fifty or a hundred years ago. The greater attention now paid to severe weather events may simply reflect three non-weather related facts:*

Currently, our best understanding is that natural internal variations of annual mean temperature may account for plus or minus about 0.2°C, and solar variations may account for perhaps 0.2°C of the 20th-century warming. So, at a stretch, it is possible that a substantial portion of the observed 0.6°C warming might have been caused by non-human agency.—Kevin Trenberth, National Center for Atmospheric Research, February 4, 1998

On a global scale there is little evidence of sustained trends in climate variability or extremes. This perhaps reflects inadequate data and a dearth of analyses. However, on regional scales, there is clear evidence of changes in variability or extremes.

In areas where a drought usually accompanies an El Niño, droughts have been more frequent in recent years. Other than these areas and the few areas with longer term trends to lower rainfall (e.g., the Sahel), little evidence is

---

* Karl, T. R., R. W. Knight, 1998: Secular Trends of Precipitation Amount, Frequency, and Intensity in the United States. *Bulletin of the American Meteorological Society, 79*, 231-241.

(1) more people live in areas that were once sparsely populated or even uninhabited; (2) local media are now able to quickly report severe weather events that are occurring, or have just occurred, in distant parts of the globe; and (3) more sophisticated weather monitoring systems and a more widely distributed population mean that extreme events in remote areas are more likely to be detected.

The number of deaths in the United States caused by extreme weather disasters declined during the latter part of the century, but the values of property damage increased. This reflects both the improvements made in systems for detecting and providing early warning of danger, and the fact that more people are populating areas where severe weather is likely to occur.

And here's a cautionary note from one of the chief contributors to the IPCC climate analyses:

It is easy to fool oneself into thinking that an unusual number of extremes has occurred. Conversely, detecting (in a statistical sense) a significant change in the frequency of extremes is a difficult task—the changes have to be larger than one might imagine in order to get a significant result.—Tom Wigley, IPCC participant, September 12, 1995

In Oregon, there is no evidence that weather severity is increasing.

available of changes in drought frequency or intensity.

In some areas there is evidence of increases in the intensity of extreme rainfall events, but no clear global pattern has emerged. Despite the occurrence in recent years of several regional-scale extreme floods there is no evidence of widespread changes in flood frequency. This may reflect the dearth of studies, definition problems, and/or difficulties in distinguishing the results of land use changes from meteorological effects.

There is some evidence of recent (since 1988) increases in extreme extratropical cyclones over the North Atlantic. Intense tropical cyclone activity in the Atlantic appeared to have decreased over the previous few decades. Elsewhere, changes in observing systems confound the detection of trends in the intensity or frequency of extreme synoptic systems.

There has been a clear trend in recent decades, however, to fewer extremely low minimum temperatures in several widely separated areas. Significant changes in extreme high temperature events have not been observed.

There is some indication of a decrease in day-to-day temperature variability in recent decades.—NCDC

• Do changes in glacier size indicate global temperature change?

Some people say so. For instance:

The Associated Press
Wednesday, 27 May, 1998
GLOBAL WARMING SPEEDING UP GLACIERS' MELTING
BOSTON (AP)—All of the glaciers in Glacier National Park in Montana will be gone in the next fifty to seventy years, according to researchers who have been measuring the rate that glaciers are melting around the world. Those glaciers are melting faster than scientists had previously thought, according to the study by geologist Mark Meier, who presented his findings at a meeting of the American Geophysical Union in Boston on Tuesday.

"The glaciers are receding and they're becoming thinner, and you can see this," Meier said, placing the blame squarely on global warming. The melting ice caps are contributing to rising sea levels that lead to beach erosion and more severe inland storms, he said. And rivers are jumping their banks more often as a result.

On the other hand, according to the Science and Environmental Policy Project,

The AP story doesn't say (and perhaps the Meier research paper doesn't say either) how the rate of glacier recession varied over the last century. If recession was initially rapid and then slowed, then it is very likely the result of the rapid rise in temperature between 1860 and 1940 as the Earth recovered from the Little Ice Age—and not from any global warming due to higher concentrations of CO_2.

And indeed there is some evidence of that. The World Glacier Monitoring Service in Zurich, Switzerland, in a paper published in Science in 1989, noted that between 1926 and 1960 more than 70% of 625 mountain glaciers in the [mid-latitude] United States, Soviet Union, Iceland, Switzerland, Austria, and Italy were retreating. After 1980, however, 55% of these same glaciers were advancing.

As glaciologist Keith Echelmeyer of the University of Alaska's Geophysical Institute noted in September 1997 (when Vice President Albert Gore made an issue of glacier recession in Glacier National Park): "To

*make a case that glaciers are retreating, and that the problem is
global warming, is very hard to do. The physics are very complex.
There is much more involved than just the climate response."
Echelmeyer pointed out that, in Alaska, some large glaciers
continue to advance in the very same areas where most are
retreating.*

• Is sea level rising? Does that imply global warming?

Answers: 1. Yes. 2. Not necessarily.

Let us explain. The IPCC synopsis states, "Global sea level has risen by
between 10 and 25 cm [approximately 3³/₄-9³/₄ inches] over the past
hundred years and much of the rise may be related to the increase in global
mean temperature." And Robert T. Watson, IPCC Chairman, said, "We'll see
sea level rise that could displace tens of millions of people . . . and whole
islands . . . could be significantly inundated. The shorelines of America
could be severely attacked."

In 1998, the results of a study of Pacific Ocean sea levels was published in
the refereed journal *Coastal Research*; see Figure 67. Sea levels have indeed
risen in the last century, corresponding to the general warmup seen in other
records. On the other hand, sea levels a thousand years ago (during the very
warm period generally called the Climate Optimum) were considerably
higher than at present. Interestingly, if one were to fit a straight-line best fit
to the graph in Figure 67, there would be a slight downward trend over the
last 1,200 years.

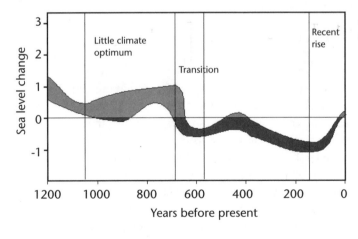

Figure 67. Pacific Ocean level (in meters), 1200 to present.

The models may be agreeing now simply because they're all tending to do the same thing wrong. It is not clear to me that we have clouds right by any stretch of the imagination.—Robert Cess, *Science,* 1997

The climate modelers have been "cheating" for so long, it's almost become respectable.—Richard Kerr, discussing flux adjustments in climate models in *Science,* 1997

The models do not agree among themselves at climatologically significant levels in their treatment of the energy balance.—ARM statement

Greenhouse warming is entirely forced by a radiative perturbation of a few Watts per square meter or less, yet neither field measurements nor radiation model intercomparisons had ever achieved anywhere near this level of accuracy, at least not in the atmospheric and climate community.—Robert G. Ellingson and Warren J. Wiscombe, March 1996

I have seen no convincing evidence that recent sea level rises are caused by human effects or global warming—Dr. David Aubrey, oceanographer and senior scientist with the Woods Hole Oceanographic Institute in Massachusetts

Scientists studying rising sea levels on the East Coast made a startling discovery. It's not just that the sea is climbing—the land is falling, too. New research shows the level of the mid-Atlantic coast is falling as a bulge formed by Ice Age glaciers slowly settles. That, combined with apparent rising sea levels, means the ocean is encroaching on the Chesapeake Bay region at a rate of about 1 inch every eight years. The findings have broad implications in the debate about sea level changes blamed on global warming. Scientists have warned that warming caused by carbon dioxide and industrial gases is melting glaciers and will raise the sea level by between 6 inches and 3 feet over the next hundred years. But nearly half the sites where sea level was measured in a pivotal 1991 study of this problem were on the East Coast of the United States, where the uneven settling of land may have exaggerated the apparent rise in water.—*Detroit News,* January 29, 1996

• Can we trust the climate models?

In 1988, Dr. James Hansen, testifying before the U.S. Senate, said, "With 99% confidence . . . the greenhouse effect has been detected and is changing our climate now." This was the statement that, more than any other, ignited the global warming debate that continues to this day. Hansen based his predictions of large increases in temperatures in the next century, perhaps as much as 8°C, on climate modeling. Ten years later, however, Hansen said, "The forcings that drive long-term climate change are not known with an accuracy sufficient to define future climate change." (*Proceedings of the National Academy of Sciences,* October, 1998)

Climate models are highly simplified representations of the atmosphere; the complexity of the atmosphere and computational limits of computers make it impossible to simulate the global atmosphere with a high degree of detail. Climate models are a useful tool for assessing and predicting atmospheric processes, but their limitations are well known. The quotes in the sidebars on this and the following pages address the issue of climate model performance.

• **Can we accurately measure the temperature of the atmosphere?**

The atmosphere is very complex and quite deep, and our ability to measure temperatures has been quite limited. In Oregon, we have fairly reliable measurements for about the last hundred years. The most common (and oldest) method involves thermometers at the Earth's surface, mostly manually read. The biggest advantage of surface thermometers is their long period of record; they are also useful because they are collected where people live. But there are several major disadvantages of surface measurements:

Urban Bias. The effects of urban activities—including transportation, space heating, and industry—can be quite strong locally, and can bias surface temperature measurements (in nearly all cases, the bias is positive).

Quality Control. Much time and effort goes into quality control of atmospheric measurements, but there remain many factors that can bias temperature measurements, including instrument problems and operator error.

Manual Nature of the Measurements. The bulk of observations are collected by unpaid observers who read thermometers and record the observations manually. This can lead to consistency problems, gaps in the data, and reporting errors.

Spatial Inhomogeneity. Globally, the vast majority of measurements are in or near population centers. While Europe and North America are quite well covered, other areas (oceanic areas, tropics, poles, underdeveloped countries) have far fewer measurements.

Surface Only. Most weather systems affect the entire troposphere (surface to about 40,000 feet), but surface measurements monitor only the "skin" of the troposphere. Weather forecasters generally focus on the upper atmosphere (5,000 - 20,000 feet above sea level) because surface weather measurements are not representative of large-scale conditions in the atmosphere.

Changes in Technology. Temperature measurement has changed significantly in the last hundred years. Early in this century, mercury-in-glass thermometers were typical, but it was found that over time they shrink slightly (causing positive

It is clear that we are not yet in a position where we can predict global warming effects with any real accuracy.—John E. Harries, Chair of Earth Observations, Imperial College, London

We believe the problem resides in the computer models and in our past assumptions that the atmosphere is so well behaved. These models just don't handle processes like clouds, water vapor, and precipitation systems well enough to accurately predict how strong global warming will be, or how it will manifest itself at different heights in the atmosphere.—Roy Spencer, NASA

Not surprisingly, there are many problems involved in modeling climate. For example, even supercomputers are inadequate to allow long-term integrations of the relevant equations at adequate spatial resolutions. At presently available resolutions, it is unlikely that the computer solutions are close to the solutions of the underlying equations. In addition, the physics of unresolved phenomena such as clouds and other turbulent elements is not understood to the extent needed for incorporation into models. In view of those problems, it is generally recognized that models are at present experimental tools whose relation to the real world is questionable.—Richard Lindzen, Massachusetts Institute of Technology

Climate models are recognized as being rather poorly validated primarily because of (earlier) lack of computer power and a continuing lack of adequate observational data (Gates et al., 1990). Although both issues are steadily being solved, it seems unlikely that very high levels of confidence in climate model projections are achievable within the next decade.—MECCA Analysis Project, 1997

bias in measurements). Gradually they were replaced by alcohol instruments. In recent decades, automated instruments have gradually replaced many of the manual observations.

Fortunately, other types of temperature measurement can be used to augment or replace surface measurement. The two most significant are data collected by weather balloons ("Rawinsondes"), launched from weather stations worldwide, which report conditions from the surface to the top of the atmosphere; and data from NASA polar-orbiting satellites, which report integrated temperatures through a deep layer in the atmosphere.

The biggest advantage of these forms of temperature measurement is their ability to report temperature in the upper atmosphere, not just at the surface; for that reason, urban biases are not a problem. In addition, the measurements are consistent and less affected by manual operations. On the other hand, they have been collecting data for only about forty years and twenty years, respectively. Table 51 summarizes the three temperature measurement techniques.

In addition to these three direct measurements , there are ways of inferring atmospheric temperatures from other data. For example, ice cores, tree rings, and other "paleoclimate" data can provide useful information which can augment direct measurements and extend them back many years in time.

Table 51. Comparison of methods for measuring the temperature of the Earth's atmosphere

Platform	Advantages	Disadvantages
Surface	• long period of record • where people live • in-situ	• urban bias • poor QC • manual • spatially inhomo-geneous • surface only • changes in technology
Satellites	• global • homogeneous • entire troposphere	• short period • remote
Rawinsonde	• entire troposphere • fairly long record (40 yrs) • in-situ	• not homogeneous

• Can we find out anything about ancient climates on Earth?

We can learn quite a lot from ice cores. It is clear that climate has changed significantly in the past, long before human activities became significant. Ice cores collected from Vostok, Antarctica, show data from the last 160,000 years. By analyzing air bubbles in the ice, and the various chemical isotopes in the bubbles, scientists have been able to estimate temperatures and carbon dioxide for the entire period. Some charts (see Figure 68) purport to show a direct relationship between carbon dioxide and temperature and suggest that:

1. Carbon dioxide increases in the past have coincided with temperature increases;

2. It is almost certain that carbon dioxide will increase in the future;

3. Therefore, temperature is likely to rise.

Recently, scientists have published reports that address short-term changes in carbon dioxide and temperature in the ice cores. The conclusion: temperature changes have occurred first, and carbon dioxide increases have apparently followed (and thus been caused by) temperature changes. Figure 69 illustrates this relationship.

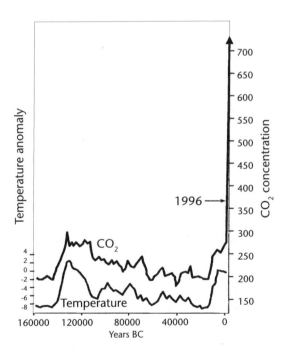

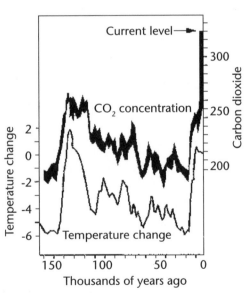

Figure 68. Relationship between temperature anomalies (°C) and CO2 concentration in the atmosphere (parts per million). Data from Antarctic ice cores.

Figure 69. Relationship between temperature change (°C) and carbon dioxide (parts per million) in Antarctic ide core.

What effects would global warming have?

• Would global warming cause more droughts or floods?

It depends on whom you talk to. On the one hand,

> *[If global legislation is not passed, the world will see] more record floods and droughts. Diseases and pests spreading to new areas. Crop failures and famines.*—Vice President Al Gore, Kyota, December 1997

On the other,

> *Nobody can say today with any authority if droughts or floods follow from global warming. It simply cannot be done.*—Dr. Ingeborg Auer, Austrian Central Institute for Meterology and Geodynamics

According to the IPCC,

> *As the world warms, some extreme climate events, like the frequency of heat waves and very heavy precipitation, are expected to increase, but it remains uncertain whether or not to expect changes in the frequency of some other extremes. Moreover, it is important to note that it is not possible to link any particular weather or climate event definitively to global warming.*— Common Questions about Climate Change, United Nations Environment Programme, World Meteorological Organization (Web site)

• Is there any evidence that global climate change would produce more El Niños?

Some researchers have opined that we may move into a "permanent El Niño" situation if global warming occurs. Dr. Tim Barnett, one of the world's premier El Niño researchers, puts that matter to rest quite handily: "As you increase CO_2 [in the atmosphere], you don't see any increase in El Niños."

NCDC says that El Niños are not caused by global warming. Clear evidence exists from a variety of sources (including archaeological studies) that El Niños have been present for hundreds, and some indicators suggest maybe millions, of years. However, it has been hypothesized that warmer global sea surface temperatures can enhance the El Niño phenomenon, and it is also true that El Niños have been more frequent and intense in recent decades.

• **Would diseases become more prevalent in a warmer world?**

Some health officials have warned that a warmer planet would cause increases in certain tropical diseases, such as yellow fever and dengue fever, by increasing the area of warm climates favored by disease-carrying insects and other organisms.

> *"A case of malaria," Mr. Gore noted darkly at the [White House global warming] conference, "showed up in Detroit during a month when the average temperature was a full 6° warmer than the thirty-year average." But the Detroit Health Department's records show that although five cases of malaria have been reported in Detroit in recent months, not one was contracted locally. In all five instances the patients contracted the disease while traveling in Africa or other tropical regions.*—Detroit News, October 19, 1997

> *If temperature was the main factor, we would see epidemics in the southern U.S. We have the mosquito; we have higher temperatures and constant introduction of viruses, which means we should have epidemics, but we don't.*—Duane Gubler, Director of the Division of Vector-borne Infectious Diseases at the Centers for Disease Control and Prevention (CDC)

> *Gubler adds that the evidence to date suggests that lifestyle and public health measures such as mosquito control far outweigh any effects of climate. Epstein, for instance, attributes Latin American dengue epidemics in 1994 and 1995 in part to El Niño and the more gradual rise in global temperatures, both of which might have favored the spread of the mosquito. But dengue experts at PAHO and the CDC say the epidemics resulted from the breakdown of eradication programs aimed at Aedes aegypti [the mosquito responsible for sperading the disease] in the 1970s, and the subsequent return of the mosquito. Once the mosquito was back, they say, the dengue followed.*—Gary Taube, Science, November 1997

New Scientist

Letter to the Editor: "Don't blame the heat"

By Dr. Paul Reiter

"Human disease is emerging as one of the most distressing indicators of climate change," claims a box in your article on the weather in 1998 ("Can't stand the heat," 19 December 1998, p. 33).

I am concerned with the inaccuracy of this box. You write: "As temperatures rise, mosquito-borne yellow fever has invaded Ethiopia." Not so. The disease is endemic in the region, and the world's most devastating non-urban epidemic occurred there in 1960-61, killing 15,000 people.

"Dengue fever is spreading through the Americas and has reached Texas," you continue. True, but there is no reason to blame climate change. The principal vector, *Aedes aegypti,* was eliminated from 22 countries of the Americas during an eradication campaign in the 1950s. The mosquito and the dengue virus are simply reclaiming their old territory.

In the past two centuries, Texas weathered eight major dengue epidemics. In 1922, there were an estimated 500,000 cases. By contrast, there were only 46 confirmed cases between 1980 and 1996, although in the same period, 50,333 were reported in three Mexican states that lie along its border. We attribute the rarity of dengue north of the Rio Grande to better living conditions and lifestyle (piped water, mosquito screens, air conditioning, TV dinners), not the weather.

Lastly: "Flood waters caused Rift Valley fever, a cattle disease, to jump the species barrier and kill hundreds of people." Again, nothing new. Numerous outbreaks, typically during excessively rainy periods, have been documented throughout Africa. Human cases have usually been evident, sometimes with significant mortality.

A continued increase in global temperatures may well affect the transmission of insect-borne diseases, but to date there is no evidence to support the claims you quote.

Paul Reiter
Centers for Disease Control
San Juan
Puerto Rico

• **Are there possible beneficial effects of global warming?**

Some researchers point to a possible longer growing season. Others suggest fewer crop failures in a warmer world. Here's a concise statement:

> *So, would global warming be good or bad? Probably both; but overall, warming is definitely better than cooling. It is certainly better for agriculture and therefore for basic human existence. All historical evidence shows that during the warm periods of the Middle Ages (around 1100 AD) people were better off than during the hard times of the Little Ice Age (1450-1850), when crops failed and people starved.*—Fred Singer, The Science & Environmental Policy Project

What do the experts say about climate change?

The Intergovernmental Panel on Climate Change (IPCC) was established in 1988 by the World Meteorological Organization and the United Nations Environment Programme to assess the available scientific, technical, and socio-economic information in the field of climate change. The IPCC is organised into three working groups: Working Group I concentrates on the climate system, Working Group II on impacts and response options, and Working Group III on economic and social dimensions.

The IPCC released its Second Assessment Report in 1995 and continues to produce technical papers and develop methodologies (e.g., national greenhouse gas inventories) for use by parties to the Climate Change Convention. The Third Assessment Report will be completed around the year 2000.

The major conclusions of the 1995 report are as follows:

1. **Greenhouse gas concentrations have continued to increase.**

2. **Anthropogenic aerosols tend to produce negative radiative forcings.**

3. **Climate has changed over the past century.**

4. **The balance of evidence suggests a discernible human influence on global climate.**

5. **Climate is expected to continue to change in the future.**

6. **There are still many uncertainties.**

It is simply impossible, with today's state of knowledge, to predict what will happen in a hundred years.—Dr. Michael Kuhn, head of the Institute for Meteorology and Geodynamics at the University of Innsbruck

It is clear that we are not yet in a position where we can predict global warming effects with any real accuracy.—John E. Harries, Chair of Earth Observations, Imperial College, London

• What do the State Climatologists say?

Table 52 shows the results of a summer 1997 survey:

Table 52. Percentage of state climatologists agreeing with various statements on global climate change.

Statement	Percent in agreement
Recent global warming is a largely natural phenomenon.	72
Scientific evidence indicates variations in global temperature are like to be naturally-occuring and cyclical over very long periods of time.	90
The overwhelming balance of evidence and scientific opinon is that it is no longer a theory, but now fact, that global warming is for real.	36
Actions by developed nations to reduce man-made carbon dioxide emissions by 15 percent below 1990 levels will prevent global temperatures from rising.	40
Current science is unable to isolate and measure variations in global temperatures caused only by man-made factors.	89
Weather events in their states in the past 25 years have not been more severe or frequent.	72

State climatologists, for the most part, are "data people" rather than modelers. That is, they study data records, assess cause-and-effect relationships, and analyze trends over time. They are also quite familiar with data quality issues, and are unlikely to treat all data equally. Interferences to measurements, such as urban heating effects, may cause them to reject or disregard certain information. While state climatologists can and do use climate models, they tend to be cautious about making recommendations based on model results, especially when model output differs from measurements.

Author Taylor, as President of the American Association of State Climatologists, has discussed this issue frequently with colleagues. The survey above, conducted by a national survey institute, appears to accurately reflect what seems to be the prevailing opinion among state climatologists: global climate trends are largely natural in origin and, while human impact on the planet is unmistakable, human-induced global warming will likely be of much smaller magnitude than the natural variations.

• What are the political ramifications of global warming?

It's unfortunate that the political aspects of this issue even need to be addressed, but one quickly reaches the conclusion that there are strong political motivations for each side of the global warming issue. As so often happens, extreme points of view tend to dominate the media and influence public opinion. One extreme suggests that the world is heading for oblivion, largely through the activities of the human race. The other extreme seems to adopt the attitudes that (1) human influence on the environment is minimal, and (2) economics and commerce are more important than the environment anyway. We disagree with both viewpoints, suggesting instead a balanced strategy that would encourage emission control while maintaining a strong economy (assuming that a vigorous economy is better able to afford and implement emission control measures). The following are some politically oriented statements made by others in regard to this issue.

A global climate treaty must be implemented even if there is no scientific evidence to back the greenhouse effect.—Richard Benedict, State Department employee working on assignment from the Conservation Foundation

We've got to ride the global warming issue. Even if the theory of global warming is wrong, we will be doing the right thing—in terms of economic policy and environmental policy.—Timothy Wirth, former U.S. Senator (D-Colorado)

Fossil fuels are a bad idea, whether they are related to global warming or not.—Luke Alexander, CNN post, December 8, 1997
To me it doesn't matter if global warming is real or not.—Ruth Brown, CNN post, December 5, 1997

The trouble with this idea is that planting trees will not lead to the societal changes we want to achieve.—Unidentified Kyoto delegate, December 5, 1997

I think that we, as the United States, must push for a global warming treaty so other countries will do the same. If we don't, it may lead to global destruction and the end of the human race.—Travis Scott, November 8, 1997, *The Examiner*

What should be done? The ideal approach would be scrap the whole fossil fuel economy, lock, stock, and parking garage.—Joseph Petulla, *San Francisco Examiner*, 27 October 1997

The real threat to Mr. Gore's Kyoto dreams is if Americans begin to doubt there's any real threat. If no one can be sure that humans are causing the Earth to warm, or even how much of a problem it is if it does warm, what's the point of breaking a political sweat? This is

why Mr. Gore and his aides are so dismissive and caustic toward anyone who doubts their claims or disputes their evidence.—Paul Gigot, *Wall Street Journal*, December 12, 1997

Knowledge about climate change is so uncertain at present that the argument in favour of reducing greenhouse gas emissions such as to compromise the economy and society is based on very precarious information indeed.—Dr. Brian Tucker, former head of the CSIRO research group on the greenhouse effect.

To capture the public imagination, we have to offer up some scary scenarios, make simplified dramatic statements and little mention of any doubts one might have. Each of us has to decide the right balance between being effective, and being honest.—Dr. Stephen Schneider, NCAR, in interview for *Discover magazine*, October 1989

The issue of the "greenhouse effect" has assumed a peculiar life of its own. Politicians, government officials, and various policy specialists cling with remarkable tenacity to the notion that this is a proven and intolerable danger about which there is scientific unanimity. At the same time, one has no difficulty hearing the muttering in the corridors of any meteorology department that this is an issue that has gotten out of hand, that the claims are insupportable, that the models are inadequate, and the data contradictory.—Prof. Richard Lindzen (MIT), May 1989

Would you walk down the road towards a policy which people have rightly said requires an economic restructuring of the world, knowing that the world was doing the opposite to what the basis for that policy said?—Prof. Patrick Michaels, University of Virginia, 1991

It's easier to get funding if you can show some evidence for impending climate disasters. In the late 1970s it was the coming ice age. Who knows what it will be ten years from now. Sure, science benefits from scary scenarios.—Dr. Roy Spencer, NASA, 1990 TV interview

A lot of people are getting very famous and very well funded as a result of promoting the disastrous scenario of greenhouse warming.—Prof. Sherwood Idso, University of Arizona, 1990

My suspicion is that if you have a crisis like this, it's easier to gain funds for the profession as a whole.—Prof. Reginald Newell, MIT, 1990

PART 7

Appendices

Climate "Normals"

At various places in this book, climate "normals" are listed. The following discussion, provided by the National Climatic Data Center (NCDC), describes the basis for climatic normals, how and when they are updated, and which parameters are included.

Introduction

Climate is an important factor for agriculture, commerce, industry, and transportation. It is a natural resource that affects many human activities such as farming, fuel consumption, structural design, building site location, trade, analysis of market fluctuations, and the utilization of other natural resources. The influence of climate on our lives is virtually endless. NCDC, which is part of the National Oceanic and Atmospheric Administration (NOAA), inherited the U.S. Weather Bureau's responsibility to fulfill the mandate of Congress "... to establish and record the climatic conditions of the United States," an important provision of the Organic Act of October 1, 1890, which established the Weather Bureau as a civilian agency (15 U.S.C. 311).

This mandate has been combined with guidelines established through international agreement. The World Meteorological Organization (WMO) set the end of a decade as the desirable term for a thirty-year period from which to calculate climatic conditions. The average value of a meteorological element over the thirty years is defined as a climatological normal. This helps in describing the climate and is used as a base to which current conditions can be compared.

Every ten years, NCDC computes new thirty-year climate normals for selected temperature and precipitation elements for a large number of U.S. climate and weather stations. These normals are summarized in several publications that will be discussed later. Every thirty years, climatological standard normals are computed as part of an international effort led by the WMO. The most recent standard normals period is 1961-90.

Interpretation of Climatic "Normals"

The term climatic "normal" has faced a dilemma since its introduction a century and a half ago. As noted by Guttman (1989, p. 602), "Climatologists generally understand that a normal is simply an average of a climatic element over thirty years ... a normal value is usually not the most frequent value nor the value above which half the cases fall."

The general public, however, tends to (erroneously) perceive the normal as "what they should expect." Dr. Helmut E. Landsberg, who became Director of Climatology of the U.S. Weather Bureau in 1954 and, later, Director of the Environmental Data Service, summarized the dilemma quite well four decades ago (Landsberg, 1955): "The layman is often misled by the word. In his every-day language the word normal means something ordinary or frequent. ... When (the meteorologist) talks about 'normal,' it has nothing to do with a common event... For the meteorologist the 'normal' is simply a point of departure or index which is convenient for keeping track of weather statistics.... We never expect to experience 'normal' weather."

It might be "normal" for the weather to swing radically between extremes from day to day and year to year, but the climatic "normal" is simply an arithmetic average of what has happened at such a "swinging" place. This is why it is important to use a measure of the variability of climate (such as the standard deviation and extremes) in conjunction with the climatic normal when studying the climate of a location (Guttman 1989).

Overview of the 1961-90 United States Climate Normals

The 1961-90 U.S. climate normals are summarized and published in several publications; the four primary publications are designated CLIM81, CLIM84, CLIM85, and CLIM20. Each publication contains the normals appropriate for the application and users for which it was designed.

The normals that are most commonly computed are thirty-year averages for precipitation and maximum, minimum, and mean temperature for each of the twelve months, plus an annual value. Monthly and annual average heating and cooling degree days are also important. The CLIM81 publication (*Climatography of the United States No. 81*) contains these monthly normals, plus monthly median precipitation and median mean temperature, for several thousand locations across the country (4,775 temperature stations and 6,662 precipitation stations).

Daily normals are computed for 422 National Weather Service offices and principal climatological stations for the following six elements: precipitation, heating and cooling degree days, and maximum, minimum, and mean temperature. The daily station normals are summarized in the CLIM84 publication (*Climatography of the United States No. 84*).

The contiguous United States, Alaska, Puerto Rico, and the U.S. Virgin Islands are divided into 360 geographical units called climate divisions. Monthly and annual divisional normals for mean temperature, precipitation, and heating and cooling degree days, as well as the corresponding standard deviation for these four elements, are published in the CLIM85 publication (*Climatography of the United States No. 85*). Monthly and annual normals for the corresponding states and territories, nine census regions, and national values for the contiguous United States, are derived from the divisional data and published in the *Historical Climatology Series 4-1, 4-2, 5-1,* and *5-2* publications.

Normals statistics that have useful agricultural applications are published in the CLIM20 publication (*Climatography of the United States No. 20*). These statistics include freeze date probabilities; normal growing degree days; monthly number of days with temperature, precipitation, and snowfall beyond various thresholds; monthly precipitation probabilities; temperature and precipitation "runs" statistics (consecutive number of days beyond various thresholds); and temperature, precipitation, and snowfall extremes, as well as the CLIM81 monthly normals. CLIM20 summaries are being prepared for approximately 2,900 locations in the United States.

The 1961-90 normals appear in several other NCDC publications, including the *Local Climatological Data, Annual Summary; Comparative Climatic Data; Climatic Averages and Extremes for U.S. Cities;* and three supplements to the CLIM81 publication (*Monthly Precipitation Probabilities, Annual Degree Days to Selected Bases,* and *Maps of Annual 1961-90 Normal Temperature, Precipitation, and Degree Days*).

NCDC computed 1961-90 normals for several additional elements for several hundred U.S. stations as the U.S. submission to the WMO global standard normals project. These elements include monthly mean wind speed and wind direction frequencies, atmospheric pressure (mean sea level), relative humidity, sunshine duration, cloud cover, wet bulb/dew point temperatures, and number of days meeting specified criteria, including: thunderstorms, rain/drizzle, freezing rain/drizzle, snow/hail, fog/mist, smoke/haze, blowing snow, and dust storm/sandstorm.

Normals from Earlier Periods

In the United States, normals have been computed for 1961-90, 1951-80, 1941-70, 1931-60, and 1921-50. The normals from 1931-60 to present are in NCDC's archives. The 1921-50 normals, the first normals set prepared according to WMO standards, were published in 1956 as *Weather Bureau Technical Paper No. 31 (Monthly Normal Temperatures, Precipitation, and Degree Days)*. This technical paper is available from NCDC only on microfiche.

Earlier normals have been summarized in previous editions of the CLIM81, CLIM84, CLIM85, and CLIM20 publications. In addition, a comprehensive *Climatic Atlas of the United States* presents the 1931-60 normals in large map format; the 1951-80 freeze/frost probabilities have been summarized in a separate volume; and selected normals summaries have been collated into individual state volumes.

Statistical summaries which further describe the climate of the United States have been published as CLIM82 and CLIM90. These summaries are based primarily on hourly data and present tables of means and frequency of occurrence of selected climatic elements.

Normals are best used as a base against which climate during the following decade can be measured. Comparison of normals from one thirty-year period with those from another thirty-year period may lead to erroneous conclusions about climatic change. This is due to changes over the decades in station location, in the instrumentation used, in how weather observations were made, and in how the various normals were computed. The differences between normals due to these non-climatic changes may be larger than the differences due to a true change in climate.

References

Greville, T.N.E., 1967: "Spline functions, interpolation, and numerical quadrature," *Mathematical Methods for Digital Computers, Vol. II*, A. Ralston and H.S. Wilf (eds.), pp. 156-68, Wiley, New York.

Guttman, N.B., 1989: "Statistical descriptors of climate," *Bulletin of the American Meteorological Society*, Vol. 70, pp. 602-7.

Irvin, L. (ed.), 1993: *Encyclopedia of Associations: International Organizations, Part I* (27th Edition). Gale Research Inc., Detroit.

Karl, T.R., and C.N. Williams, Jr., 1987: "An approach to adjusting climatological time series for discontinuous inhomogeneities," *Journal of Climate and Applied Meteorology*, Vol. 26, pp. 1744-63.

Karl, T.R., C.N. Williams, Jr., P.J. Young, and W.M. Wendland, 1986: "A model to estimate the time of observation bias associated with monthly mean maximum, minimum, and mean temperatures for the United States," *Journal of Climate and Applied Meteorology*, Vol. 25, pp. 145-60.

Karl, T.R., C.N. Williams, Jr., F.T. Quinlan, and T.A. Boden, 1990: "United States Historical Climatology Network (HCN) Serial Temperature and Precipitation Data," Oak Ridge National Laboratory Environmental Sciences Division Publication No. 3404 (ORNL/CDIAC-30, NDP-019/R1), 377 pages.

Landsberg, H.E., 1955: "Weather 'normals' and normal weather," Weekly Weather and Crop Bulletin, 1/31/55, pp. 7-8.

Reek, T., S.R. Doty, and T.W. Owen, 1992: "A deterministic approach to the validation of historical daily temperature and precipitation data from the Cooperative Network," *Bulletin of the American Meteorological Society*, Vol. 73, pp. 753-62.

Steurer, P., 1985: "Creation of a serially complete data base of high quality daily maximum and minimum temperatures." Unpublished technical note available from the Global Climate Laboratory, NCDC.

Thom, H.C.S., 1952: "Seasonal degree-day statistics for the United States," *Monthly Weather Review*, Vol. 80, pp. 143-49.

Thom, H.C.S., 1954: "The rational relationship between heating degree days and temperature," *Monthly Weather Review*, Vol. 82, pp. 1-6.

Thom, H.C.S., 1959: "The distribution of freeze-date and freeze- free period for climatological series with freezeless years," *Monthly Weather Review*, Vol. 87, pp. 136-44.

Thom, H.C.S., 1966: "Normal degree days above any base by the universal truncation coefficient," *Monthly Weather Review*, Vol. 94, pp. 461-65.

Thom, H.C.S. and R.H. Shaw, 1958: "Climatological analysis of freeze data for Iowa," *Monthly Weather Review*, Vol. 86, pp. 251-57.

U.S. Department of Commerce, Bureau of the Census, 1991: 1990 Census of Population and Housing, Summary of Population and Housing Characteristics, Puerto Rico.

U.S. Department of Commerce, Bureau of the Census, 1992: 1990 Census of Population, General Population Characteristics, Series CT-1 (Alabama through Wyoming and U.S. Summary).

Vestal, C.K., 1971: "First and last occurrences of low temperatures during the cold season," *Monthly Weather Review*, Vol. 99, pp. 650-52.

World Meteorological Organization, 1984: Technical Regulations, Vol. I. WMO Publication No. 49. Geneva, Switzerland.

Glossary

Air mass. A mass of air which has similar horizontal temperature and moisture properties.

Air pressure (also *atmospheric pressure*). Pressure exerted by the weight of the air above a given point; most often measured in millibars (mb) or inches of mercury (in. Hg).

Aleutian low. Subpolar low-pressure area on mean sea level pressure charts centered near or south of the Aleutian Islands.

Anemometer. A device that measures wind speed.

Anticyclone. A surface high-pressure area around which the wind blows clockwise in the Northern Hemisphere and counterclockwise in the Southern Hemisphere.

Apparent temperature. The "feel" of the air for various combinations of air temperature and relative humidity.

Atmosphere. The gases that encircle a planet, captured by the planet's gravitational force. The Earth's atmosphere is mainly nitrogen and oxygen. See also *Stratosphere, Troposphere.*

Atmospheric greenhouse effect. The warming of the atmosphere caused by its absorbing and reemitting infrared radiation while allowing shortwave (ultraviolet) radiation to pass through. The gases mainly responsible for the Earth's atmospheric greenhouse effect are water vapor and carbon dioxide.

Atmospheric models. Mathematical equations or physical models used to simulate the atmosphere's behavior.

Autumnal equinox. The equinox around September 23 when the sun passes directly over the equator. This represents the beginning of autumn in the Northern Hemisphere and spring in the Southern.

Barometer. Instrument used to measure air pressure. Two widely used barometers are the mercury barometer and the aneroid barometer.

California current. The southward-flowing ocean current that runs along the entire west coast of the United States down to Baja California.

Carbon dioxide (CO_2). An odorless and colorless gas present in the atmosphere at a concentration of about 0.035% (350 ppm) of air at sea level. CO_2 is important in the earth's atmospheric greenhouse effect because it selectively absorbs infrared radiation. CO_2 in its solid state is called dry ice.

Celsius scale. A temperature scale, designated by °C, where zero is assigned to the temperature at which water freezes and 100 to the temperature at which water boils (at sea level).

Climate. Weather events or measurements averaged over a period of time.

Condensation. The change of state from a gas to a liquid, e.g., water vapor to liquid water.

Cooling degree-day. A number representing the difference in degrees between an actual temperature and a base temperature, used as a measure of the amount of space cooling needed. For example, for a base temperature of 65°F, an average daily temperature of 70°F would represent 5 cooling degree-days. On the other hand, a temperature of 60°F would require 0, since the temperature is below the threshold. See also *Growing degree-day, Heating degree-day.*

Cyclone. A violent storm in which the winds rotate around a central area of low pressure. In the Northern Hemisphere the winds blow counterclockwise and in the Southern Hemisphere clockwise.

Daily range of temperature. The maximum temperature minus the minimum for a particular day.

Dendrochronology. The study of past climate conditions using the annual growth rings of trees.

Dew point (dew-point temperature). The temperature to which air must be cooled (at constant pressure and constant water vapor content) for saturation and condensation to occur.

Doppler radar. Radar which uses the Doppler shift to establish the velocity of falling precipitation either toward or away from the radar unit. The National Weather Service Doppler radar is known as WSR-88D, or "NEXRAD."

Drought. A period of abnormally dry weather sufficiently long to cause serious effects on agriculture and other activities in the affected area.

Dry adiabatic rate. The rate of temperature change with elevation in an unsaturated air parcel. The adiabatic rate (cooling or warming) is about 5.5°F per 1,000 feet.

El Niño. A situation in which the water off the coast of Peru and Ecuador warms more than usual, generally coinciding with cooler ocean temperatures in the western Pacific. This causes a shifting in wind and moisture patterns, causing significant changes in weather in the U.S. and worldwide. Major El Niño events occur irregularly, about once every three to seven years. In Oregon, El Niño events produce generally mild, dry winters.

Evaporation. A change in state from the liquid phase to the gas phase, usually through warming of the liquid.

Fahrenheit scale. A temperature scale, designated by °F, where 32 is assigned to the temperature at which water freezes and 212 to the temperature at which water boils (at sea level).

Ferrel cell. One of the three circulation cells that explain the general circulation of the atmosphere. A Ferrel cell is characterized by rising air near about 50-60° latitude and descending air near 30° latitude. See also *Hadley cell, Polar cell.*

Greenhouse effect. See *Atmospheric greenhouse effect.*

Growing degree-day. A form of degree-day the threshold temperature of which is established for different types of crops. See also *Cooling degree-day, Heating degree-day.*

Hadley cell. One of the three circulation cells that explain the general circulation of the atmosphere; it is characterized by rising air near the equator and descending air near 30° latitude. See also *Ferrel cell, Polar cell.*

Heat. Energy that is transferred through objects due to differences in temperature.

Heat index (HI). A way to express how the air actually feels, based on a combination of air temperature and relative humidity; hot days feel hottest when humidity is high.

Heating degree-day. A number representing the difference in degrees between an actual temperature and a base temperature, used as a measure of the amount of space heating needed. For example, for a base temperature of 65°F, an average daily temperature of 60°F would represent 5 heating degree days. On the other hand, a temperature of 70°F would require 0, since the temperature is above the threshold. See also *Cooling degree-day, Growing degree-day.*

High. See *Anticyclone*

Infrared (IR) radiation. Electromagnetic radiation with wavelengths longer than visible light and shorter than microwaves. IR radiation is generally associated with heat transfer.

Insolation. The incoming radiation from the sun.

Intertropical Convergence Zone (ITCZ). An area of rising air and unsettled weather that separates the southeast trade winds (to the south) and the northeast trade winds (to the north). The ITCZ is usually near the equator, but moves northward and southward following the sun's zenith position with the seasons.

Jet stream. High-speed winds near the troposphere that flow in a concentrated band. Generally represents the boundary between warm subtropical and cool polar air. Often known as the "storm track," since storms tend to follow its path as they circle the globe.

Kelvin. A unit of temperature, denoted by K. A unit of 1 K equals 1°C. Zero K is absolute zero, and equals -273.15°C.

Kinetic energy. Energy that results from motion within a body or substance.

Knot. A unit that measures speed and is equal to 1 nautical mile per hour (1.15 mph).

Koppen classification system. A climate classification system based on seasonal and annual averages of temperature and precipitation.

La Niña. The counterpart to El Niño, which also causes weather and climate disruptions worldwide. Ocean temperatures off South America are cooler than normal, and temperatures near Indonesia are warmer than normal. In Oregon, La Niña winters are generally cooler and wetter than normal.

Marine climate. A climate that is influenced mostly by the ocean. Temperatures are generally mild throughout the year and humidity high.

Maritime air. Air that has developed over a body of water and is generally mild and moist.

Mean annual temperature. A location's temperatures averaged over a year.

Mean daily temperature. The average of all hourly temperatures, or of the maximum and minimum temperatures, for a 24-hour period.

Meteorology. The study of the atmosphere and everything in it, including weather and weather forecasting.

Millibar (mb). A unit of atmospheric pressure. Standard sea-level pressure is 1,013.4 mb.

Monsoon wind system. Winds that switch directions between winter and summer. Most of the time the wind blows from land to sea in winter and from sea to land in the summer.

Ozone (O_3). A gas form of oxygen found naturally in the stratosphere. Stratospheric ozone absorbs some of the sun's ultraviolet light and thus acts as a shield for the earth's surface. In the lower troposphere, however, ozone is a harmful air pollutant formed by chemical reactions involving pollutants emitted from fossil fuel combustion.

Ozone hole. A decreased amount of ozone in an area over the polar regions in the springtime.

Pacific high. Same as *Subtropical high*.

Parcel of air. A "section" of air that can be used to study or explain the characteristics of air.

Polar cell. One of the three circulation cells that explain the general circulation of the atmosphere, characterized by rising air near about 50-60° latitude and descending air near the pole. See also *Ferrel cell, Hadley cell*.

Precipitation. Water, in any form, falling from the sky and reaching the surface.

Prevailing wind. The most common wind direction at a given location and period of time.

Radiosonde. A balloon equipped with a device that measures air characteristics and sends the data to a station at the ground.

Rain. Liquid precipitation consisting of large drops (as opposed to drizzle, the drops of which are very small).

Relative humidity. The ratio of the actual water vapor in the air to the amount the air could hold at the current temperature and pressure.

Ridge. An area of high pressure in the atmosphere.

Saturation (of air). A situation in which the maximum possible amount of water vapor is present in air, for a given temperature and pressure.

Sea-level pressure. The pressure of the atmosphere at mean sea level.

Semi-arid climate. A dry climate that is not as dry as an arid climate. Short grass is the usual vegetation.

Semipermanent highs and lows. Regions of high or low pressure that stay at a certain latitude throughout much of the year.

Snow. Solid form of precipitation consisting of ice crystals.

Soundings. Observations taken at different heights in the atmosphere that produce a continuous profile of temperature, humidity, or winds at different heights.

Southern oscillation. An alternation of surface air pressure in the east and west tropical Pacific Ocean associated with El Niño and La Niña conditions.

Standard atmosphere. Average temperature, pressure, and density of the Earth's atmosphere at various heights above sea level.

Standard atmospheric pressure. Average pressure of the atmosphere at various heights. Standard sea level pressure is 29.92 inches (measured in a barometer). In other units, standard pressure is 1013.25 millibars or 760 millimeters.

Stratosphere. The second layer of the atmosphere from the Earth, following the troposphere and preceding the mesophere. This layer extends approximately 6 to 30 miles above sea level, and is characterized by a temperature inversion.

Subtropical high. A persistent high pressure area in the subtropical belt generally centered near 30° latitude.

Subtropical jet stream. A jet stream located in the subtropics, between 20° and 30° latitude.

Summer solstice. The day when the sun is at its highest point in the sky. This is about June 22 in the Northern Hemisphere, December 21 in the Southern.

Sunspots. Areas of high magnetic energy that are linked to "cooler" spots on the sun.

Synoptic scale. The weather scale that includes large-scale storm systems, fronts, and other features, stretching over continent-sized areas.

Temperature. The average speed or kinetic energy of the atoms and molecules in a object or the heat measured by a thermometer.

Thermometer. An instrument used to measure temperature.

Trade winds. Prevailing winds in the tropics that blow from east to west, and toward the ITCZ.

Tropopause. The boundary between the troposphere and the stratosphere.

Troposphere. The lowest layer of the atmosphere, from the Earth's surface to about 6-10 miles.

Ultraviolet radiation. The electromagnetic radiation the wavelengths of which are shorter than visible light but longer than X-rays.

Upwelling. The rising of cold, deep ocean water toward the surface, usually caused by winds in the lower atmosphere.

Urban heat island. An increase in temperatures in urban areas compared to rural areas nearby, resulting from industrial, domestic, and transportation activities.

Vernal equinox. The date on which the sun's rays shine directly on the equator in the Northern Hemisphere spring (on or about March 20).

Water equivalent. The amount of water in frozen precipitation when it is melted. Usually 10 inches of snow will contain 1 inch of water.

Water vapor. Water that is in its gaseous form.

Weather. The properties of the atmosphere at a specific time and location.

Weather elements. The aspects of weather that describe the state of the atmosphere (precipitation, winds, temperature, and so on).

Westerlies. The winds that dominantly blow from the west in the middle latitudes.

Wind. Air movement caused by pressure differences in the atmosphere. See also *Geostrophic wind, Katabatic wind, Offshore wind, Onshore wind, Prevailing wind, Trade winds, Westerlies.*

Wind-chill factor. The combined cooling effect of temperature and wind speed, proportional to loss of body heat.

Wind direction. The direction that the wind is blowing from.

Wind rose. A graph or diagram that shows the percentage frequency that wind blows from different directions and at different speeds.

Winter solstice. The point at which the sun is lowest in the sky and over the latitude 23.5°S. This occurs around December 22 in the Northern Hemisphere, and June 22 in the Southern.

Index of Keywords

Index of Place Names

Oregon Locations

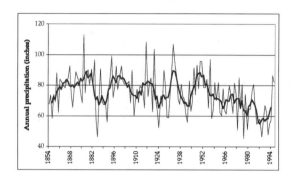